To Sedona.

— Help spread the Light.

Love Chris

Hidden Secrets

Fragments
of a Double Life

Christina Gow

Hidden Secrets: Fragments of a Double Life
Copyright ©2002 by Christina Gow

All rights reserved. Printed in the United States of America. No part of this book may be reproduced in any form or by any electronic or mechanical means, including information storage and retrieval systems, without written permission from the publisher, except brief quotations embodied in critical articles for reviews.

Published By
Christina Gow
P. O. Box 38502
Colorado Springs, CO 80937-8502
Hiddensecrets2002@hotmail.com

In cooperation with
Close Connections Publishing
P. O. Box 402
Evergreen, CO 80437-0402

ISBN 0-9670746-4-9
Library of Congress Control Number: 2002092165

Cover design and book layout by Nick Zelinger, NZ Graphics, Lakewood, CO
Cover and book illustrations by David Anderson,
1/51 Bowman Pde, Barton, Queensland 4065, Australia.
Conceptual Editing by Erika Niemann, Close Connections Publishing, Evergreen, CO
Printed by Central Plains Book Mfg., Winfield, KS

First Edition

Foreword

Ritual abuse is the great dark secret of our world. Its existence is ridiculed, ignored, and denied, which makes it incredibly hard for all those who have suffered so terribly from the impact of it, to heal. Christina's book is a brave undertaking to bring some of these dark secrets into the light.

I found reading this book both informed and horrified me. I understood for the first time, the awful predicament of those who are ritually abused that for survival they must themselves become the abusers. I understood the mind games and control these groups have over their victims.

Although there have been many excellent books on ritual abuse this book is such a personal revelation and journey that I think it is essential reading for anyone wanting to understand this form of abuse and how it affects its victims so profoundly.

This form of abuse is pure evil. It is essential that those of us who wish to win the war over child abuse accept, acknowledge and help all those who have suffered from ritual abuse. Then they can move from being captives of their childhood and living life based on fear, to living the lives that God intended for them with happiness and joy.

– Liz Mullinar, Founder of ASCA,
Advocates for Survivors of Childhood Abuse.

Liz Mullinar was one of the most powerful people in Australian TV. She started Australia's first film and advertising consultancy and played an important part in Australia's developing film industry. Her influence was recognized in the Australian Day Honors in 1997 when she received an Order of Australia.

A mysterious illness changed Liz's life in 1993. Medical tests couldn't diagnose her dramatic weight loss and debilitating fatigue of many months. Not until she uncovered repressed memories of childhood rape, did symptoms subside. During this time Liz discovered lack of support for people who had been abused as children and started an association for survivors of child abuse in 1995.

ASCA, Advocates for Survivors of Childhood Abuse has become a national voice, taking on the task of education, advocacy and support for men and women. ASCA focuses on healing, with support groups throughout Australia and a retreat in northern NSW.

Check the website, www.asca.org.au
Reference:
The Liz Mullinar Story by Liz Mullinar and Simon Hopkinson
Breaking the Silence by Liz Mullinar and Candida Hunt.
Both books available from ASCA

Dedication

I dedicate this book to the thousands of people around the world, who are in recovery from ritual abuse

Thank you to the healers who are prepared to master their own growth as they help others release fear, terror and torture. I know they are not unaffected by the trauma but are willing to confront the pain and walk in its release with the abused.

Thank you Dr Verna V Aridon Yater for your unconditional and continual support during my healing process. Your work was done in love and in belief of the goodness of Spirit in everyone. God bless you.

To those who were the victimized babies, children, adults and animals, I honor you for helping me and others, break the cycle of sacrifice.

In God we trust,
And so it is.

Author's Note

This book is a segment of my life, containing many spontaneous memories from four years of my healing process. The book also includes recollections of other people. I have altered names, personalities, shifted geographical locations, altered times and created composite characters. Any similarity between characters in this book and people known to the reader will be illusory.

However, there is a Blue Mountain Center of which Dr Verna V Aridon Yater is a co-founder. There is also an Australian organization, Advocates for Survivors of Childhood Abuse, which supports and speaks out about all childhood abuse.

Many people's lives have been diminished and traumatized by the hidden abuse that society has denied. The cult of ritual abuse is far more common than we would like to believe. People involved are programmed through horror techniques, to forget their participation. Now is the time for survivors who are ready, to speak out.

Prologue

"I'm five years old………It's my birthday………I'm having a party."

I was in a healing workshop and leaned back in my plastic chair to watch Melissa. The teenager's eyes were shut. Her face wore a quizzical expression as she sat remembering an occasion from thirteen years ago.

"I'm at Granny and Poppa's house….. The dining room is decorated with special ornaments and other things not usually there…. The lights aren't very bright….. The table looks really pretty."

Melissa paused, as if attempting to analyze the moving pictures in her head. The silence between the sentences of the brief monologue seemed as important as the words coming out.

"I'm standing on a chair at the end of the table. I feel *very* special." Melissa's body slumped as she continued. Emotions from the five-year-old surfaced and her breathing became noticeably labored.

"Granny is turning the lights down….. She is bringing in my birthday cake…. The plate is held high up above her head. I can see the candles flickering. …..Now the cake is in front of me on the table."

I glanced around the room. All twenty-two people in the group listened intently to Melissa's story. Their focused attention supported her vital memory recall. Every word she spoke came slowly, often with long pauses between them. The group waited patiently. It appeared something significant and very painful was surfacing from Melissa's subconscious. Everyone knew from experiences during the last five workshops we'd done together, that this degree of memory recall was vitally important if we were going to grow and enrich our lives as we had intended.

The energy around Melissa continued to hold our absolute attention. "Oh No!..… God, no! …. This is horrible," she continued.

Tears streamed down Melissa's face.

Somebody nearby passed a handful of tissues to her as she tried to speak about the horror she was reliving in her mind's eye. Then she lost control of her voice.

"It's not a normal birthday cake."

Terrified by something she had seen in her memory, Melissa drew in a sharp breath and held it for what seemed ages before remembering to release air stored in her lungs. This helped discharge some body tension. I shifted uncomfortably in my seat wondering what could be so horrible about a little child's birthday party.

Melissa hid her face in her hands. After a while she opened up again. Her neck and head had paled.

"It's a little baby..... A real one..... Tiny..... There are five candles around the plate. The baby is in the center. I have a knife in my hand. Poppa signals to me, I have to stab it."

Her body contorted in re-enactment of the memory. Everyone in the group felt the fear and revulsion of her family's secret fifth birthday party. Melissa dutifully put the knife through her 'birthday cake'. She knew the rules well. Total obedience or torture.

"I have to *eat* it," she screamed.

A miniature baby. Pale fleshed, translucent and recently aborted. Pre-term but perfectly formed. A human being specifically bred for sacrifice. Destined never to live.

Blood drained from my head. I watched helplessly as Melissa's body convulsed and dry-retched in an attempt to expel the memory of soft white human flesh from her mouth.

I, too, had to swallow hard to keep the bile from rising in my throat. I was even more sickened than most others in the group were, for this was my daughter's story. This was her memory of a ceremonial fifth birthday party. A family's closeted ritual.

"Dad's there, so are you, Mum," rang in my ears.

I had no conscious recollection of this and it seemed unbelievable that I could have participated in such brutality. However, so many other memories had emerged during our months of workshops together that I didn't doubt this story was true.

As I heard Melissa cry in deep grief and sadness I turned to look at her younger sister, Rebecca, who sat on the floor by her side. Frozen to my chair, unable to think and speechless, I listened.

"The same sort of thing happened to me, too," Rebecca stuttered through her tears. "I thought it was going to be a fun birthday party at night. There were balloons. Granny always made things look nice. But my cake was different from Melissa's. The baby was covered with chocolate sponge cake. ...I feel so sick." Rebecca looked at me. "It's no wonder I hate chocolate cake."

"Do you remember how many people were there Rebecca?" the facilitator asked.

"Maybe fifteen? Three times five. It had to be in multiples of five. Granny sat at the end of the table. She looked so evil. It was her eyes. They were horrid. She watched everything with those mean eyes. I was tricked again. I hate the things my family does."

I glanced at Michael, my husband. He looked askance and, like me, was totally confused. What were these horrific events our daughters had just described? They said the parties were held in the dining room at Michael's family's house. His parents, Granny and Poppa seemed to have organized these ceremonies. What does all this mean? The girls' descriptions were nightmare material, both of them. It seemed incredulous. I wished it wasn't true.

I buried my head in my hands and prayed. Oh Jesus, please help them, please help me. I believed both my children and wondered what else went on in our family we hadn't remembered.

This wasn't the first story of abhorrence we relived through these workshops. It only added to a list of brutalities we had already seen.

My body was so heavy I couldn't move. I couldn't imagine either girl would want me near her for I was there during the perpetration of these unspeakable acts. They told me so and I believed them. If I were in their situation I would be furiously angry at the participating adults and would want them to keep away from me. I felt ashamed, ignorant and false.

For the next six months during our participation in healing workshops horror after horror from our hidden lives emerged. Unbelievable atrocities.

The four of us were shocked. We were all in varying degrees of denial. It seemed impossible, and I was completely overwhelmed by the emerging truth.

It seemed we led two lives. A daytime 'nice' person life and a night time 'nasty' person life: a Dr Jekyl and Mr Hyde existence.

I always felt I was an average mother. I was there for my children. I took them to clubs, activities and what ever else they wanted. I *thought* I was supportive. I made sure they were okay at school. I provided remedial help when they needed it. Isn't that normal? Isn't that caring? I loved them. Apart from providing my children's basic needs, I felt it was my role to educate, nurture and respect the whole family. However something terrible was emerging from our past that appeared to negate so much of the goodness in our lives.

So many strange things surfaced as we worked together to heal our family. A surreal life was being revealed. It was a secret life of terror, but it was real, our bodies and emotions showed us.

I desperately wished it were past life recall for that would be far easier to bear. However, with four members of the same family recalling similar incidents I could not hide behind any masks or fabrication. This wasn't from a previous century. It wasn't a lie. The truth was shoved in our faces. We were seeing another reality of who we truly were.

My family: that was me, Christina, my husband, Michael and our daughters, Melissa and Rebecca, had been involved in multigenerational ritual abuse. This cult stretched historically back through centuries in our genetic lineage. Now we recollected memories we had previously been unaware of.

We didn't go to these personal growth groups thinking that we might uncover anything evil, anything bad. I intended to use the healing to become confident and vital. I wanted peace and harmony in my life and knew I had to change unhealthy patterns. There was no conscious thought I would uncover ritual abuse. I had never even heard of the term until recently. However, like it or not, ritual abuse was what emerged from my subconscious.

This is a story of my family's surreal life. We have suffered enormous agony and pain reliving the memories.

I have cried, screamed, beaten pillows, gone into denial, felt ashamed and thought I was going insane. I have no idea how I came to write this story. Possibly my healer suggested it. Well, I would sooner have written a book on how to save the planet, or create a backyard orchard. But that wasn't to be. Maybe this was my destiny, part of my life's plan. Now, I've had to go to the depths of the murkiest part of my being and explore the darker side of humanity.

But I am not going to hide. I want to share this story with others, in an attempt to release the darkness from our souls and collective consciences. If I can help eliminate sacrifice from the face of the earth, I will have accomplished what I set out to do.

What is ritual abuse?

This was what the facilitator called my family's experience. But what did this phrase mean? From what I'd seen so far, it appeared to be a cult of programmed members, with regular abuse of children, adults and human sacrifice. The cult appeared to gather for secret ceremonies of immense cruelty, during significant times of the year that often coincided with Christian celebrations.

Programming seemed to be a key factor. People were programmed and drugged to forget, and live their lives believing themselves to be average citizens, loving their children, doing vital work in the community without remembering the cruel and sadistic part of their life. They lived a dual life including conduct they didn't want to consciously know.

Satanic ritual abuse sounds evil and you may feel judgmental toward anyone who has been or is involved. But I want you to know, most people involved in this form of ritualistic abuse are completely unaware of their participation. Satanic abuse is a term, using a name and theme descriptive of evil. Participation creates psychological damage to human beings in a manner that pornography, violence and war also can. Fear is the emotion utilized by the perpetrators to create a life of unconscious terror, to manipulate the actions of all members. All members are mind controlled through careful programming. Techniques of indoctrination are electric shock, drugs, trauma of observing torture, death, sexual abuse and dissection with the possibility of this happening to the member, or his family. The methods are used to silence everyone and make them forget.

Cult members come from all aspects of society. Highly educated men and women, leaders of our community mix in meetings with representatives of every other strata of our culture. As incest, pedophilia and alcoholism belong to no particular class, so too, satanic ritual abuse is pervasive throughout our world.

Common themes in ritual abuse are being buried in coffins, human and animal sacrifice, torture, blood drinking, eating body parts, sexual rituals and perversion of Christian rites. Most people involved in cult activities dissociate from their body. In fact, dissociation is knowingly created by the cult for perfect control of members. Different personalities are formed in an individual by the cult to respond to a trigger. A hand signal, certain word, phrase or music gives the cult access to the person without her conscious awareness.

Survivors of ritual abuse are usually confused when memories of these strange events unfold in their mind. It is difficult for them to believe they were present for they were trained to forget all their association with the cult. Often they will suppress these recollections or think they saw them in a film, dreamed them, or read them in a book. It is easier to forget than go through the pain of recollection.

Healing is possible and vital. It requires stamina and support to move from victim to empowered human being.

"They told me I was special."

Chapter one

There was more to Melissa's fifth birthday than a ceremonial party and cake. It took many months to put the pieces of memory together – but it was important. In multigenerational satanic ritual abuse, turning five holds great significance.

Five candles symbolize five points of the satanic star. The knife stabbed into a baby, often disguised in a cake, marks the time that the five-year-old is no longer simply an abused child. It is the time the violated child is forced to become a perpetrator. Now she had stabbed a baby, Melissa was no longer different from her tormentors. She had absolutely no choice in the matter.

From birth she was highly trained through cruelty and torture to do as she was told, to respond as the cult demanded. During ceremonies she was taught to be emotionless, silent and still. Although her heart raced in terror while holding the knife, she realized the consequence of disobedience and mistakes. She already knew eating human flesh was expected and she must not become nauseated or express revulsion. Any disobedience to the cult's rules evoked tortuous punishment to herself, or maybe a sibling. Whoever they chose to torture, Melissa was to blame. Fear generated by her responsibility to protect family members was unbearable.

As Melissa dutifully stabbed the baby, a little five-year-old part of her split off as another personality compartment. This is the way she coped with trauma. Compartmentalizing and splitting personality is the psyche's survival mechanism. Her body knew it couldn't be repulsed by this travesty. The night's horror had to be stored and hidden. The split 'five-year-old birthday girl' took responsibility for the stabbing and hid the memory from the rest of the Melissa that we and she knew. This was the way Melissa learned to be normal. However, her body cells stored the memory of her action as physical tension.

Each person present at the ceremonial party was trained to forget. Further amnesia was created around the entire event by party drinks laced with drugs to hinder recollection. Participants functioned from moment to moment but forgot long term.

Melissa's grandparents', parents', uncles' and aunts' memory of the party froze in their cult-created personalities, which dissociated from their normal façade. Trauma was trapped inside their subconscious.

The next morning everyone returned to a normal life, unaware of the previous night's celebration. They were businessmen, nurses, mothers, schoolteachers and students. Each participant was an expert at hiding their personality splits for it was ingrained in their consciousness to forget from early childhood.

After her night's sleep Melissa returned to her playfulness, forgetting her hideous party. At least on the surface she seemed normal. However there was now a missing part of her personality. Her subconscious knew something her conscious mind didn't. Her little body worked hard expending energy to keep the memory of the ceremonial fifth birthday party tightly locked. Tension was set in her arm that was used reluctantly to wield the knife. She had stabbed a defenseless baby. This split personality knew she was a perpetrator. Her role was to hide away in a secret compartment most of the time. This part also knew her duty. It was to respond to special words and signals that triggered her to come out of hiding in order to repeat her child's 'fifth birthday girl' training. She was the five-year-old birthday girl in the body of an eight-year-old, or in a ten-year-old or a sixteen-year-old, depending on when her perpetrators called her forth again to do as she was trained.

As an eighteen-year-old, Melissa had to start healing her body, mind and soul so this little birthday girl could surface. There was so much spiritual pain involved in hiding this victimized child and other cult induced personalities that Melissa's life was deeply affected. Induced personality splitting gives leaders of ritual abuse control over their group members. Amnesia is common in the cult of ritual abuse. Power, sex and money seem to be the main objectives.

Ultimate power of cult leaders comes from making everyone a perpetrator. No one in multi-generational ritual abuse is just a victim.

This is a story of multigenerational ritual abuse.

Melissa, my own child, born into a family of multigenerational ritual abuse was initiated. Thank God, we are now remembering as a family.

I pray that my future grandchildren will never experience the torture of such horrific ceremonies, and that the rest of humanity begins to acknowledge and heal the effects of ritual abuse. I pray for all abuse and mind-control to disappear from existence forever.

Ignorance is not bliss.

Chapter two

What had happened to our daughters was overwhelming and incomprehensible. It appeared both Michael and I had witnessed a ceremony involving abuse on our own children. How could we be there without remembering such horror?

Surely my presence wasn't a conscious choice? Who would want their family to have to deal with such terror? Definitely not me.

Melissa and Rebecca's descriptions didn't prompt any recollection for me. Although their memory appeared to come out of the blue they certainly hadn't fabricated the event. It was true. I observed their emotion and body reactions; both girls were distressed and traumatized.

However, if I wasn't consciously involved, how did Michael and I, seemingly normal individuals, become entangled in these bizarre activities? I was perplexed, disturbed and in denial about such atrocities. For forty-five years, I knew nothing of this part of my existence.

I need to repeat that sentence to myself because it still astounds me. I lived for *forty-five years* in ignorance. That sounds unbelievable, nevertheless, I absolutely did not remember the cruelties I was forced to endure and trained to forget. I wouldn't have survived as a normal human being if I had remembered these shadow activities of my life.

It is easy to look back now and see possible indicators suggesting that something odd, could have in fact, been going on through my life.

There were little things, like excruciating pain in my legs during the night when I was a teenager. My research revealed this could have been a side effect of chloroform, soaked on a rag to anaesthetize. Another symptom was chronic anxiety on awakening every morning from my early twenties till my mid-thirties. I discovered this wasn't normal when I woke one morning after regular meditation for several months. The apprehension and pain I'd always felt, wasn't there. Another strange event was when I stopped drinking alcohol for a nearly a year. I still seemed to wake up with a hangover on weekends. Now I think that drugs could have caused the dryness in my mouth and foggy feeling in my brain. My sleep patterns were disturbed during my adult life, another symptom of stress. Then there was a most blatant symptom of trauma when I was seventeen. My vision deteriorated from reading street signs clearly as I drove my car, to only seeing a frustrating blur within three days. My optician recently told me that was not a normal genetic deterioration, based on my age and how quickly it happened. Something else must have occurred.

This happened in my first year at University. I thought I was going blind and wondered what was happening to my healthy body. Glasses worked well enough, but why my eyesight failed so rapidly had always vexed me.

At the time they occurred, these little signs seemed to come out of nowhere and appeared unrelated. Only with the wisdom of hindsight could I place their significance and meaning. My compartmentalized personality functioned perfectly, hiding critical details as it had been drilled and programmed to. Only a deep longing to resolve my inner confusion was I able to crack some of the amnesic barriers put in place. Through these cracks, memories slowly started to filter through.

The four members of our family looked on in bewilderment as the horror of our lives spilled out during these healing workshop sessions. We were the watchers and also the participants. Suddenly abuse dominated our conversations together. Anything in our lives we couldn't explain was blamed on ritual abuse. It became the scapegoat for our fears, irresponsible behavior, food dislikes and poor relationships. We all disliked chocolate cake. Had that cake flavor really been used for the five-year-old birthday ceremony? Why were Melissa and Rebecca's birthday cake memories different? We were in the grip of paranoia 24 hours a day, seemingly every day of our lives once we discovered the terror of being involved in ritual abuse.

How did we come to uncover our involvement in this power-based cult of heinous cruelty?

Our family was in a period of transition, with our children growing and Michael accepting work in Asia, followed by time in America as we did healing workshops. This relocation from our home in Australia was a vital factor in the gruesome discovery. By living overseas we didn't have consistent contact with our parents and siblings. Even our phone calls were brief and not as regular as we planned and no one had time to write letters. This way, spoken and written words we'd all been programmed to respond to, weren't heard or seen so often. We were without key words hidden in everyday Australian life that would automatically trigger and reprogram us. Australian television and radio programs were no longer available for our continual brainwashing with the common phrases selected by our mind controlled cult leaders. Our amnesic barriers began to weaken.

Also, at this point in my life, I was searching for ways to improve our family bond. Because my daughters were in their mid-teens and I was less involved in their daily care, I had more time to notice the dysfunction we were enmeshed in. I wanted to build a stronger connection between all of us before the girls left home to forge their own lives. The chaos in our family forced us to look at our behavior, fear, lack of confidence and flagging relationships.

I guess I could say my tumbling into discovery of ritual abuse in my family's life, was also part of my own mid-life crisis. It was a time of life to reflect, and I regretted much of what I saw. Once I made a decision to start working on my self and seeking help, I began a most intense journey of self-discovery. It was the first time I forbade any barriers to stop me from moving through the layers of my confusion.

I participated in a five-day healing group with a woman visiting Australia, Dr Verna Yater, who seemed to be an outstanding facilitator. She encouraged her clients to take a long hard look at many areas in their lives. Body posture, reactions, habits, likes and dislikes were all questioned. During my first workshop with her, I had a dramatic breakthrough within a few days of the group, the overwhelming recollection of childhood rape. Once I'd acknowledge that, I felt there were many more levels I needed to perceive and heal. Dr Yater offered a series of seven-day workshops run over a year in the United States of America. The process of unraveling my story began with a commitment to do this Year Long Personal Transformation Training program with her.

Although I was horrified and frightened by the abuse I uncovered in the first workshop, I was excited at the same time, for I felt like a miner as he discovered the first flecks of gold. It was an important find, which helped explain some of my behaviors, attitudes and suspicions. Through my discovery I felt the promise of a glimmering treasure that I hoped would grant me access to my soul. This very thought was the motivator that enabled me to dig even deeper to reveal the true prize. More than anything else I wanted to uncover the essence that was *me*. I believed that eventually all would be revealed and at that very moment, I would know the true meaning of my life.

My search became unrelenting. I didn't stop to consider there could be unpleasant consequences and certainly had no notion of how much agony went with the commitment to find my inner core.

The most amazing part of this pilgrimage was that my family came with me. Maybe their conscious minds, like mine, fantasized about a wonderful outcome resulting in the fabled 'happily ever after'. Whatever the reason, something within our collective subconscious knew we had to delve deep to heal ourselves. We couldn't afford to contemplate an alternative.

I looked over my life to remember and understand how clues of unhappiness, turmoil, perplexity and loneliness might validate the hidden memories I was discovering. Slowly I came to recognize that immense rage, anger and fear were so familiar to me that I couldn't see them. These emotions were by my side constantly, affecting every life decision I ever made.

Yet the story of my search for the meaning of life had begun more than thirty years earlier, after I finished high school. Back then I set out on a journey to find enlightenment, for I believed this was the goal I needed to ease my inner confusion and anxiety.

My soul searching began with yoga and meditation when I was seventeen. In those early days during the sixties, I was a 'square', too embarrassed to wear make-up or anything 'in'. I hated the popular geometric cut dresses and wouldn't wear stockings. I felt immature and gawky. My mother made most of my clothes or occasionally brought things home for me to try on. Shopping was too much of an embarrassing ordeal for me.

My experience of feeling self-conscious and deep insecurity destroyed any possibility of my full participation in life and any human interaction, particularly with anyone older than I was, made me feel flustered and immature.

I totally avoided my teenage life experience. Like an outcast I hid away from society. I was unaware of popular songs at the time, didn't follow any trends or feel comfortable with my peers. In my world of reality, I was waiting for my life to pass. I wanted to get life 'done' with so I didn't have to endure my feelings anymore. Yet at times I remember clinging to hope out of desperation. Surely there would be some good times- somewhere- along the way? I did have friendships yet I felt alone, even within the family unit. Suicide was something I thought about regularly as a teenager, along with the fantasy to murder my parents.

I don't have many exciting memories of pre-teen years, simply selections of school and extra-curricular activities. Some of my best times were with Girl Guides, at the weekly meetings and annual camping holidays. I learned music, enjoyed riding my bike, Sunday school and swimming during summer. I loved the time with our dog when she accidentally produced puppies. Each grade of primary school, the teachers and some companions hold their different recollections. I do have memories.

For some reason my sixth grade class seems significant. I was ten going on eleven and in this class we regularly used little plastic templates of Australia. We were learning about our country and our task was to draw her outline so we could fill it with the names of rivers and capital cities. I was fascinated at how some girls did it beautifully with curly blue swirls to outline the blue sea lapping around our island's coastline. We were so proud of our island continent

It was a pity the plastic stencil makers hadn't worked out a foolproof way to attach Tasmania. I wondered if any one else realized how distorted the shapes were when the little island state south of the East Coast snapped off. I created a fantasy that my imperfectly stenciled outline was the most precise map in the whole class of sixty children. Even as an adult I continued to fantasize about the world and how I fitted in. It made life far more interesting than the flat, seemingly two-dimensional outline of a life I was leading, with its missing piece.

Australian education of the 1950's and 1960's was a very authoritarian system. The cane was used in my primary school to discipline the boys. Some teachers were uninhibited about throwing chalk or dusters at their charges or even cracking knuckles with rulers. Some of this commanding anger was at times targeted at me. Spending time outside the classroom was another punishment designed to shame and humiliate. It worked. I tried to be a very compliant and obedient child.

By the time I was in high school my self-consciousness had devoured me. I couldn't look anyone in the eyes, and always felt ashamed and continually blushed. I even overheard a teacher comment, "If you even look at Christina sideways, she'll blush." I acted stupidly, unable to express my deep inner feelings. Well, I didn't know what my inner feelings were so how could I have communicated them to others? My strong fear of being judged and criticized grew. Although I mixed adequately at school with my contemporaries, during weekends and holidays I seldom socialized. I tried to remain in the background, unseen. Slowly I began to question why was I like this.

It is only recently that I became aware of some programming I received in those early days.

No one likes you.

You're not good enough.

Don't ever tell.

Keep this a secret.

You are evil.

You are a child of satan.

These were some of the messages repeated by my tormentors to enter my subconscious mind. A lifetime of variations on this theme ensured the delivery of continuous negative endorsements to prevent the reality of the abuse to permeate through to my conscious mind. The rare words of encouragement from the same tormentors maintained my dependency on them.

Throughout my twenties I tried self-help books, including Dale Carnegie's, *How to win friends and influence people*, and more Yoga. I was searching frantically but didn't know why or what for. I found my career difficult and already felt incompetent and a failure. It has taken another twenty years to understand that what I was searching for were the parts of my soul that had been fragmented. I sought wholeness. Somewhere it existed and I was anxious and desperately searching for a cure for my aching inner feelings.

In my early thirties I attended a free six-week workshop, a state funded women's only group. It met for a few hours once a week. Even childcare was provided, which gave me freedom to attend without having to explain anything to babysitting grandparents. This mental health group stirred me so much I could no longer suppress my continual anxiety. My inner doors opened, releasing emotional pain. Soon I became frantic with the dark murkiness I found oozing through my being and thought I'd be unable to cope without support from this group. Near the final class, the group facilitator called me aside after our session.

"Christina, I'd suggest you seek more professional help. If you'd like, I can show you a list of therapists."

At this time I was only just surviving. It was a relief to have someone finally see my desperation and provide the support to help me contact a psychologist. Only then did I recognize I was depressed. This descriptive label reassured me somewhat, because then I knew I wasn't abnormal and that all I felt could actually be diagnosed and I'd 'get over it' soon.

That was over twenty years ago. I chose a psychologist from a list of ten the facilitator presented. I wanted a female therapist and was interested in what was termed alternative religions. The selection included someone associated with the 'Orange People'. The nickname Orange People came from the color of their clothes- variations of orange and red. Something about this organization had already appealed to me when I saw groups of orange clad people in city streets near restaurants they ran. Six months before I had seen a BBC documentary on this new age group in London on television. The scenes had shown a mass of people in a huge and beautiful theatre. They sat, swayed and hummed together, dressed in muted red and orange colors chanting Aum. It was one of the most wonderful sounds I had ever heard.

The vibrations of the blended humming filled me with something exquisitely beautiful, I felt myself expand inside as I breathed in the sensational sound and color.

"I want to be part of that; I want to be right in that sound and energy," I had said to Michael as we sat together watching TV.

Now the opportunity to indulge my curiosity presented itself. I made an appointment with a psychologist who was a member of the commune.

I learned from her, that the Orange People had an Indian guru, Bhagwan Shree Rajneesh. He lived on a large commune in Oregon, USA. Bhagwan, who later changed his name to Osho, called his followers *sannyasins*, a Sanskrit word meaning devotee on the path of self-understanding. Many Rajneesh communes existed around the world, including one near Sydney where I went for counseling.

"You seem to be quite different from my average client," the therapist said after a few sessions. I wondered why, but was too self conscious to ask.

"Most people talk a lot about what is going on in their lives and cry from their sadness," she said. "You don't express much about yourself. Although you seem to get enough from the exercises we do, I think it would be better for you to do some group work and meditation. That will be of greater benefit to you than individual sessions with me."

The commune had meditation available every morning for anyone to join in and regularly had different workshops.

My first group was exclusively female and I will never forget how fearful I felt when we were told to say hello to each other with our feet. That seems incidental now, however back then, touch horrified me. I especially disliked physical contact with my feet. My small children often clambered to have me walk while they balanced on my feet and held my hands. They loved it, and I hated it. I felt my privacy was invaded by bodily contact. I had no idea of boundaries. Instead of saying 'no' politely, I'd become hysterical, particularly if there was sudden unexpected touch.

The foot greeting in the small group fortunately didn't last long. Quickly we moved into movement, drawing and samples of meditations.

My first experience of Dynamic Meditation was mind blowing. This meditation was created to let the western mind release its craziness and allow a space where a state of peace could be reached. I followed the process of chaotic breathing, grounding energies with the Sufi mantra of 'Hoo' and meditation, where I watched in my mind's eye, a volcano consume my thought forms. I had no idea what was happening but was fascinate by this internal picture. I felt lighter in my body and somewhere in my head I heard the words, *I AM*.

This vision showed me there was more to life than my aching three dimensional world. Along with the occasional words of encouragement I received in my head, meditation kept my sanity for I was becoming suicidal as the quagmire was stirred within.

Trust yourself above all else, even if you think the voice of God comes through others, was the most powerful message I received from Spirit during my early thirties. However, I was in such turmoil myself that I didn't know what my own thoughts or desires were. My mind echoed a lifetime of everything I heard. I was full of other people's cliches and opinions. I had no idea who I was or what I wanted. I clung to those words, *I AM*, like a life-buoy, because it was the only thing I knew about myself.

All I knew was that I existed.

Michael joined me and participated in further meditation and workshops. I felt lucky to have a partner who wanted to share these experiences with me. In many workshops over the next few years we watched together as abused people released their grief and anger. I was grateful I hadn't experienced that kind of life. It was obvious that as much as the adult's, abused child within, still hated his drunkard and cruel, thoughtless parents, there was always the other side. The inner child also still deeply loved his mother and father. Both feelings remained locked inside the adult body.

I had a caring mother and hard-working father. They were upstanding citizens and worked hard to create a responsible and good future for their children. I hadn't been abused and had no reason for my confusion and inadequacies. So I participated in regular meditation and awareness classes, waiting patiently for the healing of my inner turmoil.

Michael and I continued personal growth work in the 1990's with business training courses. *Money and You* run by Robert Kiyosaki was the first motivational four-day seminar I attended. It was riveting. Although it was essentially considered a business presentation, huge emphasis was on personal awareness. The last morning of this seminar was designed to encourage women to come into their own power, by raising sexual and emotional abuse issues. There was always one person courageous enough to talk about her own suffering and how she overcame her pain. This would provoke other females to express their childhood physical and emotional trauma. Often they were acknowledging this pain for the first time. Every participant admired the courage of these women who accepted, healed and moved into their power and leadership roles.

Not once, in all the workshops I attended over twelve years, did I suspect my own secret. Never did the energy of any abused male or female trigger my remembrances. I was lucky, there had been no sexual or physical abuse in my childhood! My parents were good to me. I thought all I needed was just some help to be a little less dysfunctional.

Certainly, I was aware of my brother being rough toward me as a child, but I assumed that was normal. So too, the sense of something sexual between us. Brothers often physically hurt their smaller siblings, especially when they are seven years older and so much bigger. I also chose to forget those funny sensations in my mouth during meditation that came with a visual image of a penis. It would make me dry retch and cough, so I eventually gave up meditation. That solved those feelings from recurring and also saved me from searching further into my true self.

I didn't know then the body never lies and stores unresolved trauma.

I was unaware that any images and thoughts we have needed to be looked at to help clear our consciousness. Likewise I had no idea that messages from our sub-conscious needed healing, and by not healing we continued to hold pain in our body.

We sent Melissa who was then fifteen, to the *Money and You* seminar. Several families gave their teenagers this chance to learn about the keys of integrity and teamwork the course promoted. Melissa seemed to gain a lot from the opportunity and wanted to do more. A few months later we arranged for her to participate in *Powerful Presentations* another three-day course with Robert Kiyosaki, focusing on speaking skills. After the second long day, Melissa came home at three a.m.

"Mum, I think I may have been sexually abused," she said.

I rolled out of bed and slowly moved closer to the doorway where Melissa stood.

"What makes you think that?" I queried, only half awake.

"We had to give two minute speeches on topics like balls, erection, screw and rocks. All had sexual meanings. I couldn't hold myself upright when I was giving my talk. I gagged on the words and could hardly breathe."

"What word did you have to use in your talk?" I asked not aware at that stage that the body never lies and certain words can trigger memories.

"Every word chosen for the speeches had a sexual connotation, Mum. The facilitators chose the words specifically to stir up people's emotions." She was irritated by my lack of understanding.

I still didn't comprehend the significance. Nor did I understand why she wouldn't tell me which word she stumbled over.

"Well, what are we meant to do about it? Did they suggest anything to you? Maybe someone will help you tomorrow?"

That sounded the best idea to me. Someone else would know better than me how to help Melissa. I still thought everyone else knew more than me and always looked outside myself and family for guidance. I would give authority to anyone who wanted to take it.

Melissa laughed, "Mum, I'm perfectly happy being in a dysfunctional family."

She released me from responsibility and so I did nothing. I didn't want to know what happened, who she thought the perpetrator was, or how old she had been at the time, as any mature mother would. She said she couldn't remember, so I didn't probe. I felt guilty and incompetent. Somehow it must have been my fault and I didn't want to be exposed. It was much easier to forget about her dilemma and remain ignorant. I didn't even know I should have just sat with Melissa and given her time to talk – or not talk, which was more like her.

Michael remained in bed, possibly asleep. We didn't discuss Melissa's problem together. It was somehow easier to pretend it didn't exist. However, I believed Melissa. Totally. I knew she wouldn't fabricate such a statement.

How strange it seems now, not to have acted on a daughter's confessions of molestation. She had such a trust in me and I didn't uphold that trust by helping or guiding her.

I spoke with a friend the next morning. He was attending the course with Melissa. I hoped he might enlighten me.

"Melissa said she was affected by the words chosen for the two-minute talks. She thinks she was molested as a child. Did anyone else react like that, or just her?"

"It seems valid to me that Melissa was abused. Her body reacted so strongly to the words that I thought she would collapse," he said.

"Oh," was all I could respond.

It seemed best to finish the discussion without digging any further. I didn't know what to do and he didn't offer any suggestions or seem judgmental. I presumed it wasn't really very important.

I didn't understand about triggering then. I think I hoped that if we denied the occurrence it would disappear. As it turned out, I was wrong, the body does not forget.

I hoped the course facilitators would suggest something that day, but they didn't. I was frustrated with myself for not going with Melissa to ask for their suggestions. I still had my own fears of authority and was too scared to ask for help. The facilitators seemed unapproachable to me so I didn't follow it up. I didn't know where to go. My therapist of nine years before had left the state and I mistrusted everyone else.

I don't know what I thought I was upholding by glossing over Melissa's memory. She didn't feel it was a dilemma, and didn't insist on finding out more. After a few days, I let it slide. Was this the cult programming kicking in, or was it my own inadequacy?

However, one of life's most important rules is, if we don't learn or respond to a lesson the first time it presents itself, it continues to re-appear until we take responsible action. The way the lesson manifests becomes more and more aggressive the longer we ignore it. Consequences worsen with denial.

Three more years passed before I was ready to face up to truth with action. I went to a clairvoyant for a reading and she honed in on my confusion.

"You had better do something about your marriage, or it could collapse. One of your daughters is in distress and may try to kill herself."

Two days later, a doctor friend of the family, who worked with young athletes in Melissa's age, warned me that her behavior indicated depression and possible suicide. Death was the reality that eventually penetrated my mind and spurred me into action. It was something I could comprehend. Although I didn't know where the starting point was, I was determined to get onto the right path.

*"If you don't take charge of your life,
your life will take charge of you."*

Chapter three

My relationship of twenty-two years with Michael was floundering. We were away from home, living in South East Asia. Both girls were in Australia, with Melissa at university and Rebecca at school. Michael and I were visiting them for a month. Things were not going well for any of us.

With hindsight it is easy to see how I tried to patch and hold our marriage together. Michael had already detached himself and sailed his own emotional boat, solo. He would return to port briefly for comforts and supplies. He didn't know what else to do with his baggage of wife and children.

I couldn't discuss what was wrong with me because I didn't know myself. I was oblivious as to how my fear stopped any confrontation with him and had no notion of how to recreate a healthy relationship. All I knew was that I felt alone and totally unsupported.

When Michael and I returned to Australia for our month holiday at the beginning of the school year, both girls were in turmoil. We'd been in Singapore for eighteen months and the part of our family left in Australia needed dramatic attention.

Rebecca urgently needed accommodation for the year. Her prior living arrangement with my sister's family couldn't continue. This was the first problem to confront us when we arrived. My sister had decided it was better to wait to tell us in person rather than suggesting I came earlier to help Rebecca settle into a different environment. After some discussions and several phone calls, a boarding school became an option. Two weeks into first term, Rebecca relocated to a new school, needing different books and another uniform. Except for the delay and distance from any family members, Rebecca felt that the boarding school was a satisfactory environment for her, although she was disappointed she missed out on the bonding and friendships that developed within the first few days in the boarding house.

Simultaneously Melissa needed support. Her behavior puzzled me. She seemed to refuse to do anything to help herself. I thought many things she did seemed inappropriate for her age. The Saturday I returned from Asia, the girls and I walked about six blocks to the shops. As we sauntered home, Melissa collapsed on the road and would not move.

"I'm exhausted. Please don't make me go any further," she pleaded.

"Get off the road Melissa. At least sit on the curbing," I said.

I couldn't understand how an eighteen-year-old would not feel self-conscious about sitting on the road. From what I observed, although we were on a back street with no traffic, she didn't seem to care enough about herself to consider any possible danger. By the look of her she was worn out and was responding immediately to her body's needs. But why did she have to make such a fuss?

It took some effort to talk with Melissa. However Rebecca and I eventually managed to coax her home. We chatted about her exhaustion and inability to cope with overwhelming emotions and for the first time I probably began to understand how she felt.

I returned to the shopping center to buy vitamins, iron tablets and energizing compounds from a health food shop. I didn't know how else to help her. She had already been subjected to a number of blood tests and diagnosed with anemia. It seemed useless to go to another doctor for the same tests and similar conclusion. The exhaustion seemed to require something beyond the capability of medical diagnosis, though I didn't know what exactly. Personally, I was relieved when Melissa returned to live in the student village, for then I wasn't confronted on a daily basis with her behavioral symptoms.

Michael dismissed my concerns and thought I worried unnecessarily, which was his usual way. He didn't contribute to the resolution of Melissa's dilemma. There was no easy solution and I had no notion of where to start. Michael didn't believe our daughters had problems they couldn't cope with themselves. He was unable to express any compassion toward us. I was torn between wanting to live in Singapore with Michael and staying in Australia to help Melissa and Rebecca. They still needed their parents around yet Michael treated my anxiety lightly.

"There is nothing wrong. The kids will turn out alright," he said. "We've provided them with accommodation and living expenses. You can visit them when you want."

Michael was indifferent about their need for psychological support. His mind set considered his contract work in Asia more important than family. I didn't understand at the time that the girls' anguish reflected our family dynamics. I bowed to Michael's beliefs and started to search for a solution. I extended my stay in Sydney for another month and Michael rushed back to his overseas job, assuring me that everything was fine and would turn out okay.

Fearful of the clairvoyant's prediction of my marriage failure and my daughter's possible suicide I decided to have marriage guidance counseling. To change myself was the only way I knew how to help my family.

One session was enough to make me realize it would take another lifetime to rectify the course I was on. A weekly session with a nice counselor listening simply wasn't the way for rapid change. I was in major predicament, overwhelmed and lost. I needed dynamic counseling to expose negative patterns that were lodged in my body. My soul cried out to expose hidden wounds.

Desperation consumed me. I was self-conscious about my inability to cope so I didn't discuss how I felt with other family members. Already my mother had commented about Melissa's inappropriate behavior and how she always seemed tired.

"Don't you think there could be something wrong with Melissa? All she seems to want to do is sleep," Mum informed me. " She didn't clean up after herself or help in the house when she stayed here. She's young and healthy and should look after herself."

I didn't want to discuss my own confusion with Mum because I thought she judged me. She scorned my spiritual beliefs. Although she acknowledged the possibility of Spirit and even saw my father after his death, she did not approve of my meditation and various groups.

Although I craved to understand the patterns of my personality that needed healing and release, I was embarrassed about my apparent failure of being the perfect wife and mother. I was frantic and slept fitfully. There had to be a fast track for change. I even prayed for help.

I spoke with an old friend, Shanti, who pointed to an advertisement in the local alternative paper for Dr Verna Yater, an American trance channel and Spiritual healer visiting Australia.

Shanti was a special education teacher and our friendship began sixteen years ago during our first meditation weekend together. Since then we had shared our spiritual awakening over coffee, meals and wine.

"When was the trance channeling with Indira we had together?" Shanti asked.

Indira was the East Indian entity that Verna channeled.

"Would you believe it was ten years ago?" I said. " I recently listened to the tape in Singapore and the date was on it. I cringed when I heard the questions I asked Indira. They are the same questions I am still asking. I don't seem to have learned much since then."

The experience of channeling had delighted us with wonderful energy and accurate reading. Indira gave us insightful information about our families. She referred to them as though they were beloved friends she knew well. Her answers to our questions astounded us as she described personality habits accurately, along with ways we could improve relationships. Indira had treated us with respect and left us pondering.

"That reading was fun. Really loving. There was so much energy around," I said.

The energy of Spirit had surrounded us strongly during the session. On our way home we stopped by the river for an hour to sit by some trees. We needed to absorb the feelings still with us and integrate the whole concept of channeling. That had been a special moment in my life.

"Why don't you call the phone number on the ad and find out where the introductory evening will be. You might even want to do the workshop," Shanti suggested.

Spirit pushes when we are ready. I was desperate for change.

Although marriage counseling didn't seem adequate enough to halt my family chaos, at least it was a step. I was ready to move forward now. The advertisement promoted an evening of channeling and a five-day workshop. I looked closely at the paper. Maybe this was the opportunity to reverse my family confusion. My holiday in Australia, already extended, gave me time to participate.

Shanti and I went to the channeling. The evening was pleasant and the few hours went quickly. I enjoyed talking with different people after the experience equally with the actual meeting itself. We met several women who had been to America for workshops with Dr Yater. I was impressed with two sisters we chatted with, Laura and Shelley. However I wasn't devoured with passion to attend the upcoming workshop.

"You'll know if this group is what you need. Ask yourself and trust the answer," Shelley advised me.

I asked myself and decided not to attend.

Until later in the night, that was. I awoke and was unable to fall back to sleep. Energy and sparkling light moved through and over my body for what seemed like hours. I wasn't afraid and lay fascinated, enjoying the feeling of aliveness. Something amazing was happening to me. I hated using the word Spirit, however something from the invisible was definitely working on me. Magic. Maybe something had followed me home as a signal to do the workshop? Definitely the change occurring was initiated during the channeling evening.

Next morning I called the function organizers and told them of my intriguing, sleepless night.

When the pupil is ready the teacher arrives.

Chapter four

Dr Yater's method of working with a group was different from any other I'd experienced. She didn't lecture rows of people behind desks like the *Money and You* motivational business course. Nor did she focus on one person then create exercises around issues raised from their experience, as I had encountered with Sannyasin groups. Instead she encouraged people to talk and experience the impact their language had on their emotions. She listened closely to their dialogue and helped them extract the deeper meaning of their words. Then she'd bring in healing energy to remove the patterns that had been expressed and heal the exposed wounds, layer by layer.

The workshop opened with a prayer of gratitude and intent, laying the foundation for the group focus. We stood in a circle, held hands and together chanted Aum. The harmonious sound we created both centered and unified the group's energy.

The chant hadn't even stopped vibrating in our circle when a participant screamed. The sound jarred me from my meditative state.

"Stay in your body," I heard someone command.

I was totally confused and looked around to see what was happening, then noticed a few people close to a blonde, curly haired woman. Her body looked rigid, as though she was unable to move. I couldn't see her face and had no notion of what was happening. I wondered if she was seeking attention.

"I'll hold your feet on the ground," another person said.

Two people beside the woman helped her move into a chair. They remained close to her.

"Let it go. You don't have to hold it in anymore."

What was she holding in? What did she have to let out? I had no idea what was meant. I had done many workshops and never witnessed anything like this. Gradually other people sat in their chairs, so I took it as a cue to follow.

"What's happening, Rhonda?"

I hadn't noticed the facilitator move close to the activity on the far side of the circle.

"They are telling me they'll get my family if I don't do what they want."

I watched Rhonda's arm contort and spasm.

"My elbow hurts," she said.

For me, it was odd watching others who had done groups before help another participant come back into her body. I presumed some of these people knew each other. They seemed to be familiar with the process and confidant supporting Rhonda. I felt shocked and nervous watching, almost displaced, as though I didn't belong. Verna stood unperturbed by the chaos. It seemed nothing unusual as she talked Rhonda through the experience. This occurrence was apparently quite ordinary. Verna appeared to be in total control.

I was on the opposite side of the room from the activity. Often the words Rhonda said were whispered so I couldn't hear everything. From snippets, I pieced together a scenario of abuse. It must have been past life with the sort of terror described. It couldn't be a new memory if it was this lifetime. No one could forget the torture I thought I heard Rhonda mention: of men in dark capes holding a knife to her throat as they threatened to kill a sibling if she didn't comply with their wishes.

The facilitator worked with Rhonda, asking questions beyond her immediate recollection to help free more memory. Laura, whom I'd met at the channeling evening, held Rhonda's feet gently on the ground. The process looked agonizing for Rhonda, yet the memory spoke of painful torture and sexual abuse, which was just as distressing.

"What's happening?" I whispered to the person next to me.

"She's remembering something that happened when she was seven."

This was incomprehensible. I watched Rhonda's body react to the terror of her recollection. She moved as though the abuse was happening right now. She shook, sobbed and looked terrified. Was this really the first time she'd recalled such trauma?

"Are you sure it's not another lifetime?" I questioned my neighbor.

"No. It's definitely this lifetime."

Verna kneeled directly in front of Rhonda.

"Look into my eyes," she said.

A change occurred in Rhonda as she responded to Verna's request. Her shaking stopped and she gradually calmed down. Laura held her hand and Verna returned to her seat in the circle.

This was my first experience of watching an adult recalling repressed childhood abuse. I found it difficult to believe someone would, or could, block brutal memories from themselves for nearly forty years

Now this episode of Rhonda's was finished, someone else in the group began to talk about his life, what was going on now and things that had happened in the past. This set the group process off with a life of its own, triggering other participants as it went. Nothing seemed structured or planned. The group brought its own dynamics and problems. It seemed as though there were individual sessions occurring within the group. However, everyone was affected.

So much anger was expressed in this workshop. I was overwhelmed by the chaos as several different people yelled simultaneously, releasing their emotions by hitting pillows and beating plastic bats on the floor. They all talked at once and I became quite nervous watching. The whole group appeared disorderly. I had had enough of anger and didn't particularly want to watch others going through the same things I'd seen more than ten years ago in other workshops. This environment wasn't what I wanted and I didn't want to be there. At the first break I approached Dr Yater.

"I don't want to stay here," I said. "Is it possible to receive most of my money back if I leave, please?"

"What is it that you want from the five days?" Dr Yater asked.

I avoided this question and commented from a totally different angle.

"Well, a friend who is a dowser used her pendulum to tell me I would only get ten percent value from the course."

"What percentage value would you be happy with? Would ninety percent be OK?"

I was surprised she offered so much.

"Well, even seventy percent would do."

That seemed reasonable to me for this kind of work.

"Stay a bit longer to see how things develop for you. You can make up your mind after the next session. If you still want to leave, I will refund your fees."

This was a very strange conversation with Verna because there really was no meaning to what I had negotiated. A breakthrough in self-understanding is priceless. How could I have thought I could put a percentage value on the course?

I was impressed by Dr Yater's total attention to me when I approached her. She needed a break like everyone else, for the work here was intense. However, she had allowed me to vent my fear and desire to run, without expressing judgment. This discussion highlighted another difference from other workshops I'd done. Verna was prepared to talk to participants outside of specific group times.

Later I recognized that my frustration and discomfort within the first few hours of the group was actually resistance to my own internal anger. A lot of my own emotion was bubbling up but I hadn't noticed the stirring. The anger I'd witnessed from others was but a smidgen of what I held inside and needed to release. However, I was totally unaware of the group process as it unfolded and dragged with it my own reluctant anger, frustration and rage. It took me nearly a day to decide to stay in the workshop. Thank God I did.

Another significant difference between Verna's work and previous groups I'd participated in was her invocation of healing energies.

"I ask for complete healing of this space and our vibrations, and the release of any debris. I invoke the presence of the many Masters of Healing. I ask that any and all blockages to full healing be released and taken into the realms of light to be dealt with. We send energy and healing to those who have asked for it. We send healing energy to those who have no one to support them. We align with healing and openness and in readiness we begin."

I sat in prayer with eyes closed, feet on the floor and spine straight. We were in the presence of Spirit, listening to Verna facilitate our healing.

"I ask for the removal of any and all patterns associated with violence."

A shudder went through my body. Then I was surrounded by warmth and safety as golden light was brought in for healing.

Verna continued lifting patterns.

"I ask for the removal of any and all patterns associated with anger."

The words she continued to ask for removal seemed to be patterns that had revealed themselves to the participants through this session. I let the words hum over me, not always knowing what they were, feeling my body's reaction and then the healing energy. I was carried off into bliss and happily sat in that state of peace, calm and eternal safety long after everyone else disappeared for a break.

These participants raised the same issues I had encountered in other workshops years before, sexual abuse, emotional abuse, anger, control and religion. But on this day, something different occurred as memories from other lifetimes began to arise.

As the discussion began, Verna asked, "Does everyone believe in past lives?"

A few people didn't. I had seen too many things during earlier workshops and in meditative visions to disregard other lives. Most groups I'd participated in previously recognized other lifetimes and believed we were still affected by things from former lifetimes.

Trisha, a lean, older woman, added, " I've only done one other workshop. That was the first time I encountered the possibility of other lives." Looking around the circle, she took a deep breath before she continued. "What made me comfortable with this completely new concept, was to imagine that the past lives, which I wasn't certain about then, were symbolic. Because we'd see ourselves in a certain situation, it meant there was something to learn for now. Rather like our dreams being a message from our subconscious. I think whatever we visualize, or feel, is a key to help us, whether we believe in past lives or not."

From childhood I had contemplated that I lived before. Maybe it was easy for me to remember other life times.

Shanti my friend who I did many workshops with, once commented, "I used to be surprised when you told me about your past lives and spiritual experiences. I was jealous and wished they would happen to me."

Even Indira, in my first channeling experience said, "In the next ten to fifteen years, you'll remember hundreds...no, *thousands* of past lives."

I had asked her for confirmation of some I'd recalled. Rather than answer my question, she responded, "Why don't you believe yourself?"

To start with, I was unsure about the memories really being from other lifetimes, for it wasn't as though I remembered every detail. Mostly I sensed feelings or saw visual snippets, which gave me clues. As a teenager I read everything I could find about prisoner and refugee escapes during World War II and was fearful that I couldn't speak German because I thought they'd 'get me' again. I was also the only person in my class who drew swastikas over the front pages of my school books.

I managed to piece together memories while I traveled through Poland on a camping trip in my early twenties. The beautiful countryside made me excited to be there. Warsaw was familiar: the streets, sights and smells I had experienced before. Instinctively I found my way around the city with very little reference to my map. I found it easy being with the Polish people. Bartering for goods was effortless and came naturally. I became convinced this place had been important for me during a recent lifetime as I felt at home and part of the crowd.

During meditation I had caught glimpses of a relationship with my brother during our World War II lifetime together. I recalled him as a Nazi officer, with peaked cap, smart uniform and shiny boots. A confident, handsome and authoritarian man. These images came to me like a movie picture of incomplete scenes: a street corner seen from the second floor of a building; a dirty hotel room with peeling wallpaper and scenes of the countryside. I often felt intense emotion with these memories. They helped me understand my present-life relationship with my sibling, and my issues with patterns of male domination and authority. The past life in Poland and involvement with Nazis seemed to be fragments of the same lifetime ending during World War II.

Another vision of a past life I shared with Michael during meditation together. It was eerie when we could relate matching images and scenes as servants in an European Manor.

Years earlier I had seen previous connections with Melissa as I recognized we had shared many lives together. I believed I even knew her as a friend in this life who died unexpectedly and returned as my daughter.

Reincarnation and past lives were not unaccepted in my life. My youngest sister, as a preschooler, surprised mum by announcing, "When I was bare air I chose you to be my mummy."

Naturally I assumed I was prepared to look at previous connections with other people. I soon discovered it wasn't easy looking at negative aspects of the past, particularly when I was not always an innocent party. I was brought back to the room by Verna's voice.

"Those of you who are not sure if you believe in past lives, just be open to the possibility it could be true. I always include healing for the past. If you allow this without judgment more healing will occur on all levels." Verna looked at everyone in the room, "Is everyone OK with this? Does anything else need to be said before we continue?"

No one seemed to have any objections and I was ready.

A group scenario had already begun. The time frame was World War II as Russell, a handsome, twenty-three year old, started to remember.

"I'm a Nazi officer. I'm important, in charge of the prison camp. I have a lot of responsibility and run this camp well."

He searched his own consciousness and re-experienced the pride of wearing the Nazi Uniform, the fine quality and the power it emanated. He became the former Nazi.

Trisha, on the other side of the room from Russell began.

"This is strange, I'm an Englishman, in the Air Force. Hmm... interesting. This seems to be World War II and I've parachuted down behind enemy lines. I don't know if I'm in the right place. Something's not right."

As she sat in a semi-meditative state Trisha exploded, "I'm hiding in a barn. I have a code for the resistance radio to hand on to someone."

There was a moment of silence before she continued.

"There is a golden-haired woman. She betrays me."

I sat open-mouthed, listening to these strange monologues.

Simultaneously Russell, remembering himself as the Nazi officer, got to his knees. He grabbed a pillow and started thumping it as he shouted, "They took my cross away. Prisoners escaped from my camp and I lost my cross."

He was raving mad and pounding the pillow with his fists.

"Starve the prisoners," he screamed. "Starve them until we get information on the escape." To lose the coveted cross, a symbol of status and honor was demeaning for a Nazi officer. "Do anything to get the prisoners to talk."

Something drew my attention to Russell's story. He was fearless. The clear recollection of his story astounded me. I was fascinated by his energy and focused totally on him as he experienced the energy of this angry Nazi. I felt a connection with him.

He continued thrashing the pillow.

"The resistance has found a way into the camp. Capture them. They've got a radio."

I was riveted to this handsome officer, captivated by his presence.

What was happening to me? My whole body was shaking. I felt weird. My energy changed as I watched Russell. I trembled in my chair, overpowered by my whole frame vibrating. All I could do was to let this energy move as I rattled inside.

Someone sat next to me.

"Don't stop breathing," he encouraged.

I took a breath. Then everything changed.

I knew him! The shouting from the Nazi I recognized, faded away as I switched into another consciousness. I stood up to let my body shake, oblivious to anyone in the room except the handsome young Nazi officer, until Verna came over.

"What are you doing?"

"I'm shaking out the fear, terror and torture."

The words flew out of my mouth without conscious thought.

"Who is he to you?" Verna asked of Russell, now the Nazi officer.

"I'm his mistress - one of many," I said without thinking.

I have no idea what happened next, for suddenly I was lying on the floor, kicking my legs and shrieking uncontrollably.

"I hate him. I hate him."

No restraints could have inhibited my scream as an image of the Nazi officer raping me blasted into my mind. My physical body distorted, stretching out like a bowstring ready to discharge its arrow of sound. My spirit was on its own schedule. It wasn't going to put up with the suppression of memories from past lifetimes anymore as the cry disengaged from the core of my being.

Who was I? I was a Polish woman raped by her Nazi lover and I was Christina lying on the floor in a workshop. I was both, simultaneously.

I knew some of my past life was as a Polish woman working in the resistance movement in Europe and of a relationship with my brother of this life. Some form of betrayal caused me to be caught, interrogated and tortured by him. However I didn't know how I came to be in Germany, if that was where I was and I didn't know there were other officers in my life. I had been aware of some of this previous life as a child and my recall, visions and recollections accelerated as I moved into meditation during my thirties.

As I lay on the floor I was able to tell my Polish memories to Verna. But the unfolding of this rape was beyond anything I had ever seen or experienced before. I was in a totally different consciousness. Nothing was in my control; my body's movements, thoughts and words that poured out, came of their own accord. I became an onlooker as my subconscious mind took over.

"Do you know anything else about this lifetime?" Verna asked me

"Yes. I had a baby that I lost in a crowd at a railway station. I've met her in this life. She's French now. We had enormous love for each other when we met, even though it took us a while to know our relationship. We couldn't stop laughing and hugging each other before we understood why. Then I saw a golden cord of light pulse between our hearts."

"What happened to your baby at the railway station?" Verna focused on the past life.

"I don't know," I answered.

"Yes, you do. Look and see. You know."

So I looked.

"There are so many people crushed in the crowd. We have no control; there are hordes of people crammed and moving together. My baby slips out of my arms in the bedlam. I can't get to her." I experience the pain of that lifetime as tears swell in my eyes. "She is trampled; her little body broken."

I lay still, feeling again the loss of my baby. I could only whisper my thoughts. "I am glad I met her again. Her name in this life is the same as my older daughter's."

My consciousness moved to this life as my attention jumped to my present day children.

"I was really hard on Melissa when she was little. I would smack her for things which didn't warrant such harsh punishment."

I took a breath as I realized I had just shared so much more than I had ever been comfortable with before. Everything poured out, even though I would have preferred to keep most thoughts to myself. Within the short time of this workshop I had already placed enormous trust in Verna. I recognized her deep respect and genuine care for her participants. I was safe. I lay still, feeling my regret and grief.

The small toe on my left foot hurt as I lay on the floor. A sharp, stabbing pain which demanded my attention, though I tried to ignore it.

"I have a secret."

The sentence popped out of my mouth of its own volition. I had struggled to keep these words to myself, knowing I didn't really want to say them, even though I had no idea what they would be. This may sound somewhat ridiculous, but the words appeared to be stored in my toe. The niggling pain forced the words from an unconscious part of me. I didn't know what was happening and couldn't stop it.

"That's from this life," Verna said.

Really? Was she right? I hadn't understood what these words meant, or where they came from. I thought they were part of the last life scenario I had just spoken about. How did Verna know?

"It is something sexual."

The words rushed out again. I felt ridiculous. I didn't want these words to escape and felt naïve and embarrassed as they formed in my mouth. Where was this information coming from? Why couldn't I control what I said?

I felt so ashamed. What had been sexual in my early childhood? A few investigations with a little girlfriend flashed into my thoughts. I remembered the time we snuck into the boy's toilets after school one afternoon to find out what a urinal was. These thoughts passed quickly as I began to see distinct moving pictures in my mind's eye; a private screening. I watched with my eyes closed.

"I am in the children's hospital. A nurse takes me to the bathroom. I see a row of child size toilets – but there is only the nurse and me. I feel uncomfortable because I think she expects me to go to the toilet without the door being shut. Then she asks if my dolly needs to use the toilet also. That is so stupid - doesn't she know dolls aren't real and don't need toilets? I see myself in a dressing gown - a plaid woollen gown. I am very scared."

I lay still, as I mused over this memory, when more images came.

"Now I see a photograph I remember - me playing with my family in the yard near the back steps to our house. It's a picture of Dad, my brother and me. I am dressed in a nurse outfit - playing cricket. I don't remember the incident – only the photograph."

I didn't know why these pictures came to mind. They seemed so obscure. I didn't understand their relevance,

"What are you seeing?" Verna asked.

The internal movie rolled on and I explained.

"I'm in the backyard where I lived when I was little. I lived in that house till I was six."

"What age are you now?"

"About three."

The answers came without conscious thought. I was on the floor, my eyes shut and I was the only person in the whole world, except for Verna. I was oblivious to everything else as my subconscious took me on a journey

My memories kept playing.

"My God…I'm seeing further down the yard. I'd forgotten about that area. We lived on a huge block of land in the suburbs, surrounded by a vast area of vacant land out the back and rows of houses on quarter-acre blocks along the front. There are Melaleuca hedges dividing the yard. I am way down the yard, beyond the hedge and see the chicken pen across from me. There is a man moving around the side of the chicken pen towards me…"

The scenes playing in my head fascinated me. I had a little control; I could open my eyes, see the white ceiling of the room overhead, then close them and go back to the point where I left the memory.

Oh no, I didn't want to see this part.

"He is undoing his fly on the khaki trousers…He's dropped his trousers…"

"Oh shit!" comes out of my mouth.

I *know* I don't want to see anymore.

"Oh shit!" someone repeated.

The repetition of my words forced me back to the man unbuttoning his fly.

"He's coming towards me."

My body took over as I pushed myself away from this man with my feet.

"Nooo....!"

Another involuntary scream rose from the depths of my being. I couldn't stop it. It just came - my body contorted as my head flailed backward.

I started to spit and my hands moved to my mouth to help clean it out.

" Spit out that semen," Verna said.

My God. Was that what I was doing? Someone had already put a tissue in my hand. I coughed and spat out everything in my mouth. I wanted it gone. How could I cleanse it? I wiped the inside of my mouth with the tissue. I also felt pain around my vagina and gut.

This was the beginning of release of trauma I had completely blocked from my mind for over forty years. I was relieved when it finally ended. The truth shocked me. How had this memory been locked inside my body all these years?

"Is this true?" I whispered. "Was I raped?'

"Yes. Do you know who it was?"

"Yes, he was a workman, employed by my father."

I knew who it was. Well, a name came to mind immediately. But that couldn't be true. That man went off to study the Bible and learned how to teach children about the love of Jesus.

Surely I had been tricked by my own mind.

My little child part, wherever she came from, said, "It is true." My adult, rational self said, "This is nonsense."

Was it possible this had been the cause of my kidney infection around that age? My thoughts were running faster than my voice.

"Do you think this could lead to kidney disease?"

"It's possible," Verna said.

"It took a long time to diagnose your kidney infection," I remember my mother telling me. "Your temperature would fluctuate daily. You'd be sick one day, then the next day you'd be well. We didn't know what was wrong." She had explained that the infection had occurred by a reflux from my bladder into the kidney.

One kidney had been severely damaged because of the slow diagnosis, but there had been no mention of sexual abuse. How could doctors ignore this possibility? I wished I could check my hospital medical records.

These events started to fill in my life picture. The discovery of sexual abuse forty years after the fact is a lot for anyone to deal with. I was furious. How could my father be friendly with such a hypocrite? I remember my parents admiring this man when he sacrificed his job to follow his calling to preach the gospels to children. They helped him. Even I loved the stories of God and Jesus he had told, particularly one about loaves of bread coming in time to feed hungry children who had prayed for food.

I was so angry about my lost innocence, furiously wild at an adult's violation of my being and the horrendous effect it had on the rest of my life.

I recalled my feelings of a few years earlier during meditation when I had felt a penis in my mouth. I *was* sexually abused as a child.

Why would I hide the truth from myself? Why did I ignore the images I received in meditation? Remembering this, I felt such deep shock and rage. I believed that I came from a normal family and had enjoyed a safe and secure upbringing. Somehow the thought lived in my mind that I was living a lie. I had often told friends I was living a lie, but didn't know what the lie was. Now I knew my life *was* a lie, or at least, had lies hidden deep within it.

So many questions were emerging.

Verna brought me back from my own musing.

"Where is your mother now? Go to your mother."

I knew not to ask her for comfort.

"No, she's unhappy. I don't want to bother her." I explained. "Anyway, I was told to keep this secret."

I wasn't stupid. The perpetrator knew where I lived. What's worse, he was there nearly every day. He was enormously bigger than me, a giant, taller than my parents. I knew he could kill or hurt me again, so I was obedient and kept my mouth tightly shut.

His payment had been a packet of chewing gum. The pretty, but tasteless gum in a cellophane packet with four small different colored pellets – orange, pink, yellow and bright green. My mother thought I stole them. Although I claimed that the fairies had given them to me, she didn't believe my explanation and marched me off to the local shop to pay for them. The shopkeeper told Mum she hadn't noticed me come in earlier.

Suddenly, more thoughts emerged as I lay on the floor recovering from my memory. Why is sexual abuse of a child called molestation? Why not just call it rape? Why hide behind that silly word that avoids the reality of an adult's penis going into the vagina, mouth and anus of a child. A non-consenting child without enough words in her vocabulary to describe such atrocities.

I was angry beyond words, furious with this man who had violated my spirit.

What pleasure could someone possibly get from ejaculating into the orifice of a toddler? How pathetic to tell a child, *This is a secret.*

This traumatic memory helped explain some of my adult behavior and feelings. It was likely that this was where my lifetime partnership with fear started.

It slowly dawned on me the impact this event had on my life.

"He took away my power."

I needed to take it back.

With my memories finished, I was exhausted and wanted to sleep on the floor.

"It's time to come back," Verna said to me. "I need to bring in healing for everything that went on before we go on break. You can lie here till you're ready to move."

For the rest of the day, I sat on my chair, disorientated, in shock. I was vague, totally immersed in my own thoughts and unaware of much happening around me.

When I went to bed that night my room-mate told me, "Your memories took several hours. Did you know you were on the floor for that length of time?"

"Was it really that long? I had absolutely no idea."

It hadn't seemed like hours to me. I had been totally centered on the images playing through my mind. Time hadn't even been a factor and I was immensely grateful for the focused attention I'd received from Verna. It gave me the opportunity to remember and release trauma. The right triggers had been there for me from the group. If the Nazi era energy hadn't come out of that handsome young man, I wouldn't have recognized him as a past life lover. He had allowed my memories to snowball. Releasing the rape energy from my past life helped shake out the memory of the childhood rape in this life.

"The body never lies," Verna continually told us through the week.

"Memory is stored forever as tension, stiffness, pain or illness until healing is brought in to release it. Trauma of the memory is removed only by healing."

It was time for healing my patterns of rape, both this life and past life.

I now grasped an understanding of Rhonda's experience of recovered memories she had on the first day of this workshop.

More unfolded several days after the surfacing of these memories when I returned home to Singapore. Sitting at the dining table in my Asian home, I wondered how to continue healing my injured three-year-old self when out of the blue, two little girls appeared. I saw them like little ghosts, in front of me. I had never experienced anything like this before and was amazed.

One of the girls was totally naked and crouched under the stairway. She was a 'spirit-child', her body covered with shining, silver-gold colored skin and a not quite human demeanor. I had never heard of a spirit-child before, but that name popped into my head as I observed her.

The other little girl I recognized as me: the three-year-old in a dressing gown at hospital. She stood apprehensive, in the middle of the room, paralyzed by fear and unable to talk.

The spirit child spoke to me.

"Heal me first," she instructed.

Wow, this is different, I thought. Is this what was meant by dialogue with the inner child? I didn't understand what was happening here at all. How could it be possible? She was 'real' and could talk to me, even though she was ethereal.

It was only the Spirit Child who spoke. The other remained silent and frozen. She was petrified and I found I had to hold her and cuddle her in my arms for almost a year before she'd talk to me. She was pleased to be held; I knew, because of her loving response.

The Spirit Child didn't speak again but stayed near. I looked at her and decided to include her in my daily activities. We even listened to music together. I started to sense how this part of myself had more musical and artistic talent and appreciation than the rest of me.

When I went to bed at night she'd come with me. By the next morning she would awaken older. I continued to let the experience unfold and after three days she was an adult. On that last night she came into my body as an integration of energy. Lights and sparks of energy surrounded us as she merged into me.

At first, I wondered, can she leave me? Instantaneously she did. But then she merged again immediately. I was astounded. What an experience this was. Now my Spirit Child had returned to me, I could start working with the other little girl.

The integration and healing of these little-girl parts of me happened after the workshop with Verna.

By the end of the workshop I knew five days of healing was not a final solution to the disintegration of my family. It was better and much faster than weekly marriage guidance counseling. During the workshop I had resurrected and healed core issues that could have taken several years to clear with individual counseling. However, I felt I still needed more clearing, and everyone in my family needed healing.

Verna offered a Year Long Transformational Program in America. That sounded like the answer for me. I imagined how much could be accomplished in weeklong groups once a month. If what I'd just gained from this workshop was any indication, think of the things I could work through in a year. It would also be exciting to live in another country. What an experience it could be.

I was impressed by the wisdom and knowledge that Laura, Shelley and others who had done this course seemed to have. There was a quality about them, a calmness that attracted me. Most of the time I felt frantic inside, reacting quickly to any stimulus whether verbal, physical or emotional. It wasn't pleasant living inside my body, always feeling tense and defensive. I resolved to talk to Michael and find out his response to undertaking such intensive self-search. He would still be able to work between workshops if he chose. I wanted massive change in my life and somehow this program seemed to promise it.

Immediately after the workshop I drove to visit Melissa at college. I was so excited. Together we called on Rebecca. I needed to say goodbye to both of them before I left for Singapore the next day and wanted to offer them the proposition of a year in America. I shared my experiences of the last five days with them and how the people I met who had participated in the year-long program, seemed to be psychic. Rebecca had displayed psychic abilities as a child and was keen to rediscover them. For me, the most important part of my daughters' education was self-understanding. Deeply knowing themselves seemed essential in making possible full, confident lives. I always wanted them to know and understand more about their spiritual selves. With a substantial grounding in accepting who they were, I felt any academic education they had would not be wasted as mine had because of my lack of confidence. This year of healing could be the beginning of a wonderful future for my family.

Although I had now confronted my own abuse, I still hadn't faced Melissa's. It had been three years since she had first mentioned it. Now I was so engulfed in my own memories I didn't delve further into hers, though I knew there were some links. My excitement over the energies in healing past lives, healing present time and finding my own core anxiety, meant I forgot her specific problems. Although I wanted to include everyone in total family healing, I knew it had to start with me. Healing myself would overflow to the rest of the family. Melissa was having counseling at college but she hadn't reached specific incidents, so we still had no idea of what had happened to her.

I was sad to leave my daughters as I returned to Asia, but a possible new path in our lives had presented itself. Both girls were prepared to consider my proposition of a year in America. Now I needed to discuss the Year-Long program with Michael.

The flight to Singapore was reasonable. At the airport, Michael and I easily recognized each other's brown hair amongst the predominantly Chinese heads. I was so glad to see him again and wanted to tell him everything about the five-day course. The drive home was full of my chatter.

"Would you come to America and do a spiritual workshop with me?" I asked.

I'd already talked on the phone about the basics of the course and Michael listened to my rediscovery of core personal issues.

"I want to see if there is more I need to know. Maybe we can help Melissa too." He seemed amenable to the possibility of doing the workshops. We faxed America for more information, with a list of questions asking how we could live there for the duration of the program.

Re-organizing our lives to start in the Year Long program was quite a project. We needed to find accommodation in America, get visas, sell off possessions. Plus we had to organize our daughters and arrange their visits during their summer vacations of December and January, if they didn't want to stay with us for the year. Like everything, there was excitement tempered by fear and trepidation and the enormous logistics of organizing a household in another country. We had five months to prepare.

Things changed though, when Melissa called me three months later from Australia.

"Mum, can you come home?"

I returned to Australia and saw the problems both girls had were not superficial and had not been solved. Particularly Melissa's. She was deeply distraught.

"Mum, the counselor at college told me I need more help than they can provide. Usually they only allow six sessions per student."

"I don't understand. Is the limit to the number of sessions absolutely definite, or can she give you more help if you really need it?"

"Well, she told me that their records indicate that of all the students who have done my course, fifty percent have had counseling and all but one of those was sexually abused. She will keep seeing me but thinks I need several years of help. She can't provide that."

I was surprised about the limit on sessions. Melissa obviously had a great trust in Karen from the University Health Clinic. It seemed best to stay with the same person she felt comfortable with.

"Do you know what happened yet?" I asked.

"I shake a lot and cry when I sit there with her, but I'm not sure what it is."

I didn't know what else to do other than just hope Melissa could keep seeing Karen while at college. Confidence and trust had built between them and both were vital in the therapy process.

My only thought was to try some alternative healing for Melissa. A trusted friend, Lynette who taught me dowsing, had previously recommended a Kinesiologist for me. I'd found this session helpful, so thought it could help Melissa.

"What is Kinesiology?" Melissa asked me.

"It is a form of therapy using the body's own memory. The Kinesiologist tests the strength of a muscle to give a 'yes' or 'no' answer to a question. The muscle is strong when the answer is yes. If the answer is no the muscle is weak and unable to resist pressure."

"I don't know how Melissa managed to do so well at college. Her energy was blocked and out of balance. I truly wonder how she functioned," the Kinesiologist told me after her session.

No wonder Melissa had collapsed on the road and refused to move five months earlier.

I didn't inquire further into Melissa's sexual abuse. I had no idea it could be related to her lack of energy. She hadn't discovered what it was yet, although she wondered if she had Attention Deficit Disorder. Maybe there is cult programming to stop questioning or deeper search. Perhaps it was because I had been so conditioned to keep quiet that I didn't know how to investigate thoroughly. I also felt shame and guilt. What had happened? What was wrong with my family? I didn't dare search deeper for the true reasons because I assumed it must have been something I did. Maybe her memories would come soon.

Melissa enjoyed her Medical Science course and found her subjects interesting. I was relieved to know that and pleased to see she achieved well in her exams. She wanted to continue her degree and enjoyed the practical work. I wondered if it might be better to sort out this other psychological stuff in a few years time when she was working.

Truthfully, I didn't want to know what happened, for I was anxious that my mothering skills would be questioned. Anyway, Melissa was a young adult beginning to detach from her childhood family. She chose what she wanted and we would support her in her decisions.

When I first went to Asia with Michael, a friend advised me, "If you want to hold your marriage together, stay by your husband's side. Your children are important but they will leave home eventually." I thought that made sense. However my life felt pretty out of control with Michael and me living in Singapore and our daughters in Australia. I couldn't deal with everyone's problems in addition to holding us together, and there was so much we didn't know about our life at that time.

Rebecca was fairly happy.

"I've always wanted to try boarding school, Mum," she told me. "I love the companionship and having someone around to talk with."

School holidays were difficult for me however because she chose to stay with her aunts in Australia rather than be with us in Asia. Michael didn't encourage her to visit us because airfares were expensive.

I think Rebecca enjoyed the time with her relations and was able to develop deeper friendships with her cousins. However, it meant that we weren't there to provide the extra help with homework and encouragement that was needed. Plus I was missing out on part of her teenage years.

My family was becoming so fractured that I decided I simply couldn't leave Melissa floundering at college or Rebecca at school in order for me to do the Year Long program in America. Everything around me seemed to be falling into the pits.

It wasn't that the kids were leaving the nest. No, we the parents had dumped our own children. Life was chaotic. This wasn't how I wanted it to be at all. Michael ignored the possibility of problems. His work in Asia was probably the most empowering job he had ever had. As a highly competent and very intelligent professional, he was recognized for his abilities. He also loved teaching younger people and was patient and thorough with them. This earned him huge respect from his Asian colleagues. The Asian way was male dominated and he felt good there.

I spent several weeks at our home in Australia with the girls after Melissa's plea for me to return home, not quite knowing what to do.

"Melissa, if I go for two weeks to the USA and do two short workshops instead of the Year Long program, could you cope?"

She assured me that she would be fine. My thought was for Michael to come with me for some of the time in America. At least part of my life could be brought together better.

"Well, when I return we'll figure out what to do about all this stuff. I'll keep in touch and be back in a few weeks."

I wanted to support my daughters. Cohesiveness of my family was more important than fanciful thoughts of a year of healing. But I couldn't help wondering if Michael would ever leave Asia. He wouldn't discuss this with me when I broached the topic. I didn't think he wanted to return to Australia and I didn't know how to hold us all together if he wouldn't. My life was in chaos and my mind was in its normal state of confusion. How I managed during this time amazes me now.

I thought there could be a possibility for Michael to come with me to do one of the weeklong workshops in America. It would be both a holiday and an opportunity to heal the rift in our marriage. I packed up my Australian house yet again, though for a shorter time. Then I returned again to Singapore and to Michael before leaving for the USA.

There is only this very moment.

Chapter five

Michael agreed to come to the Blue Mountain Center for the August summer workshop. I was delighted he was prepared to sacrifice some time from work to be with me. His job dedication often meant family matters were a low priority. For this reason I suggested he only attend one workshop and didn't even broach the possibility of us being together the whole time. I limited my thinking without considering we could have done both.

Our plan was for Michael to meet me after the first workshop for a few days touring before going for the second workshop together. I had high hopes for healing and fun together. Both were desperately needed in our relationship. Michael was sympathetic to my recently discovered childhood abuse.

"This workshop will help fix you up," he said.

I wondered why he only ever thought there was something wrong with me? He seemed oblivious to strange behavior and lack of friends in his family.

Summer workshops were held on Blue Mountain, south of Colorado Springs. The eighty acres of lightly wooded, mountainous land was 8,000 feet above sea level. The high altitude challenged the body's oxygen carrying capacity. I was warned to prevent possible altitude sickness by taking vitamin E, iron supplements and to drink plenty of water to help prevent headaches and tiredness.

I'd been surprised to find Blue Mountain labeled in our National Geographic map of the Rocky Mountains, as it seemed to be only a small mountain. Maybe it was because this area was sacred to Native Americans. Ley lines starting from the pyramid in Gizeh, Egypt and Machu Picchu in Peru connected here. Cheyenne Mountain, which housed a military base, was close by. I was informed that the military chose their sites carefully, using information such as the energy grids of the earth.

My flight arrived a day before the workshop. Three other Australian women were already in the Springs and we arranged to have dinner. All of them had done various workshops together in Australia and on Blue Mountain, and were old friends. I'd previously met the vivacious Laura, an intuitive healer and Rhonda, a woman in her early forties whose soft smile and fair curly hair gave her an angelic appearance. They'd both participated in Verna's Australian workshop a few months ago. I couldn't forget Rhonda's remembrance of childhood abuse.

They introduced me to Gail, a petite, dark-haired teacher. Her welcoming embrace made me feel as though we'd known each other forever. Having lived in the Springs at different times, the three women knew their way around the abundant restaurants. Eating out here was inexpensive and the food quite different from my previous experience. Mexican food reminded me of my own meals made from left over food, so we stuck with a more conventional American style restaurant. The huge servings were astounding and I discovered the 'doggie bag' concept was real. Unfamiliar taxes and tipping confused me, dramatically changing the cost of the meal. Cultural differences hidden behind similar appearances and common language appeared. Already I'd sensed misunderstanding from my Australian phrases and slang and was amazed at the humorous acceptance from Americans. It seemed anyone with an accent was intriguing.

During our meal, the four of us discussed the intensity of search within self we wanted to conduct to change our old patterns and ways of being.

"Information on earth changes was bantered about in the early 1980's," Laura began. "At first I wanted to become self sufficient and live in the country. It took me some time to realize that it's only our inner changes we can work on."

"I understand what you mean. We actually decided to move away from the city for that very reason," I said as I stirred my coffee. " I spent a lot of time worrying about where to live. It took me quite a while to realize I couldn't control where I would be if a disaster took place. Only recently it dawned on me that I needed to enjoy my life as it is now and not overly worry about the future."

As our meal concluded, Rhonda explained how her psychic gifts had emerged.

"I desperately needed some money for my fare here, so I prayed that if I was really meant to be doing my own healing, Spirit would help me financially. Within a few days my clairvoyance came through."

She looked at us with her soft blue eyes. They were angelic. I had presumed she'd always been psychic, but it seemed this wasn't so.

"People were delighted with my readings and started to pay me. After a month, though, I started to doubt the information I received. I thought I was making it up. These doubts came to me during a reading and immediately, the information flow stopped. I had to tell my client I didn't feel well and give her money back. Since then I always trust what Spirit gives me. That was a big lesson."

"Something similar happened to me as I discovered my gifts," Laura said. "I believe it was the clearing work I'd done over the years which enabled me to receive information. I think spending an intense year here gave me the biggest breakthrough in growth. Now I use sound and energy in my own healing work with clients."

I was impressed.

"Do you think I'll figure out my life purpose?" I asked.

"Who knows what will happen," Rhonda said.

"Well, if you're as determined as me, you won't miss any opportunity to find out," Laura informed me.

Jet lag took its toll that night and I slept late at my motel after finding the sixteen-hour time difference disorienting. This evening we were going to the mountain.

We traveled to the campsite on Blue Mountain over several miles of winding, rocky road. A four-wheel drive vehicle was vital to transport our camping gear. We traveled up and down the narrow road, clinging to the mountainside's edge. I wanted to get out of the truck and walk when I saw the sheer slopes only inches away from the vehicle's tires. My heart was in my mouth during the entire journey and my anxiety didn't diminish when we reached the parking lot either. The small, acutely sloping site was bound by sheer inclines. I was terrified the truck would roll over the edge. I sighed with relief when the brakes worked efficiently. Touching the rocky ground with my feet felt wonderful.

As I surveyed the mountain's gradient, I realized how unrealistic my expectation of a flat camping ground had been.

"Are any of the tents on an even site?" I questioned Rhonda.

"No," she joked. "You can have your feet higher than your head if you like sleeping like that."

I was so excited to be here. A beautiful calming atmosphere permeated the whole area and a sign painted, *Welcome to Blue Mountain Center* embraced my soul.

Things were definitely camp style - no electricity or hot water. But the sun shone, it was peaceful and I felt content.

"OK. Christina, you're in tent nine. That's down the path."

I grabbed my bedding and backpack and started descending the steep slope after Gail, who had already done workshops on the mountain.

"You'll get used to running up and down the track. It's definitely easier to carry your stuff down than bring it back up though," she warned me.

Gail carried a foam mattress for me to sleep on as she guided me down toward the tents. They were scattered along the winding pathway between the groves of pines and scrub oak on well graded sites. The air smelt sweet and clean.

"Here you are."

A little arrowhead sign pointed to an isolated tent well off the main path. It seemed very alone, on a reasonably level piece of ground.

"Grab your towel and wash bag and leave it on the hooks up in the bathroom."

I dumped my stuff in the tent, quickly laid out the foam and bedding and scooted back up the pathway after Gail.

"Where's the shower area?" I asked.

"Up next to the kitchen. You can see it as you walk up the path. The dining room is on the left."

I reached the kitchen and crossed the pathway to inspect the showers.

A deck with hand basins along the wall looked down a valley onto the prairie. It was the best view in the world. Even deck chairs waited in anticipation for people to sit and breathe in the glory of the miles of unheeded vista. Gold plated taps and Italian marble tiled walls couldn't compare to the magnificence of cleaning your teeth on this wooden deck.

Workshops on the mountain were conducted in a canvas dome constructed on Buckminster Fuller's building principles. A huge arched window overlooked a gentle wooded slope inhabited by squirrels and deer. Our first group session together started after dinner.

Flashlights prancing down the path, the sound of the canvas door zipper ripping up and down, propane lanterns humming, a circle of chairs, flowers on a striped rug in the center and the clear night sky, visible through the window, were imprinted on my memory. In the dome, I met the rest of the participants as we shared reasons for coming to this workshop.

We 'made a space' for dream recollection and everyone asked themselves a pertinent question for our dreams to answer. Personally, I wasn't hopeful of an answer. I rarely remembered dreams – if I actually had them. However I optimistically thought of a question. It was one of those universal questions, something along the lines of, 'What am I to do with my life'…and tried to focus on this before falling asleep. The stage was set for recollection.

Alone in my tent I contemplated the sacredness of the area and hoped to hear drumming from Takewa, an Indian Chief in Spirit who guarded the mountain. Then fear encased me. Reality struck as I realized I was alone in the dark, isolated in a tent in the middle of nowhere. A grove of trees separated me from other humans and a thin piece of canvas was my only protection from mountain wildlife. I was terrified. What sort of night creatures lived here? This wasn't Australia with fearful animals. Wild animals here killed people. Worrying thoughts circulated through my head and my senses were on full alert. Although the area seemed peaceful I sure hoped this Spirit Indian, Takewa, was willing to protect me.

I lay on my foam padding using my breath to calm myself, when suddenly a rapid wind encircled my tent. I didn't move as I listened intently for more sounds, vigilantly sensing everything. Leaves scuffled next to the canvas and something brushed against the side of the tent.

Not squirrels, for suddenly a tribe of Indians surrounded me.

A young brave come forward, knelt by me and raised his tomahawk.

"Aaaaaahh," I screamed.

My heart pounded against my chest as I was woken by my own outcry.

"What's happening?"

No one was there to answer or reassure my shaking body. If this was a dream, it wasn't normal. Those Indians were real. They weren't visible anymore – but I knew they were around. Something blew into my ear.

My God, I was scared.

Anxiously, I slipped out of the sleeping bag and moved around the tent. Who were these Indian ghosts? I didn't know what to do so changed the position of my bed. Some physical activity was needed to use up adrenaline released in my body. I had no protection from spirits in this tent. Maybe it was better outside. I opened the zipper and took a few tentative steps outdoors. No, it was too dark, I didn't know what could be lurking out there. There was nothing to do but lie inside the tent and hopefully fall asleep. I was wary, listening tenaciously for anything unusual. In my half-awake state the patient Indian with the tomahawk returned and spoke.

"Sorry to scare you, but it was the only way to get you to make a sound. The sound is the beginning for you to use your voice to speak out."

I was reassured he wasn't going to kill me with the tomahawk. Although his message seemed to indicate he was friend rather than foe, I looked forward to morning and the security sunlight brought.

Squirrel chatter greeted me with the morning sun, reinforcing that I was alive. My night's experience was still strongly with me, although I wasn't fearful anymore. It hadn't been a dream but was probably the answer to my question, What am I meant to do with my life? Was speaking out part of my life purpose? Creating a dream space in this sacred environment seemed heavy duty, not to be taken flippantly.

I ran up the pathway to the kitchen to find someone to talk with. I soon noticed I was the only person who ran up those pathways.

"Morning Laura. I had a terrifying experience last night. An Indian tribe came into my tent." I related how the young brave had spoken to me.

"I guess we should have warned you something like that could happen here," Laura said, smiling.

" I was so surprised to actually see the Indian."

"Do you think he is one of your guides?" Laura asked.

"Yeah, that makes sense. He's still here, on my left side. I wonder what he's teaching me?"

"Ask him, see what else he says. Maybe he'll tell you his name."

Although I wanted to converse with him, I was unable to hear any words and never interacted with the Indian so dramatically again. However, whenever I thought of him, he sent me love, which always made me smile.

The five days of the workshop were full of surprises from this life, past lives and the patterns carried through lifetimes. I started to grasp Verna's healing method better. By voicing and expressing our thoughts and ideas, recurring patterns became identifiable. Common patterns we looked at in this workshop included loss, anger, submission, resentment, defensiveness and abandonment. Many patterns were universally common and were stronger or lesser depending on the person. Others were cultural while some were generational. Then came family patterns. Once we started looking at our behavior we could ascertain our patterns and their recurrence, then begin clearing them.

Healing always begins with recognition of our behavior. Verna used sound healing and rays of light to help clear the inhibiting patterns. Complete removal might not happen instantaneously. As we identified our patterns they could be lifted, layer by layer. As the layers were lifted, change happened, making our bodies feel less burdened and lighter. My incarnation as a young Polish woman during the Nazi era came up again as I became aware of incidents earlier in that life involving breeding for the Nazi's Aryan Race program.

My body shook and my eyes bulged in fear as I recalled related incidents of that time.

"I'm taken from my family...I see the family lined up outside our home... I'm about twelve or thirteen... My father seemed to be fairly wealthy...a businessman, maybe a flour miller. We had a nice home...It seems to be in the country...there are quite a few children...I don't know what happened to the rest of my family when I was taken...whether they were 'instantaneously homeless' or killed... the soldiers took me away by force...they have guns."

I had no idea until then how young teenagers were used for this breeding program. When books mentioned women used for breeding Aryan children with the Nazi's, I presumed they were actually adult – not teenagers. I was alarmed remembering this life experience, for so much seemed to have happened. My skin prickled and my heart pounded as I recalled a laboratory and clinical hospital area. I was giving birth.

"How many babies did you have?" Verna asked.

What a bizarre question. A number popped into mind immediately, but it seemed so ridiculous I didn't want to answer.

"Eight."

Another workshop participant piped up.

"I was a Nazi officer there. I knew you. I remembered you had eight babies before you even said it."

Is this real? Do we keep encountering the same people lifetime after lifetime? Even though I knew this to be true, having it continually confirmed in workshops made me think I had little control over anything in my life.

I looked further into this baby producing time of my life.

"Not all the babies were acceptable ... they weren't good enough ... I felt useless. Only three were approved as Aryan ... The others were used for experimentation ... or thrown into the pits ... Maybe some were given to farming people to raise as farm laborers? ... It seems some were given away."

Uselessness, fear and loss. These were patterns of my past life I brought into this lifetime. It was time to clear them. There was loss in this life; loss of my children when they stayed in Australia; loss of my home and my pets when I left for Singapore. However, I cried with the grief of the loss of those babies and family from my Polish life. The emotion still stored in my body from another lifetime needed release too.

"I think my first name was the same in that lifetime," I told Laura later.

"I believe we choose our names. There is an energy vibration with our name. Maybe you chose the same lessons to learn this time as then."

"Well, I remember my brother from then. They were pretty bad times. Surely I don't have to learn the same lessons? Maybe I didn't learn them and need to repeat them this time. I wonder what the lesson is – and what I'm meant to do about it?"

Every workshop we had a healing from Spirit Doctors. This was always done in the evening towards the end of the workshop. Verna channeled the energies of Dr Fritz, a German doctor and Arigo, a Brazilian government worker, who built a reputation of amazing healing and was known as Surgeon of the Rusty Knife as well as other titles. More beings from the Spirit realm also came to assist in our healing, in fact a whole spirit doctor team. Participants sat in chairs in the dome, quietly and waited together. Spirit energies could be felt moving into the room. In my first workshop a beautiful perfume spread around the room like a gentle breeze as spirit moved inside the circle, ensuring the scent reached everyone. I felt a hand on my shoulder and was aware of nurturing energy behind me. Each person received some etheric surgery or body repair from Dr Fritz and colleagues, depending on what was their highest need.

As Verna touched our crown and heart chakras, an electromagnetic energy surge went through the body. It felt like warmth moving through my veins and muscles. This was the charge given for healing to really begin.

Spirit worked on the body in All Time. Although we may have thought we had healing for an hour or so, it could have been days in Spirit time. Some people experienced an etheric operation during the Spirit Doctor visit. Their body had to recover as if the operation was third-dimensional surgery, but the procedure was not as long and was without the physical trauma of a typical operation.

Always, it was the choice of Spirit as to where to focus healing. Often it was chakra clearing and heart opening.

It was my turn for the focus of healing and time disappeared. As I received the energy charge, my body wouldn't stop jerking. I'd regain my composure then the process repeated itself. This jerking centered on my mid-back and was embarrassing, annoying and uncontrollable. It lasted at least thirty minutes and I presumed I had an energy block that was being released.

I lay on the floor after this experience, exhausted, but my body wasn't going to let things end. More release of energy occurred. I started moaning involuntarily. My body wasn't listening to my thoughts. It had its own agenda and wasn't going to be stopped by my conscious mind. Here was the opportunity the very cells had been waiting for; to release more stored tensions and memories.

"What was happening to you?" Verna asked after the session.

I was somewhat confused myself, not believing everything that came into my mind.

"Perhaps it had to do with the eight babies. Drugs were used during pregnancy as part of the experimentation. Experimentation on timing of birth, trying to speed the gestation, trying to develop the baby faster... I'm not totally sure, but there was more than just breeding children. There was genetic experimentation also."

It seemed my body still carried some of these violations.

Although I felt embarrassed about my body's reactions I was grateful that release happened. This was full-on healing and I continued to feel better all the time.

Through this workshop I had learned more about the healing process and temporarily put myself before my daughters and their dilemmas. As my body was allowed to express itself I felt less stress. Something good was happening and I wanted more. I was moving in my consciousness. I had a teacher and healer whom I respected and could further help me. I experienced enormous healing in my body and soul and my whole psyche cried out to me, "Please don't stop."

At the conclusion of the workshop, Michael arrived. I met him at the motel before we spent a few days touring. We hired a car for the three days before the next workshop to drive south toward New Mexico.

The scenery around the mountains was magnificent and as I looked out the car windscreen, my mother-in-law, who recently passed into Spirit came toward me. My relationship with her hadn't been close. I didn't want to see her, even in this ghost form. Immediately the thought came, my Indian guide appeared. He knelt in front of her with his tomahawk raised and she left. I realized that I now had a protector and was thrilled.

Michael and I participated in the next workshop. I still yearned to do the Year Long program. My own healing had started and I wanted to continue at this speed.

Also, there was another factor influencing me. I didn't know how to get Michael away from Singapore. He seemed to want to stay indefinitely. I wanted my family united; for us to be together and support our children. They were still teenagers, financially dependent on us and I wanted to be available for emotional support for them. My family was in confusion and I couldn't nourish everyone. While I lived in Singapore I was unable to help.

Laura, in her forthright fashion, suggested the whole family might want to partake in the Year Long. She and her husband had participated several years before. They brought their small children and lived in the USA. It was a possibility I would consider but we were a family of adults with different paths to follow. I desperately wanted Michael to do the program with me and maybe Rebecca would come and live in America. Melissa seemed to want to stay in Australia and continue her education. It could be difficult for her to break her tertiary studies.

When I told Michael I was still keen to do the Year Long he was furious.

"You tricked me into coming to this workshop. We can't afford to keep doing all these workshops and flying between countries."

Neither of us recognized the confusion I was in and Michael didn't seem to know what he wanted. Within a few minutes he agreed to do the program with virtually no discussion about its consequences. He instructed me to stay in America till October, two months away, when I could return to Australia to see how the girls were and finish up business there. I thought the idea for me to stay alone in the United States was his way to punish me.

We made some plans. There was disorder, but a united goal within our family to move the chaos into more cohesion. Just one year in our lifetime hopefully would get us to a level of unity, mutual caring and love. I was totally optimistic.

By living in our bodies we can reclaim our power and life force.

Chapter six

On a late afternoon in early August, twenty-two people congregated at Base Camp. The Year Long program on Blue Mountain was about to begin. Scattered clouds reduced heat from the sun's rays as people gathered amongst the jumbled piles of camping gear.

Base Camp was a grand title for this small isolated area that looked somewhat disorderly. Cars in various states of cleanliness stood around the edge of the sparsely grassed area leaving a circular patch for a small truck to maneuver in. Baggage was tossed together in random piles. From the cliff like edge of the mesa, steady traffic could be seen below as it moved quickly along the highway we'd all come on. Low clumps of sage and miniature cactus grew amongst the grass, with scattered scrub oak circling the edge of the meeting area. They were tough survivors in the dry cracked ground. The absence of flies was an appreciated difference from our Australian bush.

Laughter drew my attention to a small group assembling. Rhonda was there with her husband Glen and brother Daniel. She knew how it felt to be here for the first time, so welcomed everyone with reassuring anecdotes of mountain experiences. A few people unloaded bags as stragglers arrived.

What had brought this bunch from around America and Australia together? Was there anyone who really knew why they were here or what connections we had? What was the reason for us all being so ardent in our deep personal search that we'd commit to something with an unknown outcome?

Daniel, a strong young man with thick grey hair and sun tanned skin, climbed onto the tray of the Ford truck. He was Rhonda's youngest brother. Taking the cigarette out of his mouth, he called to her in a broad Australian accent.

"Toss your bags up to me Sis. Let's pack the truck."

I moved next to Rhonda with my luggage ready to help load, pleased to be distracted from my anxiety by an activity. Glen, Rhonda's husband, sauntered over to pass the bags up to his brother-in-law.

"Here mate, I'll help. Catch."

These two men, strong muscled from years of work in Australian mining camps were used to getting a job done and worked in synchronicity stacking belongings neatly on the truck's tray.

"How did you and Glen talk Daniel into coming to these workshops?" I asked Rhonda as we watched the rest of the group gravitate toward the truck.

"That was unbelievable. I didn't intend to influence him at all," she replied. "When he arrived from Melbourne a few days ago, we took him for coffee to meet Verna. Before he'd even finished his cappuccino he said he'd come to the workshops. I don't know when he plans to finish his round the world holiday."

Daniel leaned over the edge of the truck to tell us, "You may be surprised about my change in plans, but I was really taken aback when I saw Rhonda. She's happier and doesn't argue with me so much. There's a peacefulness around her too."

" Weren't you always an angel?" I teased Rhonda.

"Of course! But I had all my brothers to defend myself against. They were pretty mean at times and often tormented me, so I gave what I got. I had to be tough."

Daniel didn't believe in spirituality or anything he couldn't see with his own two eyes. He loved to tease Rhonda about her "woo-woo" stuff. "Just between you and me, I won't do the whole year," he whispered.
" I want to see what Rhonda's doing and check she and Glen aren't being taken for a ride. I'll probably leave after a few days of this workshop and

resume my holiday."

"Is everyone's baggage on board?" Glen bellowed.

We crawled over the stacked bags and found a stable position on the piled truck for our journey. A small American woman leaned on the sleeping bag next to me and introduced herself.

"I'm Donna." She looked well prepared with a neatly packed backpack, good walking shoes and soft hat. She smiled, "I came last year for the program. I know how to be comfortable camping here."

"Why are you doing this year program again?" I asked.

"This is my *life* we're talking about. I want to be clear, remove negative patterns and know who I really am. I don't want to carry this garbage over with my consciousness to the next life. Whatever I learn will help my family, including the grandkids. There are five so far and I want them to grow up being aware of their behavior and know who they are."

She expressed my thoughts and determination, but suddenly I became concerned about the time it could take. Wouldn't one Year Long be so intense and moving I'd be totally transformed by its end? I hoped to have such self-awareness forever after one year, I would easily move through future life challenges. I turned to Rhonda.

"Will I know everything I need to be sane and loving human by the end of one year?"

She laughed, "Christina, you know working and clearing ourselves never finishes."

In a previous workshop in Australia, Rhonda uncovered memories of ritual abuse in her childhood. She remembered a favorite aunt taking her to meetings so it could be possible Daniel was also involved. As we bounced around on the back of the truck, Rhonda shared some of her discoveries.

"We moved to another state when I was about ten, so I didn't see her again. Daniel was only a tiny kid then. He might not have been involved. I've never seen him in a memory, so maybe he wasn't." Rhonda continued, "I was instructed to befriend kids at school and find out who had working parents, or parents that let their kids run free. These were the children I'd recruit for ceremonies. Any child whose parents wouldn't question their whereabouts was a target. It's surprising how many kids aren't really looked after by their families."

I thought of my own daughters and their friends. What sort of people would do these horrid things to youngsters? Had I been protective enough of my children? I didn't know this type of person Rhonda described existed in our society.

"I was trained to conduct some ceremonies. They had secret books of incantations I was supposed to learn. I didn't like them and sometimes would change the evil words into nonsensical ones so no harm could come to anyone. Mostly they didn't notice, but when I was caught they were furious because it messed up things for them."

Rhonda led two lives. There was her normal childhood of going to school, helping at home with a loving mother. Then there was the surreal cult life of ceremonies and horror story tortures.

"My Aunt belonged to the Bible study group in her Church. If I was at her house after school she'd read Bible passages to me. She was a bit of a task master, and even made me learn some of the texts."

I became a little confused.

"Really? How can she be doing that witch-craft and going to church at the same time?"

"It's all to do with mind control," Rhonda explained, "and that's another story."

Although the ride in the tray of the truck was rough, I found that every time I rode over the dirt track, my fear of slipping down the mountainside diminished. Now on my third trip on this road I even recognized turns and boulders along the way.

"What got you started doing personal growth?" Donna asked Rhonda.

"I went to a psychologist first. That was a few years ago. We talked about my family, all the boys and my dad's drinking. I was still in turmoil after several sessions, so the psychologist suggested hypnotherapy. Nothing more came up. He thought my family was typical of an alcoholic parent. Still, there seemed to be something missing. Do you remember Laura?" Rhonda asked me.

I nodded.

"Well, I talked it over with her. We ended up going to a group workshop together. I uncovered some sexual abuse in that workshop. I'll still have an individual session when I know what is up, but I like groups best."

"What is it about the group process that you like Donna?" I asked the petite American.

"I learn more being in a group. When I'm with other people, I hear their words and feel their energy. If it relates to me, I'm triggered and can clear myself of those issues. It's as simple as hearing someone laugh. If I hear laughter, I laugh too, even if I don't know the joke. Groups help me move faster. Like Rhonda there was alcoholism in my family. I understand this family pattern even better from listening to other people's experiences."

"Well, I'm hopeless at sad movies. I always cry and walk out with swollen eyes. I guess that means the sadness the actor expresses, triggers mine," I responded. " The rest of my family will come to the workshops when school finishes in Australia. I thought we'd get more out of group work. Especially with the time span. Six days together has to be better than weekly hour sessions over several months for moving through our dysfunction."

I yelled over the noise of the truck to the chain smoking Daniel.

"Do you know what you're getting into?"

"No idea," he laughed." But I like camping."

We had an equal mix of Australians and Americans in our group. I assumed most of us had been together before in past lives. Russell, the cute young guy I remembered being a mistress for in Nazi times, was here along with several other Australians I'd already met at the workshop earlier in the year. I was amazed that such young people would take a year's leave from work to pursue their personal growth. This was a working holiday with a difference.

There is something special about group energy. It is exponential, not just the sum of the individual energies. So with twenty-two people a lot can be expected. We could work together, trigger and support each other.

The logistics organizer greeted us on arrival. For many on the truck it was the first time on the mountain.

"Welcome to Blue Mountain. I'm Emily, the body behind the voice of the phone conversations we've all had. I've a list of assigned tents for everyone here. You'll soon get used to the altitude."

Emily stood on the slope by the truck and gave a brief introduction how our week would go. She set up the facilities and organized the food for each workshop.

"It's best to carry your backpacks around with you to save walking back to your tents during the day. Keep your tent closed at all times, and never store food in them. Little critters have a great sense of smell and will be in your tents searching for the snacks. We hit the gong when its meal time." She moved to turn, "Oh. Nearly forgot - when you've got your bags in your tents, there's juice and snacks in the dining area."

Temperatures varied significantly in a day and evidence of the regular early afternoon rain showed as steam rising from the tents' tarps. Dressing in layers was the best way to adjust to the temperature changes and the sun, almost on the horizon hinted at the need to prepare for the evening chill.

Blue Mountain has magic. Certain places specifically connect with other realms and dimensions. If anyone wanted solitude to meditate, the energy of Middle Earth, Extra Terrestrials and the Elohim were available. Energy of spirit is everywhere. Although our eye's band of vision is small in the realm of what exists, I began to sense, feel and intuit the multi dimensions of life around me. Past, future, present, spirit and our connections with each other became part of the invisible I experienced.

Michael wasn't there to participate in the first Year Long workshop. That was partly my fault, for I didn't push him to fly from Asia for this one week. I thought the extra airfare cost as well as jet lag both ends of the journey would have made it difficult for him. I regretted that now. My eight weeks in America had been long and lonely. I missed him and my daughters enormously and wanted them with me to share this experience. I had to wait till next month for him to join the group.

I had kept regular phone contact with my family though. Melissa in Australia assured me, "I'm fine Mum."

"Sorry I didn't come back immediately," I explained. "I felt desperate to do more of this clearing work. I keep finding more and more that helps me understand myself."

"I'm not annoyed with your change in plans. You don't have to come home to look after me."

Her crisis of two months ago had subsided.

"I'm looking forward to coming to America for my vacation. Maybe we'll have snow at Christmas? That'll be different."

Rebecca relished time at boarding school. Over the phone, her house mistress told me, "I enjoy having Rebecca here. She is mature young woman and a great help mediating problems with fellow boarders."

This didn't surprise me, Rebecca was gentle and understanding. Even as a little child she acted sensitively to people and their needs. I was proud of her awareness and consideration toward others.

I repeatedly wondered why Michael insisted I couldn't go back to Australia or Singapore after the August workshop.

"It's too expensive to return to Singapore again," he said.

This didn't make sense though, for my lodging and expenses in the United States were equivalent in cost. Often I was out of the house I boarded in when Michael phoned so I didn't get to speak to him enough. Other times we only talked briefly because phone calls were costly.

His lack of communication left a void within me. I missed him but managed to keep myself busy enough by helping friends in their greenhouse intermingled with some sight seeing. Now, I was excited to totally focus on personal growth. I wanted to work on changing my own frustration and inner turmoil.

I came back from my musing as the group gathered together in the dome for our first meeting together. We'd eaten and many of us had introduced ourselves to each other. The sun had set and gas lanterns hummed as they lit our workspace.

"Use this evening to define your goals for the program and what you want from the course," Verna explained. "I'd like you to share your reasons for coming and how you planned your life around this year's commitment."

"It seems unbelievable that I'm here at last," the handsome young Russell started. "I planned for nearly a year to come. I created a chart of my dreams, worked and saved. When I arrived a few days ago, it was such a cultural shock – and very lonely. I've been hanging out to get started. "

I expressed something of the confusion and mess in my life.

"I'm here because my life is totally out of control. I lived in Singapore for a few years without my daughters. They were in school back in Australia. Michael, my husband, enjoys being in Asia. He is respected and likes the male dominated society. It was interesting living there but I was lonely and isolated. We went back to Australia seven months ago for a holiday. It was crazy. Melissa, my elder daughter was in distress. She needed us to be closer. Michael dismissed her requirements. He didn't seem to care or understand. We're so scattered. More than anything I want my relationship with Michael to be revitalized and caring. I want my daughters to grow fulfilled and know how to be happy. I want cohesiveness and love in my family. I don't know how to get Michael away from Asia. He won't discuss his plans with me and I don't think he ever wants to leave."

Verna looked at me, "You are responsible for everything happening in your life right now."

What? I didn't want to hear that. What a jolt to be told to take total responsibility. It stopped me from saying more to expose myself for further judgement! I was in confusion. It was easier to blame someone or something else for my circumstances. I felt worthless, unlovable, and sad.

"I feel displaced, like a refugee. Where do I belong?"

Was I really responsible for all this pain and anxiety in myself?

"How can I feel better inside?" I asked.

"Only by clearing yourself of habitual patterns. " Verna's response was direct.

I took a deep breath. Dear God, this year would be tough. Total honesty was vital. I sensed that there would be nothing we could fudge about ourselves. This group facilitator was on the ball. She wasn't frightened to confront anyone.

Daniel told us he didn't believe in the three lettered "G" word of omnipotence and wouldn't even say it.

"Don't try and say that word in front of me or I'll knock your teeth out."

After that descriptive warning, Rhonda mentioned her discovery of ritual abuse in her life.

"My middle brother is schizophrenic. I'm beginning to wonder if he may have been involved in the abuse as well and if it could be the cause of his illness. I remember he and I were looked after by the same aunt who took me to rituals, when mum went to hospital. I was about seven at the time and he was a toddler. After mum took us home she'd often ask me what happened to him while she was away. She thought something was wrong with his behavior when she took him home again. I think she suspected he'd fallen on his head. Whatever it was, he wasn't the same and continually got worse till he was diagnosed as a schizophrenic when he was sixteen. He's totally dependent on welfare. I help, but a lot of the time he's impossible and yells at me to get out of his house."

Everyone contributed personal reasons for their presence. I only half listened to most. I wanted confirmation I was on the right path by spending a year here. Especially I listened to the few who had already done a Year Long. I planned to talk to them after our evening and find out why one year wasn't enough.

Every one of Daniel's paradigms were challenged, when Verna trance channeled Indira. Rhonda hadn't mentioned Verna was a trance channel to her brother. I watched him look in disbelief as Indira started to speak through Verna. He thought this was a trick. But he didn't seem to totally dismiss her message:

"You have been together as a group many times before, since the beginning of time. There are so many from Spirit in your midst and many more will gather to be with you. There will be opportunities for you to open up in many ways during this. You will find there will be opportunities to educate others, over the radio and through the printed word. Take everything moment by moment. Acclimate yourselves to each other's vibrations and to higher and higher vibrations of energy. That will be possible as you move forward. Love yourselves and be unconditional in that love. There is no paucity of love. Always there is more available."

We spent eight or nine hours a day in the dome together. We laughed, cried, worked and played. We opened ourselves and attempted to understand each other. The year together promised much change. The environment of Blue Mountain nurtured us with perfect warm summer days, followed by cool mountain evenings as we moved through our growth work.

Morning sessions began at 9.30am with a prayer and toning Aum. Often dreams were shared, or something read from a book. One particular morning's discussion astonished me. I will never forget my fascination with a story Verna told us she read in a newspaper.

She began," The story was about a young father's denial of his little boy's death. For several days the father treated the boy's lifeless form as though the child was asleep. He even visited his own father, carrying the baby's body to the car with him, strapping him in the car seat and proceeding on his way.

"My son's sleeping now. Can I put him on the bed?" he asked the child's grandfather. The two men chatted over lunch. When it was time to leave, the child was 'still asleep' so the father gently carried him back to the car.

The father's denial of his son's death was so deep, he even convinced the grandfather the child was sleeping. It took several days for the rest of the family to realize the child was dead.

This story is about denial," Verna continued. "The father couldn't cope with his son's death so blocked it from his mind. Can you comprehend how his denial also affected the rest of the family including his father?"

Everyone was quiet.

It was incomprehensible how someone couldn't see reality.

"Is it really possible that someone would block the truth from themselves?" I asked the group. " How would I know if I was in denial?

"Becoming aware, is the only way to come out of denial," Verna told me.

"That story haunts me, " I told the group. I could not fathom how someone could trick their own mind.

I began journaling everything, determined to make the most of this year. I wrote snippets of experiences to keep track of what happened.

I had memories of birth and my anger at the stupidity of the midwives thinking 'poor little thing', as they looked down at me. Although they had to revive me at birth, I was a born a capable human being, couldn't they recognize that?

I had forgotten that awareness I had at birth.

Most group work was in the dome but sometimes we'd walk to other places depending on what energies we wanted with us. There was the fire pit, with middle earth energies and favored places of the Indian guardians of the land.

Although pathways meandered over the camp area and reduced the gradient we had to climb, it was exhausting to walk up the hill. I became used to packing my backpack with journal, sweater, raincoat, water bottle, and flashlight: anything possibly needed in the day to save running back to my tent unexpectedly.

Fresh, sweet smelling air, exercise, delicious food and wonderful energies created an atmosphere for clearing my own internal pollution. I was there to unravel the tangles and knots I'd created in my life; to heal, grow and to dislodge those stuck parts so my energy would flow smoothly.

Verna appeared to remember everything we said. Well, it was sure more than what I remembered. Her focus was intense. When our comments and patterns came up during discussion they were 'on line' for healing. Spirit – part of the invisible energy- was involved in the healing process. Verna would ask for what she wanted and it came. She would call for massive golden light to enter and it did. She'd request removal of negative patterns from our bodies and they'd be lifted. I could feel patterns dislodge. It felt as though strands around my body were straightened and pulled out and I began to feel lighter in my body. My sense of the invisible opened as I learned to feel and accept Spirit working amongst us.

However, it was Daniel's uncontrollable body reactions that shocked us all. We began to sense he had been abused the same way as his sister Rhonda. On the second day on the mountain something triggered Daniel and his body went into spasm. He had no control as he gripped his chair tightly with his hands, hoping it would diminish the pain. His legs cramped. The cramp moved up both legs through his body till he could no longer contain himself. He slipped to the floor. Daniel tried unsuccessfully to take charge, but his body took over.

"Talk about it Daniel. What's happening?" Verna encouraged

"What the fuck," Daniel said through his gritted teeth.

"If you talk the pain will go."

"Fucking hell what is this?"

"Daniel, tell us what you're seeing," Rhonda encouraged. "It's your body's way of reminding you of something."

Verna walked over to Daniel as his body writhed on the floor.

"Say any word. Just say it. How it feels. It's the only way to release the pain."

It took Daniel tremendous effort to get any words to come out. We could see the cramp was agonizing.

"Stuff…. Blood and guts… That's all."

Those few words helped Daniel let go. This was the beginning for his body to release trauma. Pain he'd pushed into his subconscious and totally forgot.

Many times through our workshops Daniel's body demanded more words to disclose the memory and ease the pain. Little by little he let go. His visual memories weren't as clear as Rhonda's but his body showed the stored fear. His body memory awakened.

I admired Daniel's courage. He asked probing questions for an explanation of his body reaction.

"The body never lies," Verna reiterated. "We store our trauma in every cell. Unresolved trauma needs to be release. That is the way of healing. The shaking that comes with shock is a traumatic release. Mostly people don't allow the time for recovery from periods of shock, so the energy stays within the body. It becomes tension and can cause stress and disease."

"Let me get this straight, " Daniel asked Verna, " are you telling me, my cramping on the floor is a result of stored trauma. Does this mean my body has held the tension in the muscles and bones since I was a little kid?"

"From whenever the abuse occurred."

"So why is it coming out now. Why didn't it happen before?"

"Because you pushed the memory of the abuse away, into denial. Your consciousness didn't want to deal with the horrors going on in your life. It was easier to create a fantasy and pretend to be normal."

Something strange occurred. Daniel triggered me. Every time his body cramped or he talked about his memories of ritual abuse my body shook. My legs became jelly-like with fear. I didn't have any thoughts or memories but my body reacted. When Daniel recalled ritual abuse my heart pounded. When his body went into spasm, my throat constricted. I'd never seen anybody's muscles cramp violently like this before and every time it happened, I was affected.

"What's happening Verna? I feel scared. Does this mean I was ritually abused too?"

"No. Just wait. You'll see what it is."

The feeling of being triggered was involuntary and uncomfortable. My body responded in unfamiliar ways, including shaking. Daniel noticed my consistent reaction to his energy release. He'd check my response when he started processing his trauma. Every time! He'd wink, a moment of lightness in the pain of body memory. There was a connection between our energies, we knew there was a link.

Gradually, during Daniel's body memories of ritual abuse I started to remember a lifetime around the 1880's as a young black male living somewhere in the Southern States. Louisville came to mind. I was free but there was a feeling also that I wasn't really free. I remained bound to the white family that had once owned us as slaves.

I saw myself as a little boy employed in the main house, dressed in a cute outfit somewhat too small for me, with shoes that looked nice but cramped my toes. My feet hurt and felt squashed during my memories. I served drinks, freshly squeezed lemonade to the young people in the family. There were several girls and a young man. I recognized the young man and one of the daughters. They are married now, one of Michael's brothers and his wife. The young man didn't like me then and would complain about my work.

Every time Daniel triggered me I saw enough glimpses of this lifetime to piece a story together. I became a young man in my late teens or early twenties. I was proud of my golden colored skin and felt strong looking at my muscled arms. My body was wonderful. Soon, however my life was fear ridden, when I saw burning crosses, bonfires and white clad people on horses. It was the Ku Klux Klan. They pursued me and I was terrified - even now, as I remembered back to another lifetime.

These memories surfaced during the entire week. Often during our breaks I'd flee. Running up the steep mountain paths, through the bushes and jumping over dead branches created an illusion that I was actively trying to elude my attackers. Then I would stop exhausted and put my face on the ground, reminding myself I was Christina on Blue Mountain, not a fearful young man running from the Ku Klux Klan. I never saw how the black person I was then died but I was sure he was young.

Some of the fear from that black American life reminded me of my Polish World War II life. Decades ago I'd pondered on whether the childhood punishment from my brother was an opportunity to clear some of these energies of fear and torture from previous times. A common trigger of fear made me remember both these victimized lives simultaneously. The two lives had parallels. Both had misuse of a sacred religious symbol - the cross and swastika. During the two lives I'd suffered loss of family, my home, along with torture and early death. These were puzzle pieces and I attempted to fit them together.

Had I lived other lives in between these two? Obviously I set myself up to learn the same lesson from the two I'd already recalled. There was commonality in the emotions and patterns I experienced in these lifetimes. Clearly I still had things to learn from these experiences and came into this life with similar patterns. I was living the same life in a different setting. This time I chose to be a victim of men's sexual abuse and to clear up last life karma by coming into a family where my brother had been a Nazi lover and betrayer. The only way I knew to heal was putting victim, fear, loss of family, and Ku Klux Klan on line and have the patterns removed.

"Usually we don't remember our past interactions with each other. We forget when we incarnate. That's why it's important to respect everyone for the role they play in our lives this time. We have free will. Exercise of our free will was set up between lives. We chose our parents for the lessons they help create."

"Don't give me that Verna," Daniel responded. "Do you mean I chose to be abused as a baby? I don't believe it."

"Sure you did. You chose in full consciousness, before birth. The decisions of our interactions are made with others between lives. There we plan our future incarnation for either us or them to act out the role of bad guy, friend, teacher, parent and so on."

"But who would choose to be abused?" .

"Everything has a reason. Often we aren't cognizant of the reason. We don't remember the big picture."

"No one should abuse babies and children," Daniel persisted.

"Yes, that is true. But everyone is interconnected. Any judgment we make is a reflection of ourselves. We are all here to release patterns and negativity and understand who we really are."

I continually reminded myself I chose everything as I further unfolded parts of my life during this Year Long course. I had to take total responsibility for every occurrence in my life and recognize no one else was to blame.

Memory fragments arose relating to my feeling of being unloved and unlovable. I suspected I had been smothered as a baby. I felt myself lying in a crib, then slipping into unconsciousness. I slipped off my chair onto the floor and found the feeling of unconsciousness pleasant. Helen, a social worker and another participant, took me aside during a break.

"Christina, you know I'm clairvoyant and 'see' things. I saw you as a baby with a little boy beside your crib. He smothered you with his hands over your face. He knew what he was doing. Don't doubt what you sense."

So my brother wanted to kill me. I didn't doubt my sensation of being smothered, though it was a surprise. Maybe this started my claustrophobia?

Indira gave me a message:

Christina, we want to greet you admiringly and we say to you that indeed there were elements of smothering that were present with you when you were a wee one. Pursue this in such a way to find deeper recollection, or simply attune to it. Then you will find the energy flowing for healing. There are blockages in your body. Some are related to the smothering. When you come to grips with it five or six times, there will be dramatic changes in the ways the energy flows through your body. It will become smoother.

Indira often gave messages telling us patterns we needed to look at so we could accelerate our healing during the workshop.

Let the heart experience the pain that it is fearful of removing. There may be temporary pain but there would be so much that would be lifted that you will be amazing yourself. Then you will walk with new Light Divine...

I'd felt my heart open already from healing at these workshops. But feeling the pain of my heart? I had no notion what this meant. In a message to the whole group, Indira reminded us of the work Spirit was doing to help us move faster.

Many of you in the conscious mind are not completely retrieving what happens at night when you crawl into your little teepees. When you open up to channels of receptivity there are remembrances placed within you. Sometimes they are placed clearly within you so that you are moving even as you go into the sleep-state. Don't think you have a bit of down time. We are still there helping some of you put rays of light around yourself....enhancing the cellular alterations....dusting some of you down a bit. So you see, work goes on in the night-time.

This was a reminder of what I had heard from so many sources before. When Spirit is asked for help, it comes. Often I had been told I didn't ask Spirit enough for help. Slowly in my consciousness I was starting to grasp and experience this concept. It became part of my own knowing. My trust in Spirit increased as I felt the energy surround me, initiate changes and gently prod me. I began to accept and acknowledge the invisible presence in our world.

At the end of the week I looked forward to the next workshop. Only three weeks away. I'd be with Michael, then return to Australia. All I wanted was my family mess sorted out by the end of the year. I wanted more love, fun and honest communication with Michael and to see my daughters grow into the magnificent beings they came in to be.

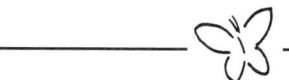

> *Most people don't see the world as it is,*
> *they see it as they are.*

Chapter seven

Melissa, Rebecca, Michael and I were driving high into the Rocky Mountains in the December snow. I was so happy we were together and on our way to the workshop.

The last month had been hectic after cleaning up households in two countries. Michael came to the second session of the Year Long program on Blue Mountain in October, then we returned to Singapore together. From there we shipped some goods to Australia for storage until our eventual return. I flew to Australia and completed our business there. Rebecca helped me clean our Australian home so we could rent it. Then we both returned to Asia when the school year finished at the end of November. We had a week to clean our Asian home and say goodbye to friends there.

Michael finalised his job and sold his car the afternoon Melissa arrived. Her exams had finished the day before so she only had an overnight stay in Asia before our journey to America together. Our luggage was copious, with clothes and household items needed during our last few weeks in Singapore. Two taxis were needed to get us to the airport.

We'd organized ourselves for the year ahead, with everyone having slightly different plans. Melissa was to holiday with us for her summer vacation during December and January. The group had agreed to allow her to participate in the December workshop before she returned to Australia at the end of January. Rebecca had decided to live with us in America for the year. She wanted to do the workshops, along with completing her Australian schooling by correspondence. We were set, my family was together and I felt content. Everything was progressing exactly how I wanted.

Despite the worries of an impending snowstorm, we managed to get out of Denver and into ski country without any problem. We had traveled for several hours, following our mud map to Aspen. Even with the poor visibility of the evening light, the marked turnoff to our destination eight miles down the road was easy to find. I used the odometer to measure the distance to ensure our accuracy in finding the driveway of the ranch. About seven miles down the track our car stopped. It was 5.30pm, but could have been midnight. It was cold, dark and snowing. We had never experienced such conditions, so sat and waited for a few minutes, not quite knowing what to do.

"Checking under the hood seems fruitless unless we can solve the problem immediately," Michael said. At least six inches of snow already covered the road, with more falling softly as we waited. Michael tried the ignition again. Nothing happened.

"Surely we couldn't be the only ones using this road," I said. "Other participants in our workshop will come by soon."

There was not a car in sight. We sat a little longer.

"What do you think we should do? At least it's not far to the ranch. We can walk if necessary."

I pulled the piece of paper with the directions to the ranch from my pocket.

"Here is the phone number of the center. I'll call them from the shop back there to see if anyone can come and help."

By the time I'd made the phone call, Michael was waiting outside the shop in the car with the heater warming the interior. After several attempts the engine had re-started. Relieved, we cautiously drove the last mile and arrived safely at the ranch.

This workshop in the ski area of Colorado was our first healing experience together as a family. I was worried about what might come up. There were now three people who could condemn me and back each other up about my shortcomings.

Naturally I anticipated my failings as a mother to be voiced by Melissa and Rebecca. I also expected Michael to talk about his frustration in the lack of communication in our relationship. I decided not to broach these subjects myself. I certainly wouldn't come out of any discussion as a very nice person and I didn't want to feel ashamed in front of this group of people.

Melissa's counseling at school helped her move quickly into the swing of things. She seemed like a professional at group work, raising her issues about childhood and university life. Rebecca was more reticent. Although I was proud of Melissa's forthrightness I winced when 'mother' issues arose.

"I remember being two and sitting in the middle of the kitchen floor," Melissa related to the group. "I was playing with bowls from the cupboards and got some sugar to tip into them. The sugar spilled on the floor and mum whacked me with a wooden spoon."

Cringe. I sat guiltily on my chair, wondering what else would come up. I didn't remember this incident specifically but I remembered having phenomenal expectations of Melissa as a child. She easily understood things asked of her and spoke very well for her age. If she didn't respond to my requests quickly, I reacted with strong discipline. I'd looked at this myself and accepted that my daughters also needed to heal their own versions of their childhood.

"I'm sorry for my ignorance Melissa. I'm ashamed I expected so much from you."

Melissa hugged me. I was grateful to her for having the courage to begin her healing by speaking out.

What stunned me most though, wasn't the 'mother' issue. That I expected. No, something else came into Melissa's memory within several days of the course. She recollected an incident of being tied up in a park. I couldn't comprehend her story.

"I'm in a park, near where we live. I'm tied up to a pole..."

Rebecca sat cross-legged on the floor next to Melissa. Her head drooped.

Melissa continued. "There is a man here ...and I have a bundle of sticks in my hand...He's telling me to hit myself. I'm bad. He says I'm bad. I have one arm free so I can hit myself with the bundle of sticks..." Rebecca lifted her head and looked at Melissa. Both girls had tears welling in their eyes. Melissa continued with the memory.

"There is a bonfire. We're both tied to poles. They told me to keep hitting myself...and I have to say 'I'm bad' while doing that. There are quite a few people around..."

Verna asked gently, "How old are you, Melissa?"

"About six."

"Can you remember where this was?"

"I'm not sure, but it's an open space. There aren't any houses around."

Rebecca pulled out a bunch of tissues to wipe her eyes. Verna questioned, "What do you remember, Rebecca?"

"I was there as well. I remember the man walking with us to the park. He held our hands. There were other kids too. If we got tired they'd whack us across the legs to make us open our eyes and stay awake."

What was this? I was stunned. Who did this to my children? The girls hadn't mentioned Michael or me. Where had we been while this was happening? I wondered if it was a dream they had both experienced. I looked at Michael. We were both confused about what had happened to our children. This sounded like Rhonda's recollections of ritual abuse. It was beyond my comprehension.

"Remember when we left the kids for a week with Sally when we had a holiday?" Michael reminded me.

"Hmm...maybe. They were about that age then. But I can't believe she would take them to this abusive activity. She had her own kids. Anyway she was one of the most loving people I knew and was very patient with children."

Something weird had happened here. If Sally didn't take them to this ceremony, who did? Did this mean we should never have left our children with other people? Was this the time we left them for the week? It may have been on a night when they stayed over with other friends. I was dumbstruck and unable to make any definite conclusion. Then I made the connection. It came suddenly to me, Rhonda had told me about this on our way to the first workshop. Children were watched and selected to take to ceremonies. Both girls remembered, their emotions were powerful - and their bodies reacted.

I'd let them down as a mother. I hadn't protected them. Where *was*

I while this was happening? Was it something to do with Sally's former husband?

Healing was brought in on this episode in their lives, but I couldn't fathom what had occurred and what impact it had on our lives now. Thank God I was with other people when this strange episode came up for Melissa. Support and companionship from the rest of the group meant I didn't feel so distraught by my inconclusive thoughts. There were several more days to follow through and hopefully discover what really happened. Imagine if we'd only had a one-hour session of family therapy - I would have felt tormented. Most likely this episode wouldn't even have been remembered in a short therapy session.

One of the most unique parts of this work was the healing energy surrounding us. The group had a force of its own that built and amplified healing. The safety of being in a group provided great support.

Rebecca had a cold, which I also caught. The recent travel and preparation had been stressful, reducing my immunity. After a few days at the workshop I felt ill with chest congestion, tiredness and a pounding headache. I planned to remain quiet through the day's session.

"Christina, why do you need to lie on the couch?" Verna asked.

"I feel sick and have a headache that won't go away." I was surprised and irritated by her focus on me.

"Why do you have a headache?"

'Why?' I wanted to say, 'Isn't it obvious? What a stupid question. Leave me alone.' However I responded more politely.

"I have the same cold that is going around here. I've caught the virus from someone else."

"No. That's not the reason. You have manifested a cold and headache. Why have you done that?"

She was nuts. I'd studied biology and knew illness was the result of infection spread by various means to other people. Medical science proved microbes and viruses caused these problems in the body. What was Verna going on about?

"Why don't you get up and go into the middle of the circle?"

Reluctantly I agreed. I moved to the center of the group and was shown a pillow. Suddenly, I started bashing it. The pillow became my punching bag. Overwhelming anger emerged from my body. I just wanted to kick and annihilate the pillow.

"I hate men," I screamed. That surprised me as much as everyone else.

I looked at Michael. He held the pillow for me to hit. I wasn't furious at Michael but my wrath towards men included my father. I lay on the floor kicking my legs. An image of my father kept appearing and I wanted to kill him.

"Get off me," I screamed, sitting upright. Lying down felt too vulnerable. I was murderously angry as I pounded the pillow.

"Leave me alone. Get away from me." The words poured out in rage, no, it was vehement fury toward men. I was incredibly, violently, enraged. I looked around the circle and threw a cushion at young Russell, yelling, "I hate you."

Instantly I regretted the outburst. Those feelings were from another time, not this life.

"Sorry Russell." I attacked the pillow again.

At last, exhausted, I relinquished the pillow, stood up and took a deep breath. My headache had disappeared. Fifteen minutes of raging, expressing hatred toward men and I was cured. How could that be? Until then, I didn't know how much anger toward men was inside me. It was unbelievable! I hated men because I saw them as sexual abusers. How could a memory of sexual abuse as a little child enrage me so much I'd become sick?

Maybe illness *was* caused by blocked emotions. Unless I took medication, my frequent headaches, compounded by nausea, would last for days. This few minutes of anger release was the best pain relief I had ever experienced.

The body never lies.

Why did I have such incredible hatred toward men? I wasn't sure, but now that I had discovered my real attitude towards men, maybe I could find the reason for this rage. How many feelings had I suppressed by not acknowledging my body's call for healing? How many times had I taken tablets to cure headaches, thinking it was just a headache? Thank God I had started to understand. Now I could ask my body why it was in pain or sick. The answers would be reasons and patterns ready for healing. What a learning experience to know I could heal myself.

At lunch I sat with Donna, the petite grandmother.

"I found it amazing to discover illness is not just the result of bacteria or viruses. What do you do if you are sick Donna?"

"I ask myself, 'What is my body trying to tell me?' When I'm unwell I use my awareness to find the reason, then work on the issues. Sometimes I avoid what's going on and get sicker. If I don't face the reasons for being ill, I become worse till something more dramatic happens. Then I have a bigger dilemma to heal."

"I've had regular headaches for many years and took two to four painkiller tablets to stop them. I didn't think to find what issues were causing them. I didn't want to believe those books that say we cause our own illnesses. Now I'll check every ache and pain."

How could I encourage people to believe me about this experience? We create our own sickness with negative patterns and beliefs. Illness is the result of our psychological state and stuffed emotions. I knew to listen to my aches and pains in the future and find the reason for their occurrence.

Sound played an important part of our healing process. A spun crystal chakra tuned bowl set its tone with a leather bound stick running around the rim not unlike running a finger around the edge of a crystal glass. The humming sound quieted our brains, bypassing the conscious mind.

Our awareness slipped into a deeply relaxed state, opening our subconscious minds. The vibrating sound produced put us 'under the bowl' and patterns we'd already put on line were verbally repeated for us to look at more deeply in our relaxed state.

The group sat, eyes closed, spine straight, feet on the floor, ready to receive healing energies from Spirit. The sound of the humming bowl took me into meditation.

"Look at 'kicking'," Verna guided us.

Immediately I felt jabs in my ribs. It was my brother. His boots kicked my body. It hurt and I yelped. Yes, as soon as the bowl started humming, I knew it was him. The sound faded as attention was directed to me.

"What are you remembering, Christina?"

"My brother is kicking me in the ribs...I'm about four years old. I'm tied up and there's a feeling of something sexual around me."

I sat upright in the chair with my eyes closed, sensing this memory I actually felt in my body again.

"Why are your hands above your head?" Verna asked.

I took my awareness to my hands. She was right, my hands were above my head, wrists pressed together. I hadn't even noticed them move there. How weird. I dropped them to my lap.

"My hands were tied together above my head. A trail of rope was left for manipulation of my arms as my tormentor desired."

I took a few deep breaths as I absorbed this information.

"What are you doing with your left hand?" Verna asked.

Huh? What was my left hand doing? I opened my eyes and watched my fingers sweeping something off my thigh.

My body was remembering more than my mind. It was leading my thoughts. Every time my attention went to where my hands moved, I 'knew' what was happening.

"I'm wiping off something moist. I think sand had stuck to the moist stuff. I'm brushing it off. It's sort of sticky."

I wondered if that little child had wet her pants, though that didn't make sense. I was lying on my back and urine wouldn't have gone onto my thigh in that position.

Michael, who was always sympathetic towards the trauma of others, asked me later whether I thought it was semen I brushed from my leg. Maybe that was true. I did think something sexual happened, but I didn't know exactly, for this memory was entirely physical, with no pictures. Whatever had happened, I remembered enough to begin to heal this episode.

At this stage of our Year Long program we were encouraged to experience bodywork as well.

"I recommend you have some form of bodywork," Verna told us. "Deep tissue work helps release stored trauma and patterns held in the body. By combining bodywork with psychological work, you will speed the process of healing. "

A Rolfer came to speak to the group to educate us more fully about what this method could do for our bodies and healing.

"Rolfing is a form of structural alignment, working on the principle that the bones are held in place by the fascia and muscles. If there is tension in the muscles and fascia of the body, the bones are pulled out of alignment. The sessions are designed to help educate your body for organized and fluid movement. Your shape can change and you will often feel taller and more comfortable moving after a series of sessions."

I tentatively booked a consultation. During the first session my Rolfer asked, "Who burned your feet? Who kicked you in the ribs? Who strangled you?" He was sensitive to people's energy and picked these images up from my body.

"Your feet feel like burned steak," he said.

I wouldn't let his hands anywhere near my head and throat unless I held them as he moved. I was scared in the vulnerable position on my back. Well, I already knew who kicked me from the previous workshop experience. That session had given me conscious awareness of my reaction along with removal of the pattern of being kicked. But I didn't know if I'd been strangled, or if my feet had been burnt.

Although I had bodywork similar to Rolfing ten years earlier, I hadn't responded with traumatic release- uncontrolled shaking- then. The deep psychological work I'd started in the Year Long had helped me release more layers of control on my body. This meant I could further let go with Rolfing. Further processing during sleep had helped release more energy of being kicked so it was easier for my body to continue to release with the bodywork. My body now had less blocks to exert energy on to control and maintain. Bodywork combined with the psychological and spiritual work sped my healing process. Each played a part in release.

Little snippets of information popped into my consciousness during this workshop. Fragments with no connections. I was embarrassed to share them for I didn't want anyone to think my memories were wrong and it was hard to believe them myself. I could scarcely utter these recollections in the group.

"I felt someone urinate on my face…and was forced to eat feces. " Where did I procure these memories? They had to be another lifetime, nothing else in this life I remembered could tie in with these visions.

"The Nazi's used these forms of torture," Verna responded.

Melissa saw a baby with its intestines cut out.

Rebecca talked about a dream where she read a book with illustrations of rhinos and burned babies.

These fragments of strange images popped into our heads. We didn't know how to piece them together or how they fitted in our lives.

Not all our group work was heavy duty, though. It was nearly Christmas and the snow was deep enough for sliding down slopes near the lodge. During breaks we'd don our gloves and hats to romp in the snow, sliding, snowboarding or making snow-angels. Many of us hadn't experienced snow before. With the sun shining down and no cars driving by, we had great fun frolicking in the pristine environment.

Katar Schoenstaadt, a healer and trance channel from Phoenix, spent a few days with the group. One of her master teachers whom she channeled, came through as Clark, a fun-loving entity from the spirit side who told jokes and stories as his teaching.

At our Christmas party I watched Katar dance along with everyone, then quietly sit down. Her head bowed, arms moved gently and within a few minutes it was the presence of Clark surveying the group. Apparently he loved to socialize at parties. This was my first experience of a trance channel walking about with eyes wide open. After dancing with us, Clark sat in a chair and shared a joke and a story. His jokes weren't as memorable as the concept of an extremely extroverted entity taking prime position in our party and throwing in his spiritual teaching that we need to have *fun*.

Only a few of us remained when someone decided to introduce Melissa to Clark.

"Clark you haven't met Melissa before. She's only here for a short time."

Clark turned to Melissa and looked deeply at her.

"No, we've met before. In fact, she knows me very well. Maybe not in this body but we've known each other in other times. She has come in as a pilot light for the world." Tenderly he added, "It's a very lonely and difficult role to take on isn't it?"

Melissa laughed. She was touched by his compassion.

When Melissa was six, I had her astrology chart drawn.

The astrologer told me, "She's a very rare being. Alternative schooling along Rudolf Steiner lines would be best for her; anything with an environment that doesn't overload her sensitivity."

Along with Clark's comments I wondered again what Melissa's role was? Well, what was I meant to be? The eternal question. I prayed to see how I fitted into this crazy universe, and my reason for being alive. Hopefully by the completion of this Year Long program I would understand.

On the second last day of our week together, Verna asked, "Melissa, would you like to join everyone for the January workshop in Santa Barbara?"

"Yep." Melissa agreed.

Huh? I was amazed by the invitation and pleased with Melissa's response. It gave me more time with her before she returned to Australia for college. I desperately wanted Melissa to be with us for as long as possible.

Indira reminded us throughout this workshop of changes happening at a cellular level, which affect our interconnectedness.

There are so many profound elements that you have discovered for yourselves. There has been the quickening and the altering even within your cells. Hence you are walking away in new bodies, with new elements of yourselves.

Always remember that each is as the other. You are as one. When it is that you move forward, you will remember, 'There go I and there go my feelings of life and of love.' Come then into your largeness, the entirety of all that you are. Simply tell Spirit… 'This is what I want to move into.' You will be supported. Beings of light come to help you. We can't make the decisions. Once you make the decisions you are supported, completely supported.

*Joy comes in different forms, a friend,
a flower, a butterfly.*

Chapter eight

My family's first task on return from the winter workshop was to organize permanent accommodation for the next seven months. We found a simple, two-bedroom apartment, even smaller than the size of our first home. Such a small place could only hold necessities: beds for Michael, Rebecca and me - and basic living room furniture. As Melissa was due to return to Australia in a few weeks we decided she could improvise with a foam mattress on the floor. With a couch, table, several chairs and a few kitchen items the home seemed adequate until Rebecca pleaded that she needed a TV. Michael obliged. He carefully chose one to function with our dual system VCR from Asia and small enough to not overpower the tiny living room.

Christmas day came. It was bitterly cold outside. Snow fell gently as people from the group gathered for a celebratory lunch. That really meant all the Australians and a few Americans without family nearby. Everyone brought a contribution to the meal, making an interesting combination of American and Australian dishes. I'd brought several packets of traditional Christmas crackers filled with trinket, hat and joke from Australia, so we sat with colorful paper crowns on our heads, eating plum pudding. The Americans thought we looked a trifle ridiculous.

In a few days we planned to leave for our trip to California. We had prepared the car, found maps and organized accommodation for the holiday. The next workshop was in two and a half weeks in Santa Barbara and our mission was to see as much of America as possible on the way there.

From the beginning the trip was incredible. As we drove past spectacular geological formations along the highways over the Rocky Mountains, I was breath taken by the stunning scenery. The snow-capped rocks colored in reds and earth tones lay soaking up the sun's rays. The views were awesomely different from every angle.

It took four days to drive across country to San Diego to see the Zoo and Wildlife Park. A day at the Grand Canyon en route was disappointing. We needed more time to explore the area. We had seen many widely published photographs taken by professionals from the best vantage points, so somehow the real thing didn't quite have the excitement we expected. The vastness of the park and cliffs was overwhelming. We missed the airport offering short flights over the canyon. In hindsight, a birds-eye view was probably the best way to spend such a short time there.

Materialistic fantasy was our trip's highlight with a week in Los Angeles - enough time to visit Disneyland and Universal Studios. The weather was perfect and it was off-season at these theme parks as schools were in session. They were pleasantly quiet, an absolute fluke in our planing but obviously a great advantage when lining for rides. We quickly scooted under the miles of crowd control barriers. Shorter queues meant more rides. This truly was a remarkable couple of weeks together. Something I would always remember.

I suspected this would probably be our last family vacation. After Melissa returned to college in Australia I presumed she and Rebecca would plan their own separate holidays as independent young adults. However, being a mother, I fantasized about having a future vacation somewhere like Bali with them, their partners and my grandchildren, in maybe ten years time.

During the trip the four of us always shared one motel room. It would have been nice to have two motel rooms some nights, for often I wanted to be alone with Michael. However the extra expense didn't seem worth it when he wouldn't talk much anyway. Most of our conversations were one-sided and it seemed he scorned anything I suggested.

Santa Barbara, like San Diego, was full of Australian eucalyptus trees. The greenery was quite different from the mid-west environment of sparse vegetation and far more resembled the tree-lined streets of Australia.

Our workshop was in a beautiful retreat, bounded by a river and long rock wall along a quiet road. Manicured lawns were around several statues near a small chapel and a small citrus orchard grew near our lodging. The environment was peaceful and I was relieved to no longer be reliant on the car for the week we were lodged there.

Through the entire holiday the car's engine continued to cut out. Always it seemed to require a few minutes rest to restart. Although this happened less than ten times through the journey we were anxious about the vehicle's reliability. Every evening we'd check at a garage to see what could be done. The mechanics seemed either unable to diagnose the problem or wanted to sell us various replacement parts. The car didn't improve with any of the changes. Michael observed several characteristics including how the car ran better with a full tank of petrol and that it would eventually start again.

A few of these power loss situations were terrifying. Once in the Nevada desert with nothing in sight, the car wouldn't start for ten minutes. The other was on one of the Los Angeles freeways. Fortunately, the car's engine restarted as we moved without power. We decided to stick to the outer lanes on the road so it would be easy to pull over to the shoulder if the engine failure occurred again.

"What are you going to do about the car?" Michael asked, emphasizing the *you*, when we arrived at Santa Barbara. I was speechless and totally unable to comprehend his anger toward me. Maybe because I bought the car he assumed it was also my responsibility to organize its repairs. Fortunately, after I found a phone book and struggled looking through the Yellow Pages, Michael took over and booked a mobile repair business specifically for Hondas. This mechanic was a lifesaver, for although various others had changed parts to 'fix' the problem, he actually knew the vehicle and its foibles.

"I'll check the odometer. With the symptoms you described…Yep – around 160,000 miles. That's it – the fuel pump. Have you had to change the transmission?"

"That was done six months before we bought it."

"You were lucky! '85 model – trouble with the left rear window yet?"

He knew these cars. He changed the fuel pump and did a minor service and the car didn't balk again.

Melissa continued her active participation in the group.

"There's something about Dad that makes me angry. I don't really want to be near him."

I added, "That's strange, because I keep thinking Michael is cruel. But that doesn't make sense to me. That's one thing I definitely believe he isn't. Why would him being 'cruel' keep coming into my mind?"

We meditated with the sound of the chakra tuned bowl and I briefly felt something sticky poured over my head – blood – but immediately forgot it as images of the girls' childhood took over. Their childhood and our home were things I related to – they weren't obscure, like anointing with blood. Neither Melissa nor I found anything that could explain our odd feelings about Michael. But we had expressed them as elements we wanted to understand and opened channels to discover why we had these thoughts in our minds.

As a group we were more comfortable with each other and quickly brought our issues into the forum. Another session opened and a woman went into her past, sobbing,

"My mother wouldn't believe me…my brothers couldn't do any wrong. She wouldn't listen to me asking for her help. They were so cruel; they knew they could get away with anything…. They would torment me…Sometimes I had to hide for my life…."

Several people wept as this outpouring triggered them. Small groups formed within the room as some people moved closer to those in process and listened, offering silent support or asking questions to stimulate more memories.

"Never put any words into anyone's head. Only repeat what they say," Verna was adamant. "Questions to ask are, How do you feel? When did this happen? How old were you? Were you alone? Never say, "Was so and so there?" Rather ask, "Is there anything else you can remember?"

In this particular session the energy buzzed with remembrances of abuse. I sat alone and watched the others, a little surprised by the number of people triggered. I pondered the amount of cruelty in the world and why people were so violent to each other. What was wrong with our society?

Suddenly my own body felt strange. My skin prickled. With eyes closed I asked myself what was happening. Was I being affected by my recent memory of being abused as a toddler? No, that didn't evoke a response. I had healed many layers of that episode. It couldn't affect me like that now…. I waited a few moments. Then in my mind's eye a strange scene unfolded.

It seemed to be outdoors, with huge boulders around. There was an entrance between some of the rocks and I could see a gathering of people…and a full-length table with a body on.

I focused on the body. Why was it there?

It had a fancy ornamental gown and shoes, a queen. I don't even know if it was male or female, but if it was a queen it is most likely female. She was a queen because she had twins …which was really special…two babies. She is probably dead…I don't know…Definitely not moving…Just above the head was a candelabra…silver with some candles.

Definitely not a standard dinner table. It has a grey top…there are some objects on the table. I see them although they don't register in my brain for I notice there are grooves along the sides of the table…

I was stunned reliving this scene. Was I making it up? No! But where did it come from? More pictures screened through my mind.

I saw other people there…they were more like shapes and forms than distinct people. I sat in a chair. I think I was tied up. It seems probable…around the hands, behind the chair…maybe my feet too. I have a robe on…maybe I'm naked underneath? The other people have robes on with different colors lining the lapel and hood, different dark colors. I *am* naked underneath. Someone to my right stands with a dark robe on…the hood over his head.

I couldn't see a face but somehow I knew it was my father-in-law, Poppa. He was holding a gold tray with gold colored goblets on it. Maybe they were bronze.

"I don't want to drink the blood," burst out of my mouth.

The words woke me out of my trance-state. My eyes flew open. Oh my God, this had to be ritual abuse. I thought back to Rhonda's experience of torture of children and ceremonies But blood drinking? Is this really true? Is it my memory? I don't have the imagination to concoct this.

"No. Don't drink that blood." Verna said.

My eyes focused and saw her striding by. Verna brought me back to the reality of the room. I was torn between sitting in the midst of a healing group and being engulfed in a vision with its accompanying shock, prickly skin and weird feelings. What had just happened?

This recollection seemed like a lucid dream where I remember the scenes and participants clearly. A very, very conscious dream...but it wasn't a dream. It was a memory, for here I was, seated on a chair in a room in Santa Barbara, USA, wide-awake.

I questioned my vision. Why would I see a body? Why was it dressed? This seemed something like Rhonda's description of ritual abuse ceremonies. I hadn't heard her describe bodies on tables. But I suspected that different groups, although similar, had different customs, and everyone who had memories had varied stories. I knew this was ritual abuse.

I closed my eyes again and felt body parts being stuffed into my mouth.

I spat into the wad of tissues in my hand. The revolting feeling of slimy stuff in my mouth wouldn't go. Nothing could cleanse that sensation. My body shook, my head jerked. Something happened to the right side of my face. It felt like electrocution on one side. Did they use low voltage electrocution? Electrocution low enough so it didn't kill, but high enough to terrorize the victim? It was hard to believe that what I saw in my mind's eye was significant. Had I seen this scene in a book? How would I feel such a part of it if I had only seen a picture? Why would I notice my father-in-law as a participant...and know I am in a chair bound and naked under a robe, at the foot of a table that had a body on it? Why would I shout, "I don't want to drink the blood."- and think there was blood in those gold colored goblets? And how did I know the blood in the goblets was drained out of the body and allowed to run down the sides of the table along a special groove?

I experienced a huge body shock when feeling, sensing and seeing these memories. I kept thinking, *This can't be true. This can't be true. This didn't happen to me. It's not true.*

My body was fatigued and my mind was numb. I looked through my eyes, completely detached from what I saw. The rest of the group was in slow motion as I observed someone sitting twenty inches away looking directly at me. I turned my head and slowly surveyed other groups in the room, then honed in on Melissa. Three women surrounded her, holding and supporting her.

The eerie sound of Melissa's scream brought me back to the room, back to the group. I returned to present reality, no longer detached, as I watched my daughter in despair and terror. I knew she had support from others in the group but I wasn't yet fully back in my own body. I didn't know how to get to help her or see what was happening.

Helen, the psychic, rushed over.

"Melissa is going through the same thing as you. Come over here, it's your whole family. You're all involved."

I couldn't think. I was in another reality…one of shock and dissension. My heart simultaneously ached and pounded in fear. Helen had to hold my hand and guide me towards my daughter. Melissa shook, cried and kicked. Her body re-enacted pushing away the tortuous implements that inflicted pain. Her vision wasn't the same as mine but the theme was. She remembered torment. Another episode of ritual abuse.

"They burned my feet," she screamed.

Did this mean we were all involved? Was this what was called multi-generational ritual abuse?

I stood in front of Melissa, very confused.

"Are you OK, Melissa?" I asked after a little while.

"Yeah, I'm fine."

Sure. Who really is fine after an experience like that? Oh, how we belittled the agony of trauma. Why couldn't we say, 'I've just had an unbelievable memory that I know is true, but I don't want to believe. I feel sick and exhausted from the feelings that came with my inner vision of torture and terror. I would love someone to hold me and nurture me and tell me I'm safe, loveable and this memory isn't ridiculous. Believe me, please.'

No, we could only respond in the way we'd been trained: emotionless and dismissive of the pain.

"Michael's father is involved. It comes from Michael's side of the family. I saw it," Helen explained her perception. She didn't know I had also seen Michael's father in my inner vision. She saw it independently. I noted her comment in my shocked brain. So, it came from Michael's side of the family. Helen confirmed my thoughts. The little energy available to my brain thought, *Well, at least that means it didn't come from my family. Helen told me it was Michael's family. Michael had probably been involved as a child if that were the case.*

Why hadn't he seen abuse in his childhood? Why did he always think there was something wrong with my family? How arrogant his family was. They always acted as if they knew everything and were always right. Women were inferior in their opinion.

My God. What did they do to their grandchildren, my daughters? Slowly I started to comprehend something of the enormity of the last few hours of memories. What did they do to me? I felt angry at the façade of Michael's father. I was wild at my involvement in this abuse because of his family. How dare they do this to my children and me!

It made me feel better to believe that my birth family wasn't involved. I chose to forget all my images of my brother's abuse and something about my father I hadn't quite got a handle on. It suited me to believe Helen's narrower vision and not where my own previous recollections were leading me. I wasn't going to suggest to her that my family were probably also involved. It all seemed too much to cope with so it was easier to ignore my hunches and images.

I looked back at what we'd recalled in the group so far. The girls had been in a park tied to poles; Melissa's feet had been burned as part of torture; they had seen dead babies. Where had those babies come from? I had seen a group of people in robes and a dead body on an altar table; I felt as if I'd been electrocuted. What more was there to see? Wasn't this horrible enough? But why would anyone do these things? Why were we involved? What were our parts? What was the whole purpose of this? How on earth did we see and do these things without ever remembering them till now.

It was all too much for me. I didn't want to know anything. I didn't want to talk to anyone…. I wanted to hide…with my no-thinking brain. I was so ashamed of myself, of my energy. Wouldn't people be able to sense horrible energy about me from my involvement in this abuse? My emotions exhausted me. What had happened in my life? What was real? I still didn't understand how someone could be involved in this and not remember. I had seen a dead body! How is a dead body disposed of? How did the person die? A queen: I couldn't comprehend how I knew what that meant. Two babies, twins: very special.

I so much wanted someone to tell me it was all right. But it wasn't.

This was insane knowledge that we were recollecting.

Nothing could soothe this disorder destroying my family's life. There were no pacifying words to placate these travesties. Is this why I felt my life was missing something…that I hadn't quite 'got' what life was about? Is this why I felt like such an immature, forty-five year old woman?

Rhonda and Daniel had remembered ritual abuse but they had known for a while. Rhonda hadn't described anything like I saw and she seemed to remember better than I did.

I had to talk to her.

"Am I making this up? Rhonda, can you help me remember? Is this really true? What is going on in my life? Am I crazy?"

"No, Christina, you're not making this up. These are your memories. It's true."

"Have you seen dead bodies on tables?"

"Oh yes. I don't say everything I see. Sometimes it seems too much to tell everyone."

Fortunately, I wasn't alone. Although everybody in the workshop moved through their own different clearing, we still supported each other. I couldn't have survived without their love and care. We ate our meals together, walked the Santa Barbara Beach and strolled along the eucalyptus-lined roads.

Although we worked on current issues and patterns in our workshops, abuse was emerging. Ritual abuse. An insidious cult that brainwashes its members to forget the travesties they partake in. Rebecca spoke to me later.

"Why is it such a big deal for you, Mum? I knew from the very beginning in December that the whole family was involved. When Melissa and I were in the park I knew it was Poppa who took us there. He held my hand and walked with us."

"Did you really know then? Why didn't you tell us?"

"I guess I was a bit shy. I didn't know anyone in the group and I'm still just a kid. It was Melissa's story and she didn't seem to remember that bit. Anyway, back then, I thought we all saw the same scenes. I didn't realize we only remembered what we were ready to remember."

I couldn't respond. There was nothing to say.

I worried about my beautiful daughters. What sort of life had we bought them into?

I was aghast about what seemed like my irresponsibility as a mother. When they were little I was often angry with them if they didn't match my expectations. All too often I would let Granny and Poppa baby-sit. I wanted the girls to have a good relationship with their grandparents. How could I fail to know about this abuse? I didn't protect them.

When my children were born I was so delighted my daughters would have grandparents around during their childhood. I didn't have mine nearby when I was a child and thought that grandparents always meant more love. But now it seems they could be a source of violation as well. Fortunately, both girls seemed more self-assured than I had been at their age. I was pleased about that.

Now Rhonda's words about targeting children for abuse four months ago had more meaning.

I was drawn to Rhonda's nurturing and loving energy. She was a tremendous support for me. Her abuse had ended when her family moved, before she was a teenager. The narrative of her memories was always so clear and detailed when they surfaced; it appeared she'd always known and wasn't recollecting for the first time. She clearly remembered what she did, what she had recited and who had been present.

This evening she remembered something else: the agony and deep distress of being forced to kill. I watched Rhonda's body shake, and heard her voice change as she recounted her story. I felt the grief with her.

"I was expected to make friends with the kids who were 'outsiders' at school, and bring them to the circle. I knew what was going to happen to them. They were going to be tortured," Rhonda sobbed. "I didn't want that to happen. I really only wanted to have friends. There was one little boy I remember, he was terrified. I could see the look in his eyes. We were all standing there together, just us kids. We didn't dare move. We knew he was going to be killed. But they were going to torture him first. I couldn't bear it. I was meant to kill him…but I didn't do it the way they wanted me to. I did it quickly so he didn't have to suffer so much pain. I thought it was my only choice."

Her adult body convulsed in the grief of the agonizing dilemma. Emotions stored for a lifetime flooded out. It was time to recognize the decision forced on a little girl: choices of life and death. I watched and listened as Rhonda cried in despair about the small boy. Death would happen anyway, so the quicker the better. Was this the reality she had to live with? What terrible choices forced on a child.

Verna began healing for Rhonda, for all of us, removing patterns, bringing in light energies.

"We have all killed in some lifetime, if not this one. No judgment can be made. Everyone needs healing."

She started a prayer for the child who died, and for Rhonda.

I didn't hear a word of the prayer. My body, my emotions, had turned into despair. I started sobbing uncontrollably. Suddenly, I knew that I too, had killed. The prayer continued as I wept. I couldn't stop the tears.

I internalized my own prayer. *I'm sorry, so sorry...God forgive me!*

I felt shame, agony, guilt and grief for my cruelty, for my inability to take the knife on myself, instead of the victim. The group's prayer finished. I still cried.

Verna turned to me, "Do you have something you want to say, Christina?"

I have to get this out, however self-conscious I feel about my feebleness and cruelty.

"I've killed someone too." I said.

"Do you know who, or when?"

"I have no idea. I just know I've done this..."

How could I ask forgiveness when I don't even know my victim? I didn't know when, or how. I will never do that again! I was a coward to go against my own judgment of right and wrong. I should kill myself first. I will never kill again. Although we are spirit - eternal - and spirit never dies, there is still no reason for forcing death on someone. I took a vow. If it came to the point of being forced to kill, I would kill myself first. Would I have the courage? I wondered.

This was crazy. I had so many questions. Why were people killed in the cult? How could I forget something so horrendous? Did the mind really suppress these horrors so we didn't go mad? How old was I? How did they get the potential victims?

Did I go to school the next day and simply do what teenage girls do, oblivious to the previous night's activities? It's odd that I write this...I thought I had no idea of my age. Why would I think about being a schoolgirl? Whatever age I had been, I was sure in denial. Just like the story I heard about the father denying his son was dead.

I lived my life as though I was a normal, law-abiding citizen; obviously suppressing the memories of the murders and rapes I'd seen. I'm still a spirit in a body, but, oh God, help me, I wish I could start again. This is not what I wanted to know, or how I wanted my life to be. Where is the Love? Where is the 'do unto others as you would have others do unto you?'

No one in the workshop commented about our being in the midst of murderers.

Once Michael had a work colleague who, after doing some in depth courses confessed in the group he thought he had killed someone in a hit and run accident. It was raining hard and he'd driven a long way. He thought he had hit an animal so kept driving along the dark country road. The next day he saw a news item about a pedestrian hit on one of the roads he had been driving on the previous night.

I wondered at that time how I would react to a murderer, but in my understanding, thought I could accept the person if the murder wasn't calculated.

How could I call myself a human being? I felt bad. Terrible. Pained. What sort of person was I? I felt alone, unloved and so hateful toward myself.

Rhonda sat next to Verna, who embraced her. She had human contact in her grief, indicating 'I empathize with your feelings. I still love you.'

I was alone in the group. Unworthy as a human being to ask someone to hold my hand. No one volunteered. Everyone seemed to be in shock. Oh, but I longed for someone to accept me, to hold me. I wanted to be nurtured too. I felt more evil than Rhonda. She had been a child. I seemed to have been involved as an adult. I should have been responsible. I have children who have been tortured. What more unknown things have I done in my life?

The surfacing of my denied, surreal life terrified me.

During a break from our group, I wandered outside the buildings and through the gardens. I came across a statue of Mother Mary. She stood in her cream alabaster form between two orange trees, arms reaching out to embrace whoever needed her compassion. I stood alone, facing her, and took in the softness beautifully carved in her face. I touched her cheek gently. I wanted to be held; be in her arms. The tranquility of the grounds calmed me. My life and my beliefs were shattered. How could I believe I was a fairly average person, a reasonable wife and mother who kept the house clean, the gardens tidy and supported my daughters and husband in their lives? Was I a good person because I cared for the environment and community? The beautiful Mother of Jesus spoke to me as I meditated on the grass before her. As I lay on the ground Spirit touched my feet. Then the scent of roses, a signal of her presence, wafted over my face. 'Mary is here. She's in two places at once,' I thought.

"I can be in many places at once," she replied. "You chose a path of thorns to cut the ties that bind you."

As Spirit held me in total love, I understood. This life of mine was Karmic. The law of cause and effect. I chose my life. It was still a hard path to tread.

The essence of Mother Mary left. The statue remained. I was to follow my destiny. But Mary had demonstrated how Spirit would come with love, when needed.

Michael hardly talked. I thought he didn't like being near me, as most of his conversation was critical of my actions. I was unable to communicate with him and felt isolated within my thoughts. I didn't know what he wanted. He was in his own world and I wanted to be alone with myself, too. Things weren't going well. We talked about ritual abuse, family…but not much else. Not about us. There was too much fear to be intimate in our conversations or to discuss our relationship. I seemed worse than him. He only remembered a little of his victimized childhood. I couldn't project beyond the immediate. Although I'd seen cruel acts from my adult self and the girls saw abuse from Michael's parents, none of us considered Michael's involvement. He seemed innocent of cruelty. I was scared. If Michael didn't love me, who would? On a subconscious level I feared abandonment. I didn't know how to voice my fears. I probably knew more than I let my consciousness see. I was in denial and if I talked, more would come out, which would further horrify me. Was I seeing things as they were, or only seeing things I had created? Either way, everything was enmeshed in confusion and disbelief.

Indira, the spiritual teacher whom Verna channeled became part of our group. I began to think her energy was with us during all our workshop time and not just when Verna went into trance. Indira's information was helpful and insightful to issues we were raising during our group time.

Her message for me this workshop was a response to some thoughts I had expressed earlier in the day. I had cut off my lower chakras, including the root, sexual and solar plexus, from my upper ones, because of the sexual abuse I had sensed.

Indira confirmed what I had been feeling.

Christina, we will hook you up completely if you like. Hook you together. Sometimes there are parts of the lower chakras you don't want to feel, that's why you unhitched yourself, like a horse from the cart. There will be different sensations that sometimes you won't want to feel ... surges of energies. When this happens, just realign them and take a break from what you have been doing.

During the workshop Verna observed a mark on my neck.

"Did you know there's a red mark that comes and goes on your neck?" she asked.

Obviously I didn't, for I couldn't see or feel it.

"It started when we discussed shackles. Try wearing something tight around your neck for a couple of days. See what reaction you have."

I did. Although I felt restricted with so much pressure on my throat chakra, no clear memory arose. I didn't like the dentist or hairdresser putting their hands near my throat or head, so wondered if I'd been strangled. More than a pillow stuffed over my face when I was a baby. Had someone tried to 'do me in' or was I just unlovable? The skin around my wrist also often broke out in a rash, and marks like slashes occasionally appeared on the underside of my arms. Sometimes they looked like rope burns. These unexpected marks started me thinking.

Our body never lies. I was learning to question my body and reactions for underlying causes. I needed to search my subconscious to find what these unexpected rashes and marks were telling me.

A fire walk was a highlight of this workshop. A huge bonfire about six feet high was lit late in the afternoon to prepare glowing coals for the evening's walk. I stood by the fire and felt the immense heat released. When the fire had died down, Michael and Russell raked the bright red coals over a designated area for our fire walk.

The group gathered around after being psychologically prepared. Michael suggested he and I hold hands and walk together over the coals. It seemed ludicrously easy. Everyone cheered and lined up to walk in groups or alone. I walked again, alone. And again. At least six times I paced barefoot over the burning coals. I could do it - even by myself. I wondered how long I could stand still on the coals and walked more slowly the next time.

The evening finished and the group dissipated. I helped rake the coals together and poured water over them. They still emanated tremendous heat as the water evaporated. I held my hand over the glowing embers and wondered how I'd walked on them. I was certain they'd burn my fingers. I couldn't do now what I had done only an hour earlier without the group energy.

Next morning we discussed our achievement.

"I see how I treat my achievements as no big deal. I walked over those coals about six times. That didn't seem anything special, but it was. Now I see what little accolade I give to my accomplishments. I dismiss my abilities and courage," I told the group.

Fire walking seemed almost inconsequential at the time. However, I don't think I could walk on the hot coals again.

After the workshop we immediately returned to Colorado. We'd spent three weeks travelling. Money was tight and we'd had enough time in the car together. I was eager to return to our temporary home.

We had three free weeks before our next workshop. Schoolwork resumed Rebecca's focus and since Melissa was going back to Australia soon, she goofed around. Michael spent his days at the library and bookshops. I certainly didn't resent that. He'd worked hard all his life and deserved a break. I spent my time helping in my friend's greenhouse. I enjoyed being with people who had nothing to do with the workshops and didn't know anything about ritual abuse.

During this break, Melissa's behavior changed. One day she walked down the street after informing Michael she might cut herself with my pocketknife. He phoned me at the greenhouse.

"Melissa needs help. I'm really concerned. She left home. I drove the car to find her and had to talk hard to get her to come back with me. I don't know what to do, she might kill herself."

I found his story hard to believe. Michael was undoubtedly exaggerating, and dramatizing the situation. When I returned home, Melissa asked to keep my knife. There was something odd in her behavior. I thought she was acting, trying us out in some way. Her eyes were strange and appeared different in some way.

"I need to have the knife with me. I like it. It is a nice size to hold in my hand."

"This is silly Melissa. Look, you can have my knife if you promise not to use it to cut yourself. But I want it back soon."

I felt confident she was sensible enough not to damage herself, even though she wasn't acting her normal self. But the whole situation was odd. I didn't know then that she had different personalities that were starting to show themselves.

Rebecca and Melissa had to share a small bedroom. This was difficult for them as their likes and habits were quite opposite. One went to bed early, the other late. They hadn't shared a bedroom for the past nine years. I thought they did well, considering the circumstances. We didn't know many people here apart from those doing the course. Basically it was difficult to meet other friends. We went to karate and church a few times. These weren't places to meet seventeen and nineteen year olds. Our course, with its monthly one-week meeting, meant there wasn't much spare time available for cultivating friendships. Melissa and Rebecca were stuck with each other as companions.

They weren't great friends. Rebecca had a good group of friends at primary school and Melissa had been more of a loner. Melissa's social life had been a void. She was often lonely and learned to retreat into herself at an early age. Books and knowledge became her companions. I was pleased she liked her university course and believed the student living environment provided good social interaction. I figured she would sort her social life out when back in those surroundings.

She was due to start back at university in several weeks.

Injustice must be made visible

Chapter nine

Melissa's vacation was nearly over so I confirmed her return flight to Australia for the end of January, a week before college started. A day later, Verna phoned me.

"I'd like Melissa to attend the next workshop. When does she start college?"

" She starts during that week so can't make it for the workshop unfortunately."

"Would it work for her to change her ticket and arrive there a few days late?"

"I'll ask," I said wondering why it could be that important for her to stay.

Melissa checked her timetable.

"I'll only miss a couple of days. I should be able to catch up easily. The first week only has introductory lectures anyway. I'll just notify someone about accommodation and my books."

Internally, I rejoiced. Did I dare show my excitement? I wanted Melissa with us longer, particularly since we wouldn't see her for another seven months. I didn't want her alone on the other side of the world for all that time. She was already an active participant in the group, exploring her spirituality and healing. Still a teenager, I admired the way she used her courage, integrity and self-trust. Another workshop would be good for her. This was the equivalent therapy that Karen, the psychologist at the student health clinic suggested Melissa needed.

I rescheduled Melissa's flight. The few extra weeks gave us planning time for support when she returned to college. I thought about what she would need. A mobile phone seemed necessary to provide security and fast contact with us and she could continue healing via regular phone sessions with Verna during her holidays. Several of our relatives lived close to Melissa's college residence. They could help when necessary. If she needed us, either Michael or I could return home within a few days. My 'limited brain' had satisfied its need to have things sorted out. I convinced myself that Melissa was well organized for her student life until we returned from America towards the end of the year.

Now I see how little I truly understood about ritual abuse. Its significance and impact hadn't yet penetrated my being. I barely coped emotionally with my own discoveries of the lie I had lived. My mind, so good at blocking out overload, was in its 'survive the day' role. I created a little box in my head which contained what I thought ritual abuse was in relation to my family. That was all I could manage. The true reality of its repercussion was beyond my comprehension.

What was the reality? As a family, we had some remembrance of Melissa's, Rebecca's and my own involvement in ritual abuse involving Michael's family. I had memories of sexual abuse as a child and some ritual abuse as an adult. Michael had accessed a fear-ridden childhood memory of hiding from the devil in kitchen cupboards as well as images of fires and chanting.

Shock overwhelmed my ability to think. Any possibility of danger from mixing with Michael's family didn't enter my consciousness and I'd completely denied the prospect of involvement in ritual abuse from my family. The comprehension of what our memories really meant hadn't filtered into my awareness. My mind blocked the most obvious conclusions.

Perhaps it was only me who was so oblivious. It is quite possible Melissa and Rebecca told me of the possibilities and I hadn't grasped how far the ritual abuse web that we were caught in, reached.

Confusion verging on disbelief was my first response to memories of ritual abuse. As I'd been in denial for my entire life it was virtually impossible to turn around with total acceptance because of a handful of memory pieces. Although violent body reactions occurred with my visual memories, I still wasn't totally convinced my memories were true. How would anyone who knew our families believe me? Where was the proof of our recollections?

Some memories were so obscure and fragmented it was difficult to link them together. Estimating my age and location of the memory was often impossible. It was rare for a whole picture to emerge. But there were enough big chunks of memory for us to know that ritual abuse undoubtedly existed in our lives. However, I didn't want to be accused of jumping to conclusions, particularly with negativity involving my family.

Always we were encouraged to express what came to our mind during the groups.

"Just say whatever is there. Let the words out. You can change them later," our facilitator continually encouraged.

There was no judgment in the group about what people recalled. Healing was the agenda and speaking our memories was a vital part.

Ritual abuse had been virtually the only discussion topic during the last few weeks at home. It cropped up when we interacted with Rhonda and Daniel. Their memories of involvement as brother and sister were growing. Often we joked and laughed about the ludicrousness of it all, especially Daniel. How ridiculous we were, laughing about the very things that we wanted to cry and scream about. The pain of remembering was too great and the consequence of being involved in something so horrendous was sometimes beyond our ability to cope. I was so grateful for these friends who trusted their memories but still looked at everything lightheartedly whenever possible.

Later, I realized they didn't really have any more understanding or assurance in themselves than I did. They believed in me and encouraged me to trust myself. I had confidence in them and inspired them to give credence to what they saw, too. Yet we were all bewildered. I thought their memories were more valid than mine. For my own reasons often I didn't want to see how my family was remembering similar incidents that were screaming for recognition and acknowledgement.

Daniel had an in-built detector for ritual abuse.

"You know, Christina, I knew from the very beginning you were involved. The first time my body went into spasm I noticed your reaction to me. After that I watched and waited for you to come up with a memory. Your body gives it away. I see it in other people too." His detector is still accurate. "I can tell quite easily. There is something about the energy of a person, sometimes a grayness, or look in their eyes that indicates ritual abuse and I get the shivers."

As we worked on ourselves the energy of abuse transformed. When a memory no longer griped us with emotion we knew we had cleared it. The value of the work we were doing in the course was to release feelings such as fear, sadness and anger associated with our recollections. These sensations ruled our everyday life decisions without our awareness of their impact. It was vital to get in touch with our deep anger so the grief could also emerge.

Still too cold for camping on the mountain, our next workshop was scheduled in Arizona, a day's drive away. We would be staying in adobe units built in the side of the red mountains not far from Sedona. I looked forward to visiting this tourist spot and experiencing the energy vortexes.

I wrote down some memory snippets procured whilst meditating during this workshop. They were powerful recollections:

I saw Melissa having to stab her baby.
I saw Rebecca tied up and forced to eat body parts and drink blood.
I saw fire.
I saw me force Rebecca's arm to do something.
I saw that although present, I was oblivious to Melissa and Rebecca being tortured. They were told, 'look, your parents don't care.'
Michael's powerlessness was linked to Rebecca.
I saw myself birthing a child.
I saw a white cloth around Rebecca's neck.
I felt myself being raped and experienced numbness in my body and legs.

Melissa saw Poppa there. He told her she had to go to other groups to learn. She was being trained for something important, a leader who needed extra experience.

Had I ever had a real life? I was furious with Verna for creating this chaos in my life. She let this all come up. Maybe she was totally neurotic about ritual abuse. I thought it couldn't be as prevalent as she said. The structure of my family was disintegrating and my own beliefs were crumbling. I had no foundation to stand on, no security in myself and no reality. I wished I'd never come to these workshops. They were messing up my life. I became very angry.

I thought I was part of a fairly average family. But with these stories of rape, abuse, cruelty and murder, I no longer knew who we were. This wasn't a fictional story, This was *my* life. It was real. What's more, it was not only my life; it was my children's lives and my husband's life.

I am only one person. How could I possibly take all this in? Everything we experienced was going beyond the OK zone. I was in no man's land. My ability to think and function was stalled at a very basic level. Part of me wasn't here with the rest of me. There was too much to contemplate.

My life seemed like a horror movie, but I didn't know I had been a star performer.

Dear God, it is so difficult to accept that my life is exactly as I chose and allowed to continue. Yes, I believe I chose this path before birth. My involvement, parents, siblings, probable partners and help I would receive, were all set in motion in the spirit realm, before my birth. Only I was responsible and I could not blame anyone else for my situation. But how could it take so long to recognize my role? Why would I have to go through all this fear and torture for more than forty years - have a confused 'normal life' and drag my own children into it, even though I know they chose their own circumstances as well?

It would be easier to blame someone else than take responsibility, then I could remain a victim. How I wished I could blame all those men who abused me, and have an instantaneous cure to the messes in my relationships. I wanted sympathy, to be told how wonderful I was to have survived all this, and that it wasn't my fault..

Compassion and love did come to me from the group but it was my responsibility to heal myself. No one else could do it for me and it was my choice to see that.

During my first channeled session with Indira fourteen years ago I asked her what was wrong with Rebecca when she was a baby.

"Indira, why did Rebecca cry continuously for the first three months of her life?"

She cried because she knew what she was coming into and didn't relish all her choices.

Rebecca had known about this abuse and her prospects, even as a baby. She chose her life before birth.

Now Indira's answer began to make sense. Rebecca reluctantly agreed to immerse herself in ritual abuse during this life and wasn't looking forward to it. The answer Indira gave was all I could have coped with then. If she had have told me fourteen years ago that I was involved in such horrific abuse I would cringe at the thought of what had happened to my children, I would have thought she was nuts. Indira had worded her answer in such a way that I could handle it at that time. How can you tell somebody something if they don't want to know? I interpreted the answer in my own way. The real in-depth answer stayed beyond my comprehension for another one and a half decades.

Not everyone in our group workshop had experienced ritual abuse, nor had everyone been sexually abused. Like a wave, abuse issues would wash over us, allow healing, clear up and finish. Those who didn't have such abuse as part of their lives were probably meant to learn about it. Nothing happens by chance.

Our workshop was in a homely building. The beautiful living area opened onto the bare red rock on the edge of a small cliff. A three-foot high statue of Kwan Yin stood in the window, watching over us. The Chinese Goddess of Mercy seemed appropriate energy to be immersed in as we released our human suffering.

Verna was working with Cassandra, who lay on the floor shaking. The normally vibrant woman was pale, with tears welling in her eyes as she spoke. I watched a few people move closer to support Cassandra as her body released energy from stored childhood abuse. They formed a circle on the floor around her.

My body wouldn't let me sit quietly. It shook. I had no thoughts, just energy moving through me. Rhonda, always loving and supportive, moved to sit next to me. I wanted tenderness and to feel safe. She hugged me; what a sensitive friend she was. Waves of energy moved through my body from my feet up.

"Breathe deeply, Christina. Come back into your body. Let's walk around so you don't stop the energy from flowing." Rhonda was aware of people's energy and feelings and noticed a change happening with me.

I wanted to disappear and leave my body, leave this room, as I had during times of abuse. This defense mechanism worked back then to reduce pain and protect my psyche.

"If you walk with me you'll stay in your body." Rhonda walked me around the room. There were small groups of support through the room. "Stay with the feeling of the trauma. Feel it in your muscles."

I really didn't know what was happening to me this time. I was surprised Rhonda came to support me, because I didn't know I was going into memory. Usually I would see clear visual images, smell, or feel something to link my feelings to an explanation for my physical reaction, This time the only sense was the unfamiliar, yet strangely familiar, energy moving through my body. No images came to mind. I didn't know what caused these odd sensations. They were weird: shaking, shivering and jerking – all of it discharge but quite uncomfortable and uncontrollable. I could feel the little bolts of energy flash through my body as a low degree of pain and unpleasant sensation.

I stayed with the feeling in an attempt to let my body integrate. It wasn't easy. There was no word to identify what I felt. Slipping out of body was simpler but I needed to feel the emotion of the trauma for complete healing. I'd grasped the importance of this concept during our workshops together and consciously kept myself attentive to my task of clearing myself. I needed reminding that pictures didn't always come with trauma release. However as Rhonda walked me around the room, the movement took me into memory.

"That's not a good place to put salt," I shrieked, when someone put some on my lips. "Get this stuff off ." Furiously, I wiped my face.

"I've got to get everything off. Here, take my watch."

I had no idea why Verna suggested Helen should put salt on my body, or that it would trigger such a reaction. I ripped my sweater off. I wanted to get everything off my body, even my hair! Rhonda held my arm. It was good to have a friend by my side.

"Rhonda, I feel so strange, I want to take all my clothes off. I know not to do it, but there's something on me and I want to clean it off." I was agitated.

"You're safe here, Christina."

"I'm covered in crap. There's a rope tied tightly around my body, like a mummy. I'm wrapped from head to foot in rope." Rhonda held me firmly. I felt safer. "My throat's aching, burning down to my stomach."

"Why is your throat aching?" she asked me.

"I don't know."

"Yes you do."

"I don't want to know why."

I wonder who I thought I was kidding. We know ourselves. I knew what had been done. I just didn't want to say it.

"It was the shit they were feeding me that caused the burning sensation: blood, body parts and feces."

"Spit it out."

"We can't be sick, they made us eat everything we vomited."

Someone gave me a bottle of water. I held it in my hand. Though I was thirsty, I couldn't drink. My mind associated the bottle with things forced down my throat. A cup of water was acceptable and controllable by me. I felt safe to drink the same water, from the cup.

My throat constricts and I feel sick thinking about it, even now.

I was exhausted. Every time my body played its part and released trauma, my mind would later go round and round, analyzing, questioning if the memory was true. There seemed to be a watcher part that responded to questions from someone outside. Mostly the memory controlled everything happening within my body. My body guided my mind in desperation to release the energy. If my mind decided to block the energy, trauma wouldn't be released. Rhonda helped me leave my mind at rest while I stayed with the energy. She encouraged me to remain with sensation and not dismiss the feelings.

Often we posed questions to another person who was processing to help bring more memory fragments to the surface. This helped in release. Also, we learned it was vital to not touch the person once they entered into memory. Physical contact changed the energy, losing the healing impact of feeling the memory. A traumatized person surely wasn't touched gently during abuse. I wanted to understand everything – why, how, when. I wanted to know how it fit into the part of life that I remembered. I wanted to comprehend how I could possibly lead this second enigmatic life - but it was difficult. After spending a few hours in the group we'd complete the session with healing energies.

"We remove all patterns of eating body parts, from the physical, the mental, the emotional, the intuitional, the atmic, the monadic, the egoic, the lagoic and the twelve levels above the lagoic and beyond...and let massive golden light enter.

"We remove all patterns of having sex with dead bodies, from the physical, the mental, the emotional, the intuitional, the atmic, the monadic, the egoic, the lagoic and twelve levels above the lagoic and beyond. Let massive golden light enter..."

Oh yes, my body recognized these patterns. I let go of everything possible. I didn't want this stuff affecting my life anymore. I let the energy strands be pulled from my body and felt the lightness as they came out. My exhaustion diminished when the golden light entered.

Necrophilia! What on earth does the cult think it is doing? I didn't have to ask what that word meant, I knew. It was revolting. Feeling the pattern drawn out of me and taken to the highest realms for cleansing, I thanked God that I was safe in my recollections with my family and a supportive group of people. Please help me sort out these horrors by the end of the year, I prayed.

Lethargy swamped me. I felt as though I carried the burdens of the world on my back as well as having to care for my family. Michael still hadn't seen his adult part of the abuse. He was sympathetic when we remembered something awful but he didn't share his voice in group. He kept any feelings and visions to himself. No one knew him. He was withdrawn and I began to comprehend how difficult his internalizing made our relationship.

Over time more memories emerged. I saw a dead body hanging from rafters, suspended by a thick rope. The legs and arms were tied together and the mid-back was the part closest to the ground. The head flopped back. I didn't even know if it was human or animal. A hideous thought came: it had been skinned. Not only did they murder but they skinned bodies as well. Who did this skinning? Why would a group of people have sex with dead bodies, kill people and skin them? How could sane people conduct these travesties in churches, community meeting halls or country sheds? The cult perverted every doctrine.

Skinning: what an agonizing way to die. God help those poor people so tortuously murdered. Imagine the pain of every strip of skin removed, sliced with sharp knives. Imagine the terror of anticipation. The victim needed to be able to dissociate to deal with the agony. Children were taught this evil art and their training wasn't on plastic dummies.

This is our society I am talking about, the 21st century. Our world of the new millennium: a technological, modern society. We've put men on the moon. Yet there is still this depravity in our mist, happening somewhere, this very moment. Pray for the children.

Some women in the group pointed out it was a full moon and they would like to have a Goddess ceremony, offering a lighter side of group work. Ceremony didn't appeal to me. I wasn't prepared to contribute but tolerated people's different ways and went along as part of the audience.

Behind the adobe building where we had our sessions was a well-built fire-pit, suitable for the ceremony, without fire. The circular pit was surrounded by about another eight feet or so of dirt with another circular row of bricks beyond. A circle within a circle. I sat on the outer row of bricks, watched the singing and dancing and remembered how I disliked ceremonies. Pompous church rituals, school speech nights, graduation, prayer vigils. I became agitated watching this show. Donna read some poetry, then a participant moved out of the fire pit with a candle in her hand, raised above her head. I suddenly experienced an overlay of another vision, fire everywhere. The flames hissed high and the devil emerged with a rod in his hand. Goose bumps spread over my body. I was nauseated and fearful. No wonder I don't like ceremonies around fire pits.

A week long workshop goes surprisingly quickly. Near the end Michael called me over to talk. Verna, Rhonda and Melissa stood with him.

"Christina, we don't think it is wise for Melissa to return to Australia."

What? What were they talking about? My brain was already in confusion and numbed from our experiences.

"Melissa needs to finish her degree," I said. "What life will she have if she doesn't have this training? How will she earn her living?" My brain could function with practicalities.

"Don't you see what has gone on? Melissa has been programmed to do her Medical Science course," Verna said.

"What? Programmed to do a course? Why? "

Apparently Melissa knew this already.

"Mum, I was programmed to do it. I was training to be high priestess. The knowledge of dissection, the access to drugs, laboratory animals, knives and incinerators is important to the cult. Knowledge of anatomy, access to certain buildings. It's all part of the conditioning."

I knew what she was saying at a simplistic level, I just didn't quite get it. I knew the words and their implications, but couldn't tie them together. Was this abuse still happening? Is that what they were trying to tell me?

"Melissa was still involved in the cult until she came here. You can't let her go home. Her life could be in danger. She will be continually programmed. Now that she's uncovered some memories, she could possibly go insane if exposed again. Any future involvement with her conscious memory open as it is now, could possibly kill her."

I understood Verna's words but couldn't comprehend how we were part of the story.

I thought of the time Melissa had filled in the application forms for tertiary education. She loved problem solving and had considered computer science. A few months before she finished high school, she suddenly changed her mind and decided to do medical science.

It came out of the blue. I knew she was capable of the study but where had the idea of medical science come from? I hadn't considered that she might be interested in it but I guess the cult had. They knew that degree was one of the best for their plans.

On the surface, it appeared Melissa had made a good choice for her career path. She'd be able to work part time if necessary and would always find work, whether voluntary or paid. One so trained could travel the world and do research. It promised to be a very interesting course, opening to a fascinating career. I had no notions of the interest the cult, then unknown to me, had in Melissa's future.

I let it go. My brain was plain overloaded. I couldn't tie in the possibility of danger for Melissa completing her studies with the killing and torture I had remembered. A plan slowly showed itself to me.

"Maybe Melissa could go to another city in Australia and finish her course."

It was possible we were paranoid about anything to do with ritual abuse. How could we still be involved with something that we had just only begun to remember recently? Weren't these all childhood occurrences? I already had forgotten abuse I'd seen on my children.

Then Melissa remembered the terror of being in the wrong place.

"I remember driving to a meeting place, forgetting there was a change of venue. When I got to the original place I remembered where I was meant to be and drove to the new location." Her body shook in fear and she sobbed through her tears, "Mum, they punished me for being late."

Melissa had only had her car license for a year. This was a recent occurrence. The intensity of our discussion sharpened.

"Are you trying to tell me that Melissa's life is in danger if she returns home?" I asked.

"Yes," Rhonda acknowledged.

I was frustrated that I had only just 'got it'. Even so, I hadn't really understood. Throughout my life, I'd created barriers to protect myself, and now these barriers were affecting my ability to reason.

"You need to protect her," Verna said. "She needs to stay with you for the rest of the year and continue healing."

I needed everything repeated for my overloaded brain to comprehend. More decisions. Life wasn't as calm as I hoped it would turn out, but I was capable of taking some action and suggested to Michael that we call Karen, Melissa's counselor at College. She might be able to assist with Melissa's deferment from University.

It only took minutes to be connected to Karen. We didn't tell her the details or mention ritual abuse, only our desire for a year's deferment.

"My experience with Melissa is such that I think it would be a good for her to stay in the USA with her family. She needs to be with you and keep on with counseling. I believe it would be appropriate for her to defer her study and I can help you by writing a letter to the secretary of the Science Faculty."

I still believed we would all be 'healed' by the end of the year and Melissa would return to college with us together as a family in Australia. Not a bad idea except I didn't know what Michael was lining up. He kept his own counsel and wouldn't commit to returning home for work. I didn't want to go to Asia again. I wanted to be together as a family, even if we had to move closer to Melissa's university.

I was creating a fantasy again; planning for something better and happier without focusing on the turmoil we were living in. I couldn't cope with much beyond my narrow vision and had no idea of the time required for the healing process. Forty plus years of abuse with brain-washing doesn't disappear in one year's worth of healing. We started to resolve some confusion and by the end of our workshop we planned to move to another state in Australia when we returned home. Melissa could go to school there. We contacted several universities and decided to base where we lived on which university accepted her. There were a few places where she had the possibility of continuation. Some of them replied quickly, telling us she would have to start her course again. What discouragement, but with all the other turmoil in our life, it was just another blocked path. There were many different ways to go and none of them looked promising. This part of our life wasn't going the way I wanted. Our stability was being shaken at its very roots and I had lost control.

I imagined my body going into nuclear explosion. How I wished it would for I wanted to die. I wanted to disperse into oblivion so every atom and subatomic particle that was part of me disappeared forever. Then my brain would never have to think again. Every one of my beliefs about myself was shattered. I couldn't see any future and there were too many decisions to be made to create one. I was overwhelmed and worn with struggle.

With the workshop completed we drove silently for twelve hours through the night, in front of a snowstorm. Now it was time to call our families and inform them Melissa would be staying in America. Michael called his parents.

"Hi Dad, wanted to let you know that Melissa is staying with us for the rest of the year. She's taking a year off her studies."

We sat together around the phone, ready to say our own hellos. But Michael's face turned white. He placed the receiver back on the hook.

"What happened, Michael? Why did you hang up?"

Michael's eyes were glazed and bulging. He was in shock.

"The devil has spoken," he said.

"What did he say? What happened?"

Michael couldn't answer. He'd been betrayed. The phone had been slammed down in his ear. We didn't bother calling back. In fact, we never discussed it with his father again. What cowards we were. It seemed best to complete this responsibility of informing our families. I called mine. It wasn't easy. How could I tell them what we were discovering? We didn't have a detailed picture, nor did I want to accuse anyone. More than likely they wouldn't have believed us anyway.

It took Michael six months before he could repeat his father's words. Perhaps more was said, but the anger behind the words, 'Melissa is a stupid bitch' was horrific.

Melissa, Rebecca and I often saw Poppa in our cult memories. He was a leader, but at what level of leadership, we didn't know. He was an intelligent man and generous to his grandchildren in normal life. It was also obvious from listening to him, that Poppa stored enormous anger from his own childhood. Did this vehement response from Poppa mean he knew of his own involvement in the cult? Was he aware in his day-to-day life that Melissa was being groomed for leadership? He was involved in her training, so it appeared her year away would affect the leadership grooming. Maybe her changed plans would throw a wrench in his plans and use for her and there were ceremonies planned for her that she would miss. Our life continued. I knew that this too would pass, but the passing wasn't easy. Hopefully the other side had more joy. We cancelled Melissa's return ticket. It was wonderful to know she would be with us, but the reason behind her staying was horrendous.

*Imbalances in our body are
expressions of our hidden feelings.*

Chapter ten

My family didn't journal consistently. I realize now that detailed diary entries may have been helpful in searching for dates over the years, to show patterns in our behavior. I wished I'd recorded times such as when I was physically tired, called on relatives, or had visitors. That way I may have discovered clues or consistencies indicating how our surreal life impacted on us.

I had friends who regularly recorded their feelings and thoughts. But as an ordinary mum with two young children I was busy and definitely too tired to be bothered writing. I didn't develop the habit of writing. I believed I would remember the significant events I experienced during groups I completed in the 1980's but probably forgot plenty. I bought a book to write down my workshop experiences with Verna but my entries became less detailed as time passed, particularly when my issues became emotionally exhausting. Rather, I'd jot down visual snippets but not feelings. This stopped me from delving further, probing and finding more. I didn't know journaling forced the writer to look more closely at different aspects of specific issues. Maybe I couldn't have coped with more anyway. My brain was in such a fog; I could barely manage with anything beyond the immediate moment.

Healing while living a 'normal' outward life was taxing. It appeared safer and more nourishing to spend time with people I knew, rather than being by myself. Basically, I was surviving, not living. Too many memories lurking about could drive me into overwhelm. If I let myself feel everything stirring in my body, I thought I would go crazy. So I held myself together the best I could. Michael never wrote a thing. He always relied on memory and treated me with disdain when I suggested recording notes. Rebecca wasn't one for keeping diaries either. Her goal for the Year Long was to open her psychic skills. Believing she was only here short term, Melissa didn't plan to keep a journal. She had made a commitment a few years earlier to record her dreams and kept that going daily.

We began to wonder if we had been programmed to bury details of events - how we felt and the sort of things that would highlight inconsistencies in our life. If we had kept detailed diaries, we might have seen a pattern of tiredness or illnesses at certain times. It would have been a monitor on our daily lives and maybe revealed more than biorhythms. When we cleaned our cupboards in Australia after the Year Long, Rebecca found an entry in a mostly vacant diary of four years earlier.

Sunday: Auntie Claire and Uncle Patrick visited unexpectedly. They brought some food for lunch; Mum thought that was odd, as they've never done it before.
Monday: I didn't want to get up this morning. I was so tired although I didn't do much on the weekend and went to bed early on Sunday. I could hardly stay awake at school.

The entry was close to Easter, a time of cult ceremonies. Were we drugged with the food to attend a ceremony that evening, making us tired the next day? Why would they have come to visit with food? That was unexpected. More clues from diary records might have given an accurate picture.

I didn't keep dates of menstruation. I always presumed I had a regular twenty-eight-day cycle because that was 'normal'. But Indira once told me; *your belief of regularity wasn't so. You had plenty of missed periods.*

The only irregularity I remembered was when I was seventeen and missed periods for four or five months. I put that down to stress.

Melissa continually suffered with menstrual pain. For at least one day every month she would be in such agony she couldn't function.

Rhonda suggested a brand of painkillers that worked for her.

"I have the same problem Melissa. These are the best American substitute I could find for the Australian brand we both take."

The medication reduced the pain, but didn't remove it. I hadn't any idea that Melissa languished like this because she had lived away from home for two years. Although she had told me she took medication, I hadn't associated that with her current suffering. Hearing her tell me about agony over the phone was different from being there and seeing how she felt.

"Sometimes I'd miss my morning lectures because I couldn't even get up with the pain," Melissa told me.

Lying in a warm bed, Melissa talked about her discomfort. I massaged her feet, not knowing how else to support her.

There was more behind her symptoms. It wasn't just menstrual cramps causing her suffering. Something from her past was making her consistently relive a particular memory. Ever since my headache disappeared after my acknowledgement of sexual abuse, I wouldn't let anybody get out of looking at the psychological reason for illness. I wondered what had happened to her through our cult association.

By Melissa's second bout of period pain, we better understood that it was a message from stored trauma, so I arranged a healing session with a friend. They covered past lives and other experiences from this life. This helped somewhat, but the next month Melissa was again writhing in torment from cramps. We called one of our group support people, Kathy, an intuitive healer, who helped Melissa heal through the layers of pain.

"I see something inserted in your vagina by Michael and his father. Does that make sense to you?" Kathy said.

Melissa rolled on the floor, clutched her abdomen and moaned.

"Yes. They forced an abortion."

Kathy spoke gently, "What else do you remember Melissa?"

"I'll never have another baby. My baby wasn't meant to be aborted then. They always abort babies early but mine was planned for a later ceremony. They didn't have enough babies for this ceremony and needed mine. I wasn't prepared…they had to get it out quickly…. I feel like I'm dying. I want to die…I've had enough… "

Loss of blood, drugs and shock took Melissa close to death. Massive support was needed to revive her. A death like this just couldn't happen. One of their own young members with school records and a family couldn't disappear - especially someone with the extra training she'd received. Her discipline took years, with special instructors from other states coming for those chosen to become leaders. After nearly killing her, Michael and Poppa fought to keep Melissa alive.

Kathy spent an hour on the phone. As Melissa spoke her memories, the pain decreased.

"I'm infertile. This was the only baby I had. I won't be able to have any children," she sobbed.

I thought these were strange thoughts for a healthy nineteen-year-old.

"Mum, teenage girls were used as baby breeders. The pregnancies were planned to fit in with ceremonies. Remember how Rebecca and I had irregular periods between the ages of twelve and fifteen?"

This made sense. A young girl in the cult could easily be unconscious of being pregnant. She wouldn't know the signs. Sore breasts and nausea could be explained as growing pains or something else ambiguous. Most girls abused in the cult would be unaware of having had sex because of the brainwashing and amnesic drugs, and would certainly never suspect pregnancy. Now I started to understand their plan. If babies were aborted during early gestation for ceremonial use their juvenile mother's pregnancy wouldn't show. As soon as the fetus looks like a baby, it suffices for ceremony. After about eighteen weeks gestation, a fetus looks normal, although its size is not much larger than an adult's hand. The external signs of pregnancy wouldn't show on the young mother at this early stage which was perfect for the baby-breeding cult.

Rhonda remembered even more.

"There was a time when children could be procured from some institutions, for ceremonial use. People in charge there were part of the cult and could fudge records of the missing children."

"Well, why would they bother aborting pre-term babies now?" I said.

"There were investigations and changes in the system," Rhonda told me, "So it became almost impossible to get the right number of babies for certain ceremonies. That's when they 'grew' their own supply from cult children. They had to make do with the fetuses, although live children would have been more powerful. Sometimes twelve or thirteen children were needed for a ceremony."

That was a lot of sacrificed humans. I shivered at the thought.

Conclusions about what happened in the cult didn't just rush into my mind. They came after days and months of pondering. The emotion associated with memory exhausted me. Melissa's recollection of her abortion affected each of us. Healing for each of us affected the whole family. We were interconnected. And our bodies took time to integrate changes initiated through healing.

We continually delved for more mysteries of our lives to prove to ourselves that we really were involved in ritual abuse. Irregularity of menstrual periods during our past appeared to be another signal. We often pondered these clues in an attempt to create a picture of our hidden life. It was confusing and devastating to build a new image of ourselves with our emerging surreal biographies. These crazy, fragmented parts were not enough to complete the puzzle and there were so many more questions we couldn't answer.

How did we stay free of sexually transmitted diseases if the cult engaged in communal sex? Were we programmed not to 'catch' infection? This was a high probability. People with multiple personalities can have a condition such as asthma or allergies in one personality and not in others. So it seems possible there could be programming to be resistant to infection. The mind had power to control anything in the body and the cult leaders knew how to use this for their evil purpose. Ritual abuse was certainly something of a conundrum

Part of our Year Long program was to undertake a project of excellence. Something we hadn't done previously that made us passionate. Rebecca decided to learn the guitar, Melissa took singing lessons and Michael contemplated a history of transport in the area. I wasn't sure what to do but had come across Earthships, houses built out of tires. I'd always been drawn to self-sufficiency and projects requiring a minimal use of resources. I fantasized about building a home using these principles.

We needed this different focus between workshops to expand our knowledge. It also helped take our minds off abuse. I read books on Earthships and was impressed with the philosophy of the system - passive solar design with one wall of southern-facing windows in the Northern Hemisphere. These windows ensured maximum winter sun. I looked at the Earthships with an eye for the area I came from, a Southern Hemisphere, sub-tropical type climate. I decided to look at some of these homes and the only place I knew was Taos, New Mexico, a three-hour drive.

Living in another country made it easy to say, 'I'm going for a six-hour drive today.' Maybe having no work commitments and a desire to tour as much of the country as possible before returning home were big factors in deciding to take off and follow my inclination to see these houses in person.

Michael volunteered to drive with me. I was surprised and pleased with his offer. We left early in the morning and he drove most of the way. I can't remember everything we talked about. Obviously it wouldn't have been about our relationship: that was taboo. I would have initiated any conversation anyway. I talked about Earthships and whether we could build one on our Australian property. Of course Michael didn't commit himself to anything I suggested, but it was enjoyable riding with him and chatting. His energy output was of resignation, not of light-heartedness. I had no idea of his thoughts on these buildings. However I was pleased that he volunteered to spend the day with me.

Taos was arid, desert-like and the Earthship structures blended well into the landscape. I was thrilled to see them nestled in the mountains of the region but somehow they didn't seem appropriate for our land in Australia. Our landscape was covered in trees and the greater rainfall in Australia could challenge the Earthship's water run-off capabilities. The predicted earth axis tilting due in the next twenty or so years could also affect the suitability of the Earthship, with only one set of windows facing the possible wrong direction for winter sun. I pursued information, watched videos and listened to talks. I liked the way they emerged from the mountains but felt incapable of the huge amount of work required to build one.

Melissa enjoyed her singing lessons. She felt good about what she learned and planned to sing two songs at our graduation celebration. Song opened her throat chakra, another part of her healing. Rebecca proceeded with guitar lessons, building a small repertoire of popular songs. These projects took our focus away from the constant emotional processing of what we were uncovering from our workshops and added levity to our lives.

"The only mail we get is work for Rebecca," Melissa commented one day. The correspondence school kept a steady flow of work for Rebecca. Her tasks were well planned but it wasn't an easy year for study.

"I prefer a classroom," she told us. "It's easier to learn. Besides, it's lonely not having friends to talk and do things with."

She felt as if her life was being tossed to the wind, with spiritual workshops, no peer contact from her course, no direct teaching and living in a foreign country. Michael was supportive of Rebecca's work but she struggled. It was difficult teaching and disciplining herself. We'd fax off completed assignments and more would turn up in the mail.

"This letter asks where I'll be for my exams." Rebecca looked at me.

"We will be back in Australia in November won't we?"

I expected to be home by then, even if we moved to another state of Australia. There was no doubt we'd be back for completion of her schooling.

"I'll put my name down at the school near Granny's house. That way I can stay with her if I need to." Rebecca's practicality was phenomenal.

Melissa had decided to stay with us for the remainder of the year. She had only brought enough clothes for a short winter holiday and needed suitable summer attire for a trip to Mexico in April. She didn't have anything 'special' with her, little things she'd have brought if she knew she was staying longer than the original four weeks: some books, her tape player, more clothes, jewelry and shoes and even something familiar to decorate her room. However, we discovered a bead catalogue and she became a creative earring and necklace maker. We weren't bored. So much here was new. Shopping malls, scenery and the climate were all different. We didn't get to know many local Americans, so birthdays, Australia Day and any party opportunities were grabbed as chance for celebration with our group. With the rest of the turmoil happening in our consciousness, fun was essential.

Michael and I made a trip to Yellowstone Park and met up with some Australian friends touring the States. We used any excuse to sight see and explore this incredible country. One year free from work commitments gave us the opportunity of a lifetime.

When I let go of past hurts, the need to forgive disappears, for then there is nothing to forgive.

Chapter eleven

I'd now spent eight months in the United States with the brief trip home to Australia to sort out our business, clean up my household there and bring the girls back with me.

All this time in the States, I'd totally focused on personal growth and healing myself. Changes had happened and I could see them in the etheric child I met during my first sexual abuse memory, nearly a year ago. Any time I called her, she would appear. This little entity was more confident, no longer frozen in stark fear. She wanted to be held and often smiled lovingly as she sat on my lap. I went along with this as creatively as possible. Although I had heard people talk of their inner child I couldn't remember what they actually did with the experience. I hadn't understood what people really meant about inner children until I found these two of mine.

It was strange, yet touching, to have this little child along with me, like any little pre-school child, waiting for love and healing. I figured this was my adventure. She was 'me' and I didn't need anyone else's help to heal her. What I didn't know was that this child was actually in charge and would appear when it was time for me to be taught about her integration.

She whispered, 'My brother pushes me over a lot.' Instructed by the adults in her life not to tell anyone, she hadn't, until now. There was something else she tried to inform me of, though I continually ignored her attempts, because in my subconscious I already knew – and deep inside, I didn't want to know.

Am I going crazy? was a question which often arose for everyone during the course. Sometimes it seemed a viable alternative to the pain and responsibility associated with healing. Our group meditated on this phrase under the crystal bowl and people remembered a diversity of connotations of what 'going crazy' meant for them. Several people remembered past lives in asylums, and babbled nonsensical words as their bodies contorted in strange movements. Someone else recalled her parents' domination and control, and how this made her feel crazy as a child, because she wasn't allowed to think for herself.

I watched the others until I felt how deeply the words affected me as my inner little girl in the dressing gown appeared in my vision. She grabbed me and violently shook my body. She was 'going crazy' because I continued to ignore her latest pleas of the past two months. Acknowledgement of her information was paramount for my healing and she compelled me to listen by demanding my attention. She showed me a picture in my mind's eye.

There was a group of workmen at her childhood home, watching her and laughing amongst themselves. Their behavior nauseated me. They knew what was happening in her life. Most of them were involved in the activities with her father, and he had no shame about his actions. This child was fair game for them to abuse, and some of them had.

Next she showed me a picture of me in my father's office as a baby, maybe five months old, in a pram. There was sexual abuse in the pram. I felt a penis in my mouth. My hand went into spasms and fear. The pictures stopped as the little child spoke to me.

"My Daddy used to come in at night and hurt me. He didn't like Mummy and used me to get at her."

Phenomenal anger exploded within me as I comprehended what this message meant. Immediately I jumped up to hit Bluey, the human-like punching torso, which was sometimes used to vent our anger on. I had tunnel vision as rage engulfed my actions and I smashed the blue form to the floor. How could my father be such a bastard?

How could a man do this to his own child! How could anyone do it to any child? I was furious at my father's violation of my body and soul.

I smashed a plastic baseball bat over Bluey the human torso. I kicked him, swore and screamed. Frightened by the fury I expressed, others in the group stood back. I was deeply hurt, even shocked by my own anger and the fearful reaction from the rest of the group. I didn't remember my father coming in to my bed. My little girl had to tell me. She held onto that memory for a lifetime. I had to help her - and me - release the incredible rage held inside.

Dad's incestuous expression of 'I'm in charge here', contributed to my mother's anorexia, depression and sense of hopelessness as she denied the reality of the true cause. This vision seemed to explain so much of my parent's relationship.

I have to admit that several months earlier I had contemplated whether my father had sexually abused me, as little thoughts floated through my mind. They appeared like bubbles, only to burst as soon as I saw them. I didn't want to believe it then, but it simmered on the backburner of my mind. I even talked about it with Cassandra, who had discovered her father's sexual abuse about that time.

"I knew my dad was physically abusive to me," Cassandra said. "What a shock it was to find he basically slept in my bed. He betrayed and manipulated me. I'm just as angry toward my mother for not stopping this. She must have known what went on. "

Cassandra's words stuck with me. Although both our fathers were dead, our feelings for them were still very much alive. My father hadn't been a drunkard and violent like Cassandra's. She knew her father was rough and capable of physical and verbal rage. My dad had been responsible and provided well for his family. He didn't shout and yell or get drunk. Carefully, I had blown my bubbles of incestuous thoughts away. What I'd wanted to believe, and the reality I now discovered, were polarities of each other.

The man I called dad didn't have sexual boundaries, my body and my 'little girl inside' remembered. Financial background, education or class provides no barrier to incest. It happens across a broad spectrum of our society. I wondered how the statistics on childhood sexual abuse were calculated. If it was from reported incidents, adults, like me and several other men and women in our group who were breaking down the denial of their family's perversions as adults, wouldn't have been included. How large was this recovered memory group of abused children in our culture?

I really thought I had come from a normal caring family and I didn't want to be part of such statistics showing the depravity of our society.

Another forgotten piece of memory came between workshops as I parked in front of an American friend's house. A partially restored vehicle on blocks in the driveway grabbed my attention. Its shape was the same as the car I had seen a few months earlier in an image of being trapped, when I saw my father negotiating something,

"What type of car is that?" I asked.

"A 1953 Chevrolet."

Goosebumps covered my body. The image I had seen of my father being in a garage near some cars wasn't past life. Here was the proof of it being this life. I was born before 1953, so the car in the garage in my memory wasn't made until after my birth. What was going on? What was this puzzle I seemed to keep finding pieces of?

I re-read my journal and found previous insight.

We looked at being in small places. During this deep meditation, I saw my small space as a huge garage, where I was put down through a trap door in the floor- into a pit, but I could just poke my head over the floor level to see what was going on. I saw two cars on the right and one on the left with about a car space in the middle. In this space there were three men including my father. They had dark coats on and I felt they were negotiating something. I don't know if this is this lifetime or past lifetime.

The car on blocks proved it was this life. What was my father doing there, negotiating?

Several pages on I read,

We went under the bowl looking at 'not enough' and I felt deep, deep sadness. Was that because I didn't have enough love or nurturing? Feels like that to me. Then I saw a flashback of the cars in the garage again. I know where it is! It's the garage next door to where we lived when I was a little kid There is more to the 'pit' I thought I was in. There are rooms in the garage. I think we have to go downstairs to get to the smoke-filled rooms…underground rooms?

A few weeks later more of the enigma unfolded.

More went on in that underground room. I am sure pictures of some sort were taken…it seems like naked pictures, but in what situations? I don't know. I always feel as though I am naked in this room, sitting on a wooden workbench with tools around.

Often I'd been cautioned to add 'yet' at the end of my statements. In this case, it would have been better if I had said, 'I don't know yet,' to give me better opportunity to let the flow of memory consciousness surface easily. It came. More and more of what happened in those rooms surfaced over the next eighteen months... piece by piece. Something in my mind protected me and ensured sanity as I remembered. Bit by bit was all I could cope with: physically and psychologically. Time was needed for each part of the trauma to be released. If there wasn't enough time, I would go into overload again.

Regularly I was confronted by my past. Knives and swords had particular significance. Watching a ceremonial sword dance set me off into a coughing fit – a common reaction of mine to memory triggers. I sensed the use of these implements in rituals. A memory with no visual recall, just the knowledge that I had seen a variety of knives used for torture and killing. I didn't have to justify or remember any detail to clear a layer of the stored fear.

The same happened when a friend's rifle fell from his car onto my foot. My body reacted with shock, nausea, severe heart pain and a debilitating headache for a day. Even though I took a large dose of pain suppressing tablets, the feelings wouldn't go until I acknowledged memories of threats and death with guns. I discovered how immensely practical the cult leaders were. By torturing and killing someone in front of the group, we learned immediately the danger of not obeying orders. I had a vision of a close range bullet fired in someone's hip as he lay next to his grave in the bush. That was enough for me to be totally obedient. No wonder I've had such fear of authority and did what I was told during my life. These patterns restricted my creativity and vision of what I could bring into being in my life.

Often as I closed my eyes for meditation or recollection during our workshop, I'd see eyes. Moving eyes, animal eyes, human eyes. Everywhere I looked in my mind's eye they were there, floating by across my internal vision.

"Does anyone else see these eyes?" I asked. "Every time I close my eyes for meditation, that's what I see. They're driving me nuts. I can't get away from them."

"Yeah! I see them," Daniel replied. "Watching us. We're never out of their sight. That's what they mean."

Rhonda remembered, "They placed them in orifices – to make sure we knew we were watched from every direction. We even had to swallow them. I think they pretended to insert them inside us as well, to keep us scared. That way we'd always do as they wanted."

It seemed we would never get away from the cult.

Feel what the heart wants us to know.

Chapter twelve

One night at home between workshops, I woke up terrified by a nightmare. My heart slammed against my chest as I recalled my dream of being pushed - as a child - into a ship's ventilation pipe. The images were so real I could even smell the paint. A few men were on the deck next to my father as he shoved me into the constricting cylinder. My body was held tightly in the tube and I couldn't even wiggle my fingers.

Even lying awake in bed and knowing it was a dream, I felt trapped and couldn't move. There seemed no way out of my convoluted thoughts. The bed, the room and house clutched me. Nothing physical tied me down, but I was mortified by feelings.

"I can't leave this country," I whispered to Michael. "I'm stuck here forever. I'm too scared to go on a ship. Airplanes are claustrophobic - I can't ever fly in one again. I can't breathe and feel confined and squashed in the little seats. "

I was sweating – but didn't dare move, even under the bedcovers. I knew my thoughts were neurotic but I was confused and irrational. The rising sun filtering through the venetian blinds brought a sense of safety and eventually the sound of music from the girls' bedroom brought me back to reality. My fear gradually dissipated as I lay next to Michael, who reassured me that it was safe to move freely.

I'd had a similar experience during a holiday on the East Coast of Malaysia eighteen months earlier. We'd gone as a family to a beachside retreat popular with locals and backpackers from around the world. Although there was a moderately priced hotel close by, we stayed in more simple accommodation: traditional-looking two-roomed huts attractively scattered through a grove of coconut palms. Our concrete-floored rooms were sparsely furnished with mosquito nets over the beds and small side tables.

We sat quietly on the front verandah watching seagulls run back and forth as the ocean waves gently rolled and retreated on the sand. It was peaceful on this unsophisticated tropical beach. Rebecca set up a game of Monopoly on the table. Tension from the trip unwound as we bought utility companies, land and houses for several hours. This felt like family communion, a sacred time of talk and play.

When we became hungry, we took a pleasant stroll along the waterfront to a Chinese restaurant built over the water's edge at the end of the bay. The meal was delicious and the whole occasion felt special, so Michael and I each indulged in a can of Tiger beer. There wasn't any nightlife here or even television to watch, so we prolonged our stay at the table, playing guessing games and chatting, surrounded by the sound of water lapping against the pylons supporting the restaurant's wooden floor and Chinese voices.

Droves of mosquitoes emerged as the sun set. Back in our hut we slathered ourselves in repellent and lit mosquito coils in an attempt to drive the incessantly buzzing insects from our rooms. The four of us sat cross-legged on the bed under the fine netting, playing cards. The cadence around us came from insects, the ocean, our chatter and laughter.

During the night I awoke in terror. Being alive in my body in this small room and humid environment frightened me. I couldn't bear the enclosed feeling. Gently I prodded Michael awake.

"Michael, I can't breathe. I'm scared. Everything seems to be constricting me. I'm going to die."

I was desperate for human reassurance and contact, to ensure I wouldn't be alone in my death.

"Come outside and walk," Michael suggested, and helped me out the door to the beach. The familiar gritty sand under my feet felt odd and dirty. Everything around me appeared unreal.

"What's going on? I know I see cars parked over by the office but it feels as though we're alone, dumped in an alien environment with no escape. I don't know how to get away from here," I told Michael.

It all seemed so surreal.

"Breathe deeply as we walk." Michael had one arm around my back and pointed heavenward with the other. "Look at the stars, the moon, the ocean."

There was space; I was free to move. I had to see there was more than the suffocating wooden walls and mosquito netting in our room. I surveyed the ocean, it went on forever and spilled over the endless horizon – the earth was flat! I knew it wasn't round. I stared into the unpolluted sky. The twinkling stars were an eternity of nothingness away. Unreachable. Where did I belong? The smell of the thick, salty air and the heaviness of the humidity still made me feel claustrophobic. I felt like a fat ant randomly pinned to the earth.

"How do I get off this planet? Am I imprisoned here forever?" I cried.

Michael couldn't answer my unanswerable question.

The continual walking and support from Michael helped diminish my panic and disorientation. Eventually I felt safe enough to return to our cabin. I dozed sporadically for the rest of the night, but for the next several days couldn't shake the feeling that something wasn't right. I was desperate to go home to familiarity, to a place without this associated fear. I didn't fully enjoy the rest of the holiday.

We explained away that episode as the combination of beer and monosodium glutamate in the Chinese meal. Maybe the mixture was harmful for me. I avoided MSG because it always made my heart rate increase and on both these nighttime terror episodes, fear followed a speeding heartbeat.

"You looked terrible, Mum," Rebecca commented later. "Even though I didn't see you till the morning, your face was grey and I was concerned. It was hard to believe that claustrophobia could affect anyone so much."

Claustrophobia was looming again in my consciousness and some reasons for my fear surfaced. I'd learned during our course to be alert to the signals of issues rising and look for possible causes. I had always felt claustrophobic. Small spaces and elevators made me feel anxious. I easily panicked if I didn't see an escape route. I figured these dreads came from childhood torment by my brother. My dreams of being stuck in small spaces were signals for me to look for further reasons for my fear.

Needless to say, when I dismissed my dream of being trapped in a pipe the fear passed. Within a few weeks I was able to fly to Mexico for our next workshop.

Our gathering in Mexico was on the Baja coast. This trip to another country was perfect timing to renew our six-month entry visa to the USA. The small, isolated hotel was situated on a long, white sandy beach and the beautifully tiled rooms opened onto an enclosed courtyard with a small swimming pool and tropical garden. This was luxury accommodation compared with anywhere else we'd stayed in North America.

Michael and I even had a room to ourselves, which seemed something of a waste for there wasn't much communication between us. Michael could reassure and comfort me when I was in distress, however he hardly said anything and disregarded my attempts at conversation with him unless there were other people around. Our relationship hadn't improved as he continued to build an impenetrable barrier around himself. Being among so many friends diffused my frustration and anger at being treated this way. The issue of abuse continued to take our attention away from relationship issues.

I enjoyed the companionship of so many other people. It had been seven weeks since our last group and everyone was ready for adventure in Mexico. This was our sixth workshop together and we knew each other well. The group energy was strong.

Early in the week, Daniel, who still hadn't skipped from the course, chatted about his proposed project of excellence.

"I've been doing nothing much over the past few months. I expected to be on holiday, visiting tourist spots around the world. But here I am, so I thought I'd teach myself woodworking. I bought some power tools - a sander, power-saw and other stuff I need to make toy boxes. Once I've figured how to make one, I can work out a production process. Rhonda and Glen can decorate them. Then I'll have a garage sale out the front of the house and flog the toy boxes."

This sounded enterprising. I thought he had an appropriate project and the woodworking would occupy him during our three-week break between workshops. Selling toy boxes could pay for his new hobby. My attention was with Daniel when Michael tapped me on the shoulder and pointed to Rebecca. She was crying, quietly, rubbing her leg.

"What words triggered you Rebecca?"

I was constantly amazed at the speed at which Verna picked up on what was happening in the group.

"My right leg is killing me and my stomach is aching. It started when Daniel said he was flogging the toy boxes." Everyone's attention turned to Rebecca. "I was in a little box and people came and hit me. Granny, Poppa, Dad, uncles. They were all told to hit me. Punching me in the stomach, hitting me with twigs. I couldn't do anything about it. I was stuck in the little box."

"How old were you?"

"Four or five."

Oh God, something in my gut told me I'd put her in the box, positioned her ready to be flogged by these people. Was it because of Rebecca's trust in me that I was ordered to take her in my arms and betray her? She was young, a preschooler. Is it possible that I could be so compliant and harm my own child? Was my cult-programmed mind so robotic that I was unable to protect her, or had I been threatened with something far worse if I didn't obey? My arms shook as I hid my head in my hands. Betrayal and abandonment of my own child.

Rebecca sobbed. How could such brutality have been perpetrated on a child – and by those she loved and trusted? Why does the cult force these heinous acts on its children? What is the plan behind this?

What other suffering have I unwittingly helped inflict on my children? I was in despair. How could my family have been totally unaware of what had gone on in our lives? Shame at my life, my mothering, my anger and my seriousness engulfed me. I loathed the person revealing herself to me. No wonder I had denied everything for my entire life. Participating in this year of deep personal growth forced me to acknowledge my reality. Obviously I'd been involved and hadn't protected my children. Where had my mind been as these acts were committed? Where is that part of me that is the perpetrator? I hadn't seen it yet, although I knew it existed. How much agony do I have to endure to dig this part out, to have it deprogrammed and integrated?

Another two years passed before that cult-loving part of me, exposed herself. For a fraction of a second I saw how proud she was of her skillful use of knives. She thrived to torment someone else. That was her moment of power, her opportunity to avenge the cruelty that had been perpetrated against her. She didn't recognize the cult leaders' manipulation. This brief taste of power was given as a stimulant to keep her going. It was part of their mind control – build her esteem momentarily, then crush it again, so she'd hide away and let another part take the torment.

This brief flash, enough to know this cult-lover existed, came in meditation as I looked to comprehend my abhorrence of cigarette smoke and sweating bodies. To the cult-loving part of me this was the aroma of dominance she lusted for. For me it was the stench of depravity.

The process of remembering events could take months as forgotten fragments emerged from our memories. It was like a jigsaw puzzle. First there would be a few seemingly unrelated pieces, which were confusing and didn't seem to fit together. Later some new parts would appear, linking together with some original components. A few more months might pass before further parts revealed themselves, which fitted to build a distinguishable picture from the pieces. My early childhood emerged for me in this manner.

Several months earlier I had remembered watching my father negotiating with other men in the car yard. Then, I recalled underground rooms at this garage. This seemed to make sense because the large building was on a significantly sloping site. The back area automatically became underground to the front level. Light from the lower level of the building would be unnoticed at night from the highway the garage fronted. I was confident that pictures had been taken there. During this workshop in Mexico, images from the underground room came up.

"There's an animal lying on a white surface with its skin pinned back. I see a man using a scalpel. He has a white coat on. Other men seemed to be there, with white coats. There are odd, white, soft-cloth hats on the wall. I see the Freemason symbol - the compass and the set-square. It's on the wall near the door. It must be a veterinarian with the scalpel; he is skillful, very carefully incising the animal down its ventral surface. It looks like a dog being cut. No, it is a small fox. I see a bushy tail. I have no doubt it is a veterinarian performing the dissection. It looks precise and well done. Watching him, I am impressed with his skill. He has a large overhead light shining on the animal helping him see. He cuts out the heart. They are doing something to me with the heart. I hear the men laughing. I'm sitting on a bench behind them watching – naked. While I feel safe watching, I'm not free to move. The room is filled with smoke. This is someone's workshop. I'm sitting on a workbench with tools around me."

The heart still had unclotted blood inside it, which they used to draw a symbol over my heart and forehead. Did I eat the heart? I was surprised at how tiny it was.

I feel a lump in my throat, even now.

When I was small we had a fox trap next to the chicken coop, way down in the back yard. The snare would grab the paws with its metal claws when the unwary animal stepped on it. I imagine it was very painful, but not lethal. Was this where the fox had been caught? I suppose the men thought it was good sport to skin this fox and use the fur draped over my naked body for photographs of me. I felt the head of the animal over my head, with the pelt hanging down my back. Every time I think of this incident, I get the image of a canvas backdrop painted with rocks and some trees. It seemed it was used for a photographic scene. Were pictures of my brother and me taken in front of this? I saw my brother with a skin draped over him standing over me with a spear in his hand. The powerful man keeping the female in her place. No wonder my brother felt free to abuse me as he pleased.

My memory then shifted to my father carrying me home in his arms, through the backyard, up the stairs and putting me into bed. This gentle moment together had a high price tag. I'd done my night's work.

Initially I found it difficult to find a place for the fox dissection in my memories. It was obscure. I had seen sexual abuse from my father but it seemed ludicrous that animal dissection would fit into this scenario. Later we discovered animals were often used in ritualistic abuse.

Small animals like newborn kittens, baby mice and bugs we were forced to ingest. Household pet-sized animals; dogs and black cats were used for skinning practice and torture. Bugs and legless lizards further frightened children as companions in boxes and graves.

I remember them all. Perhaps the friendly veterinarian provided some. Beware stray dogs. Don't come near us, we were not kind to animals.

Larger animals such as goats and calves were dismembered and placed over children in ceremonies. The heavy weight, smell and texture of fresh fat, muscle and blood on my body filled me with desperation and I struggled to wiggle out from underneath.

I was familiar with the Freemason symbol. Dad was a member, though when I asked my mother, she was adamant he didn't have time go to meetings.

My family left my first home when I was about six. I noticed most of my childhood memories seem to involve that house. For the next ten or so years I didn't seem to have much evidence of this hidden life, though I am sure it continued. I do remember being so afraid at night that I'd edge my way to my parent's bedroom. This happened until I was at least ten years old. Mum would let me hop in her bed and I'd snuggle and feel safe with her.

Gradually I began to remember why I was claustrophobic. Enclosing children in boxes is a common cult practice. There was Rebecca's 'beatings in a toy-box' and Melissa's recollection of going to a cemetery and being left with dead kittens in a grave. She was made to kill the kittens before being left alone with their carcasses.

My own conscious recall showed me where some of my claustrophobia may have originated. My father played games with us, which included putting me in the trunk of the car. It was brief. I accidentally shut myself in a dark, cool room recently without knowing how to release the door and emerged in deep shock five minutes later, after someone had wondered where I was and released me.

A few months later, another memory was released in general conversation with a group of colleagues studying bodywork with me. We discussed trauma and how people cope with it differently.

"The speed in ice hockey almost guarantees broken bones."

I wasn't familiar with this game but it sounded fast and violent and the concept of broken bones gave me the shivers; splintered bodies sounded gruesome.

"Physical trauma from torn ligaments and bones can be minimized by consciously relaxing the body. I've seen it work, there's no swelling and faster healing."

"There was a study done on the schoolchildren kidnapped in

California. They were buried underground in a bus. One of the children who had actively tried to dig his way out had less trauma than the rest."

My concentration on the conversation suddenly evaporated as my body went into shock, shaking uncontrollably as part of the story triggered me. I put a hand to my head, hoping that fingering through my hair would calm my body. It didn't. The shaking wouldn't stop. My body demanded acknowledgement.

"I think this happened to me too. I was buried."

It was obvious something was going on in my body memory in relation to these stories.

As I shut my eyes, I remembered emerging from a box after the tightly fitted lid was lifted.

I needed to climb out and balance on my numbed legs. It was cold and musty in the box, like the dampness of being underground. I was squashed and didn't dare move while I was trapped. I'd lain still on my side, curled up with my knees pulled towards my chest, creating a fantasy world in my mind to attempt to keep the terror at bay.

When the lid was lifted, I realized the box was alongside my home. I emerged and looked around and saw a shadowy row of people, appearing as silhouettes in a semi-circle, watching me. I saw the melaleuca hedge in the background behind them. I recognized the shapes of my mother, father and several men. Although I wanted to be held and nurtured by someone, I didn't move towards the group. Adults were not reliable. Why are they in a row, observing me? It seems like a greeting – a 'congratulations, you made it' occasion. A sort of initiation that I managed to go through. What are they going to do to me next?

"Find the part of you that kept you alive," someone said to me.

With my eyes shut, I searched inside. My shaking diminished as I discovered what had sustained me.

" It seems to be an energy that glows from the core of my being out beyond my body at least a foot. I can feel it. It is warmth, calmness and fearlessness. It is my inner strength!"

I opened my eyes and looked at how far my hands indicated this energy radiated. It was more like two feet beyond my body. As I allowed myself to immerse in this strength, my shaking ceased. Nothing can hurt me when I've found my own resource and am surrounded by this energy.

Looking around the recalled scene I noticed a little black baby on top of the box. It wasn't a real baby, just a little ghost person I'd created to hold the torment and pain. I thought she was dead. Her body totally floppy, with no muscles and bones, like an old rag doll carelessly tossed over the edge of a bed. I investigated this more closely with my adult eyes. She was part of me – so could not be dead. This baby needed healing from the torture of being trapped in a box.

More months passed as I nurtured this little baby. Pink skin color gradually emerged as her body grew muscles and bones and a heartbeat. It was a slow process awakening her.

In the enclosed box episodes I wasn't always totally alone. Sometimes the box was filled with crawling insects that invaded my mouth and nose. Other times, legless lizards, which I thought were snakes, were my companions, wriggling and moving around me.

Claustrophobia, lack of trust, inability to ask for help or nurturing and feeling unloved, are patterns that develop from this experience. All have left their indelible mark on our family.

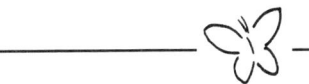

Traumatic life experiences are relegated to an altered state where common awareness is blocked off.

Chapter thirteen

The seasons had changed, it was summer again. The mountain snow had melted and it was warm enough to camp again on Blue Mountain for the next workshop.

Rebecca told the group she could read people.

"If I tune in to someone's energy, I can tell what happened in their past and some things that may happen in the future. I know what they're feeling. Either I feel what they feel or it's a knowing. Sometimes even pictures come in my mind."

"Often holding an object worn by the person who wants a reading makes it easier when you start," Verna said. She helped Rebecca to begin reading using psychometry.

"Ask them for a piece of jewelry, then focus while holding it. Information may come more clearly."

Rebecca practiced on everyone in the group during breaks, expressing pictures and feelings she got from their rings or pendants. The response to her insights was positive and her accuracy was encouraging. She gave a message to her father.

"You may receive a job offer to work in Saudi Arabia. Deeply consider how much you want this because Mum wouldn't like to be there."

Within three weeks, her prediction was confirmed. Her childhood psychic skills were awakening.

Our week of workshop every month continually deepened our personal insights. The regularity ensured we had no chance to fall back into patterns of complacency between meetings. It was like school, hammering awareness into our consciousness through repetition, until we grasped it for ourselves. Continual support from the group was assured if we needed it during our break time.

Although we were committed, sometimes it was painful, relentlessly searching for our patterns. Often it seemed preferable to sleep during sessions and avoid the inexorable clearing. Resistance still loomed around us.

This warm afternoon in the dome was one of those times nearly everyone lacked enthusiasm. Most of us didn't have personal growth as our goal for the day. I slouched in my chair lazily, paying little attention as more patterns were put on line for clearing. Somebody was alert enough to repeat common words like poverty and loneliness and how it was affecting her. Then Rebecca added swimming pools.

What? Instantly I sat up as I heard one of the most unusual words ever raised. It almost seemed ludicrous. I wondered what triggered Rebecca to throw this word in.

"I dreamed last night about back yard swimming pools. Dad and I were there and he was saving me from the cult," Rebecca explained.

We went under the bowl on swimming pools. The humming tone of the bowl took my mind quickly to a scene. In my minds eye I saw Poppa ducking people under water in our own swimming pool. He was walking around the concrete pathway on the edge of the pool. It was night. I presume our verandah lights were on, for there was enough light for me to see clearly. A full moon maybe? Poppa, cloaked in his black robe, ensured people in the pool couldn't surface long for a breath. He controlled the situation. Immediately a head bobbed up for breath, he pushed them under again. The people were gasping. They were terrified. The water was choppy as they splashed about in desperation, fearful of drowning. Water spilled onto the concrete around the pool. Poppa stood at the edge of the pool's deep end. There was seven foot of water and no chance for any victim to rest on the bottom of the pool. These people had to actively keep afloat. This picture was chaos in a pool filled with fear.

The bowl's humming stopped and I came out of my meditative state, astonished at this memory.

"I saw Poppa throw our dog into the pool and he was pushing people underwater," Rebecca said.

What? I could hardly contain myself from jumping out of my seat and shouting 'me too'. But I didn't want to bias anyone else's vision. I cautioned myself, not to rush this coincidence.

In immediate response to Rebecca, Melissa said, "I saw Poppa in our pool area, pushing people's heads under water…he was in his robe."

Can you believe this? We all saw the same scene. I could barely contain my astonishment. Chills rushed through my body. And then it struck me. My place. Were things going on in my *home*? Using my pool. How could my residence be used for these activities without me remembering till years later? What else went on there?

"I saw the same scene," I blurted out. I checked with Melissa and Rebecca.

"What did you see exactly?"

We agreed Poppa was in a robe, standing at the edge of the pool, pushing people's heads underwater. His location around the pool varied for each of us but he could have been in several places during the process. Our memory from those curiously powerful words, 'swimming pools' was astoundingly similar on this cult-perverted christening. What confirmation this was for the three of us to see the same scenario. Although Melissa and Rebecca had previously experienced parallel memories, this was the first time the three of us had been so specific.

Although Poppa was a swimmer in his youth, I only saw him swim once at the beach many years ago. Yet here he was, visiting our home for an organized pool ceremony. Not my conscious choice. Our place was used without permission for someone else's perverted pleasure.

I was so *angry*! What cruelty, terrifying people and pushing them to death's door, then saving them within an inch of their life. Rebecca reminded me of how fearful of water our dog became, even though initially he wasn't. Even my pets weren't safe from abuse. Who were the other people there? Where were their cars? I didn't see anything else to answer my questions.

My main worry now was what else had happened.

"Can you remember anything else occurring at home?" I asked

the girls.

"Don't you remember?" Rebecca responded. "You'd drive a group of kids down the road, drop us off and we had to run and hide from the adults. We were the prize for whoever caught us."

I have no recollection of this at all.

"It was pretty scary, trying not to be caught. We learned to hide well in the bushes, be super quiet and run quickly to save ourselves."

What could I say? I almost became reluctant to maintain my search and clearing. How could I get this torture and hideous perversion out of my life? I was sick of seeing my enmeshment in these abominable situations. I felt as though I was stuck in molasses. As much as I wanted to get free, there was always some strand of stickiness pulling me back. If I cleared one arm the other was still covered. Wailing and crying cleared my mind temporarily, letting go of immediate frustration. Cleaning the molasses of ritual abuse from my body took time and lots of help. But I wanted it done with *now*, instantly. I simply could not describe the grief and pain I felt about this abnormal life; the shame and anguish involved in acknowledging my involvement.

Occasionally, I recognized that inner healing could only take place if I knew what happened in the past. Although I would have preferred to forget it all, I believed it was vital to know my own story. It was important for me to remember. Firstly, I wanted verification of my involvement in abuse. Secondly, by recollecting patterns, specific healing could be initiated. Thirdly, there was too much programming involved to carelessly neglect memories and dismiss what happened. It was far too easy to be recalled by the cult if I didn't have control over my past and destiny. Being alert to the possibility of danger was necessary and having deprogramming appeared vital.

Michael didn't remember this pool scenario. His memories were slower to be revealed and his teenage and adult life hadn't come up. He saw enough to know we were on the same track and he was also involved. We sensed and saw him in our memories and internal pictures.

The mind-control cult was insidious. It permeated every profession. Michael had a cousin who was a Pastor. This man preached the exact opposite of his nighttime activity. I am sure he wasn't conscious of the dichotomy in his life. We also saw our friendly family doctor and a schoolteacher. Was the whole of society involved? Who of our friends were safe? I became afraid to mention my memories to anyone in case they were part of this obscure life and would report us to the cult. Repercussions surely could follow.

It was so confusing. My family, those people involved in these perverted acts, were people I loved. Poppa, the Pastor, Granny and other in-laws. What was I meant to do? How could I get away from it all without cutting my life and friendships into little fragments?

Constantly I was amazed at how we functioned reasonably in our daily lives while living a duality. Michael was highly competent and respected in his profession. I kept our house organized and managed our financial affairs, along with a small flower business. Melissa did well at school and Rebecca balanced her academic work with a good social life. These memories in our subconscious had to bear some effect on our every day living processes, yet we presented as normal individuals. It appeared we were 'good' members of society. We were on school committees, sponsored a child overseas and didn't appear anti-social in our attitudes and behavior. Our lives seemed well managed.

The body never lies. Our physical bodies held memories as tension, so somewhere, somehow, part of us had a notion of our other life, however cleverly hidden. I hadn't remembered anything I could piece together until this Year Long, yet there was always part of me that felt something was missing. It was the deep, continuous healing work that dislodged memories which had been hidden by drugs and programming.

"Do you know what sort of drugs were used?" Verna asked Melissa. "I remember being about eight and having a powdered drug. I was given it in a little packet and had to hide it until the appropriate time to sprinkle it on our meal."

Who would believe their own children could sabotage their family? Apart from drugs in food or drink, some drugs were injected into our bodies. Many needle sites that weren't obvious included between the toes, into the big toe, in moles, in the back where we couldn't see for ourselves, under fingernails, behind the ears. Not always the easiest places to inject a drug, but secretive and obscure. Our involvement in ritual abuse was becoming more complex and the whole set-up was showing itself as a highly organized group of programmed individuals…including us.

Drugs were used to numb, paralyze, anaesthetize, cause amnesia and help increase the pleasures of sex. Men's egos were boosted with drugs to increase their erection time. It appeared we were all involved in drugging each other. Grandparents drugged their grandchildren, then gave drugs to the children to drug their parents and parents drugged the children to take them for programming and torture to their grandparents. Such intertwining and convolutions. What was the meaning and benefit of this torture and cruelty? Who benefited? So far I could only see it as sexual pleasure for men.

My body convulsed, releasing the effects of marijuana residuals. Tossed on the fire at ceremonies, marijuana smoke lulled everyone into the euphoria created by its mind-altering properties. Never have I consciously taken marijuana. I thought my body was drug free but have since discovered it is full of residual toxicity. Chloroform too.

"What is the white powder I see in the cigarette papers?" I asked.

"What else do you remember about it?" Verna responded.

"It's not nice. I want to avoid it. I don't think I want any of this white powder. My body wants to move away from the direction it comes from. The cigarette papers were used to control the amount sprinkled…I think up the nose, maybe around the eye, under the bottom lid. For some reason cocaine comes to mind. My right nostril bled a lot…not a little nosebleed…a pouring-out bleed. I can feel the sensations now. The powder was a mixture…acid?"

I paused as I searched inside for more information.

"Was there something also called 'acid' used to take the skin and fascia off the skulls? A powder was spread over the head and then another substance was added that burnt off the flesh to leave bare bone. I remember one of Dad's friends had a skull as an ashtray. I see someone, legs tied together, hanging upside down. They are white…deathly white. I wonder if they received too much of the white powder – and were revived by hanging upside down? Doctors had to be involved…there is a fine line between 'just enough' and 'overdose' with these drugs…"

I even surprised myself with what I said.

"I wonder what pleasure this drugging gave them? Do you think this could have been a paralytic combination, causing our bodies to appear dead? Maybe this was what my memory of sex with dead bodies is about?"

"Is there anything else?" Verna asked.

"My head is aching. It feels as though all the bones are moving, and the contents are under enormous pressure. " I wanted to cry from the pain which had been bugging me on an off for months.

"We'll do some healing on those parts. Removing the effects of these drugs can make someone go into a form of withdrawal for a day or two. I'll take that into account when healing, but be aware that you may feel unwell for that time. We can do more healing if that happens. Just be aware."

Friendships, family and the here and now became more important to me as I saw the lack of control I'd had in my life.

One recurring pattern of mine was to spit out saliva I felt in my mouth and throat into a tissue.

"Do you know you do that lot? What are you spitting out?" Verna asked, after a few months of workshops. I hadn't considered it until that moment. Then the words poured out of my mouth.

"I'm spitting out blood and guts and stuff. Body parts. I had a baby I had to eat."

Who said that? It wasn't consciously me. I didn't know anything about having babies. But the words had come from my mouth. They were stored in my body, waiting to come forth.

Oh no! Please, no more. As a teenager I remember coughing and wanting to clear my throat a lot, a habit which greatly annoyed my mother. Could that have been the beginning of my reaction? Well, blood and guts I accepted but I didn't consider the baby, not at all. There was no more searching into that though, it was far too difficult to face that prospect now. If I didn't consider it, I could ignore the pain that would accompany the memory.

It took another year or so to accept the concealed pregnancies and tremendous grief I felt for the loss of my babies. Babies I had birthed only for their ceremonial killing, and was never able to hold or express my love to. Eventually my bereavement and pain forced me to acknowledge their reality.

Teenage pregnancy. Pregnancies induced pre-term. Tiny babies, sacrificed. No wonder I didn't prepare much for my living 'planned' children's births. Some diapers, tops, blankets and a cot was all I had. I remember buying them in case the baby survived. I actually thought I may die, hence prepared more for that possibility, rather than for the baby living.

The five pregnancies I have now recalled include an episode like Melissa's pre-term abortion. I went close to death. For five hours my family fought to revive me. At least there is some degree of caring for their own, in this cruel cult.

As a fourteen-year-old I fantasized grabbing one of my tiny babies and cradling it in my arms in defiance of the adults there. In my imagination I created another reality and called out, "Dear God, baptize this baby." I saw the beautiful black child as we sat together by a stream. I anointed him with water and brought rays of light into his presence.

When I came out of my creative fantasy I saw the reality of a dead white baby with its abdominal contents removed, lying limp in my arms.

Indira came again in our presence. I asked her how I could improve my eyesight.

Allow yourself to see other levels, the buried levels of abuse. The second way to assist is by cleansing the digestive system. This will have a positive effect upon the vision. It is all tied in together. As you cleanse, you clear the vibrational level, then the emotional level will let go.

I knew the reason for poor eyesight on a metaphysical level was because the person didn't want to look at things. Naturally, I didn't believe that applied to me, until recently when I actually 'saw' my life wasn't really what I believed to be true. However, doing an intestinal cleanse seemed a practical step that was relatively easy to do. I tried Egar Cayce's apple cleansing diet – nothing but water and apples for three days, finishing with a half cup of castor oil.

Nothing in my vision appeared to change with the diet. Things in the distance remained blurry and my right eye remained worse than my left. I felt disappointed that no magic cure had emerged, but still clutched to a thread of hope something would happen to improve my sight.

It was another languid afternoon in the dome with general discussion. During the year we'd learned to listen better to each other, discern body movement, watch reactions and hear specific words. We checked our body reaction to what was happening around us. Everyone's intuition was surfacing.

I noticed Melissa moving uncomfortably in her chair. She sat sideways, so she didn't look directly across the circle of people. Then she changed seats with another woman, the red-haired Cassandra. They had whispered between each other, making some type of arrangement. What was happening? Energy buzzed, although I didn't know why. Something was about to happen.

Everyone's attention turned to Melissa.

"I can't bear to look at Dad because he sexually abused me outside the cult," she said. My eyes popped open, I froze.

I believed Melissa….
Michael wouldn't do something like that…
I believed Melissa…
But Michael wouldn't do that …
I believed Melissa…
But surely Michael wouldn't do this!
I could barely move.
Melissa, somber, said nothing more.
My ears could no longer decipher another word spoken.
The group took a break.
Where were my thoughts? My brain was empty.
The broken record inside my head was going on and on,
"I believe Melissa, but Michael couldn't do something like this…"
Someone hugged me.

No more, please. I can't take much more. Horrified by words alone. I was in such an appalling state. Confusion reigned. I hugged Melissa, then went outside to touch the earth and see the trees. The sun was still there, where it should be.

I believed Melissa. Where was I when this happened? My brain wasn't functioning. All questions were unanswerable. Any answer would be just too much for me to cope with.

I saw my body as a battlefield, with bombs exploding and psychic gunfire. No one wins. There was only death. Death all around. Any structure in the way of the battle, razed to the ground. Total devastation. Oh, how I wished this wasn't happening.

I was totally shattered, bewildered and overpowered. Where was I? What is this 'I' part of me? Who am I? Am I really real?

This was way too much. Just when I thought I was getting something together, it was scattered to the wind again. Another lie in my life. I was horrified.

It was difficult for everyone in our group, including Michael, to comprehend Melissa's statement; our brains were so good at blocking out abhorrent things we'd done or experienced. We had been well trained to lock away so many memories.

Every person in the group was thinking about this last episode in the dome. Most of them didn't believe Melissa. Surely she had made this up. Michael wasn't that type of man. I started to wonder about Melissa too. No, I believed her. I was letting other people influence me.

I still thought about it the next morning. I believed it was true. Melissa's father had sexually abused her, both in and out of the cult circles.

I knew I didn't want to know.

"Nearly everyone asked me if it was really possible that Dad would abuse Melissa," Rebecca reported the next morning. "I told them it was true. For both of us."

Cassandra in her up-front style, confronted me on the pathway.

"You've got to believe Melissa! No one believed me either when I said my dad abused me. It was true though. He did. I wouldn't make that up. I believe Melissa. She needs to be believed."

I believed Melissa.

I hadn't considered the carry over of our cult perversions into 'normal life' till now.

Slowly thoughts filtered into my head that Michael and I, as adults, were sexual abusers.

Somehow the words 'perpetrator' and 'victim' had hidden from me some of the abhorrence that we had done. Doing this healing work, I still felt like a victim myself. Anything I did to others was a part of my victimhood. Now I had to face up to the truth. I performed these acts, not as victim, but as me, Christina, the adult perpetrator. Not just any perpetrator either, but as a sexual violator and torturer.

My recognition of this layer of myself was brief. I had 'got it' but couldn't hold the thought long enough for expansion. I still didn't know what I had specifically done. There was too much guilt to face, too much pain to endure. The thought just floated on by. It wasn't yet time for me to acknowledge being a perpetrator.

During the break from workshops we tried our best to be normal. We couldn't discuss all our revelations constantly and some, like Melissa's accusation of incest, were virtually untouchable. I couldn't cope with the implications it had for my future or past.

Rebecca frequently had nightmares. She asked me if we were safe from cult activities in America. I couldn't reassure her, so suggested we wrote down the car mileage each night and checked it the next morning. I didn't know what else to do. She did this for a few days but lethargy set in again. Our observations weren't scrupulous enough and we let the possibility of knowing slide

Rebecca's terror of going to meetings passed without really looking at it and I didn't dare ask Indira if we could possibly be attending ceremonies whilst in this new country. It was too terrifying to know who I really was or what we were really doing. There was so much clearing of my subconscious mind that my body and conscious mind had difficulty integrating everything immediately. I could only go slowly, baby-step by baby-step.

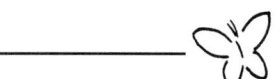

All pain is a chance to grow.

Chapter fourteen

The Year Long moved closer to completion. With only a few workshops left there seemed little chance of getting through all the clearing I had hoped for.

A year simply wasn't enough. I felt desperate as we continued to remember different episodes and wondered if the horror of recall would ever end. As my body battled along with my mind to release traumatic memories, I felt anxious about my ability to cope emotionally back in Australia without the support of these friends I had here. I didn't want the group energy to dissipate before my own inner reliance had strengthened. I wanted the anguish associated with healing to diminish.

The eleven months of my course in America had demonstrated that I was working on far more beginnings than completions. When new memories arose, it seemed as though more injustice had been perpetrated on my being and sadness and grief would threaten to swamp me again. So much confusion surrounded me, often with blame on the perpetrators for ruining my life. My thoughts and body were in a whirlpool, continually spinning with no way out and I was desperate for my self-doubt, anxiety and bewilderment to disappear. The very foundations of my life were shattered and I didn't know how to reconstruct a fresh beginning for my family.

We were back on our magic mountain for the second last workshop.

We belonged there, in the haven of safety, familiarity and nurturing. The warm July sun brought an air of lassitude into the dome. A few insects buzzed around the clear window and outside a squirrel ran through trees, knocking pinecones off the branches. Everyone was sleepy – except the squirrel and Verna. She pushed the semi-reluctant group along. Discussion was low key and it was the perfect time for me to talk with Michael about our life together. I didn't want to examine my relationship within the group. I felt embarrassed to have people listen - especially Melissa and Rebecca. Michael and I needed more deliberation on our own.

Subservience was a word which repeatedly surfaced throughout sessions for me. It would pop into my head until I looked at what it meant in my life. I was subservient to my father, brother and Michael. There were past life experiences in Japan, where I saw myself as Michael's daughter, totally obedient to him. I still felt inferior to him and presumed it was because of my own shortcomings that things weren't going well in our relationship. He implied blame and I accepted his accusations. I guessed I didn't do enough for him. It was me who got angry, so it was my fault. Michael didn't think he was angry but now I saw how he controlled and manipulated me by withdrawal. Anger brewed inside him without his acknowledgement. He displayed classic passive–aggressive behavior.

As an eleven-year-old Rebecca had expressed our family's dysfunctional situation clearly.

"When you two get divorced, I'm going with Dad."
I thought her comments were strange, for we weren't the sort of couple who would divorce. However, I had been hurt. I did a lot for my children. My family was the most important thing in the world to me.

Both Melissa and Rebecca now say they were sometimes afraid of me. My anger would burst like a bomb, with no warning and very destructive.

"You did lots of good things for us but I often didn't know how you would react," Melissa said.

"I knew how to press your buttons, Mum. I didn't really intend to go with Dad. I just thought he would buy me more things, " Rebecca commented.

I was reluctant to speak my feelings or express my desires because my own reactions frightened me. I wasn't capable of kindly asking someone to do something to help me, or gently confront issues, so I kept quiet. When I couldn't hold my frustration anymore, things would boil over. I had no idea about setting boundaries or how to protect myself. I was not even aware that I had worth.

When Rebecca told us she was leaving home when she turned sixteen, I didn't understand this was a reflection of her dislike of our home life.

"You can't legally leave home then unless you can support yourself," I told her, thinking she was just going through a stage.

She had school friends who planned to share a house together.

I understand now her statements were cries for sanity and notification for the family to check their relationships. How ignorant I was of the clues perpetually signaling for help. So many messages of chaos had manifested through the girls' lives. For example, I had sought help from the primary school psychologist when Rebecca was nine and seemed miserable.

"Rebecca is very unhappy this year. She doesn't like her teacher or class. I don't know what is going on there."

"She's a perfectly normal second child. There is nothing to worry about," the psychologist told me.

I felt these comments inadequate for the situation, but didn't know where to look for further advice, or how deep one had to go to discover the source of unhappiness.

As the lie of my life continued to expose itself in each session of the workshop, I felt cheated again and again. It wasn't that I thought the deception was someone else's fault, it was more the realization that I'd actually hidden so much from myself. My own self-betrayal by denial. To see how I lived such a superficial life by my own creation brought out immense grief from my soul. All I could see was a life of wasted opportunities. At least now that we'd found the core family problems my children would have more awareness in their future choices.

People's reactions to their trauma memories can be quite different. I often felt surprised, sad and betrayed. These senses came as a physiological shock. I shivered, left my body, altered breathing patterns and sometimes my heart rate increased. Often I felt physical pain where torture had been perpetrated, or would have debilitating headaches for several hours. Mostly I was shocked, furiously angry, then in grief.

Always my body would jerk uncontrollably and coughing repeatedly came with release. Discovery of hidden emotions and reactions were essential for healthy integration and trauma release from my body. While the shocks seemed never ending, recovery had started, though it was hard to appreciate and believe while still immersed in the process. It appeared to take forever to release everything. Gradually it became less violent on my body and easier to endure.

The fantasy of my life continued to disintegrate. I had numbed myself to believe everything given to me was perfect and that my childhood had been full of opportunities and experiences. But I had been trained not to question the control I lived under and to accept everything given to me as exactly what I needed. I had gone along with the created lies in my life and gradually started to believe they were reality. It appeared my life was good and wholesome and any problem was my own selfishness.

There was a layer of truth in this, for I had a kind mother, a good education and encouragement to believe I could do anything I wanted. Consciously I believed I was a capable person but lacked the confidence needed to fulfill my part of the creation. Subconsciously I knew I was worthless and useless: a failure and no one would like me. The suppressed lies made me angry, but being angry wasn't part of my family's expression. My hostility was repressed and all the reasons for my rage were stuffed further and further away from my awareness. My body reacted and by the time I was twenty-one, I was on medication for high blood pressure. The doctor told me the cause was from my kidney, damaged in childhood. Stress wasn't considered. It took me several years to throw the pills away.

My body was strong and healthy, except for my vision and damaged kidney. I didn't look like a victimized female. My poor eyesight still niggled at me though, and occasionally I would ask the group why they thought I was shortsighted.

Inevitably the answer would come as, "There is something you don't want to see."

My imperfect eyesight frustrated me. Even though I had now confronted many issues I didn't want to see and had done the intestinal cleanse earlier recommended by Indira, I was baffled why there hadn't been obvious visual improvement. Glasses, which I wore from age seventeen, were progressively getting stronger. In addition I now needed reading glasses. Nothing seemed to help my vision improve.

I remember exactly when my eyesight began to deteriorate: mid-May, the year I started university. We had huge lecture theaters holding hundreds of people with layered seating. It was quite a distance from the top back seats to the front podium. When I started my course two months earlier I could sit at the back of the hall, see teachers clearly and copy notes from the blackboards.

One Monday I couldn't see from my favored back position and within three days I couldn't even read writing on the board from the front of the lecture theatre. I thought I was going blind.

A friend suggested calling an optician for an eye test for prescription glasses. Very logical and practical, yet the possibility I needed glasses hadn't entered my mind. Fear numbed me and secretly I believed my eyesight would return with the same speed it deteriorated.

I didn't discuss this problem with my mother, and my father and I barely interacted. The only course of action was for me to go to an optician. My eyes were tested and glasses prescribed. The problem was solved. I could see again. Only, there was no consideration as to why my eyesight failed in three days. I didn't even know that was unusual then. I disliked wearing glasses and didn't see things as clearly as people with good sight. There was also another factor to my poor vision: it was obvious I didn't want to see things, so I didn't look at them. I had created a block between what I saw and what my brain comprehended. This improved somewhat when I became aware of my habit of looking but not seeing.

However, the rapidity of vision failure as a seventeen-year-old bugged me for thirty years, along with several other odd things. The time of the failed eyesight was associated with not having a period for about four or five months, gorging myself with food in the afternoons and putting on so much weight I increased a clothing size.

At that time it was easy to blame the lack of menstruation on stress. I was unhappy, life wasn't fun and only by my focus on a goal such as achieving my degree, was I able to maintain momentum. I was totally unaware of who I was and how to interact in the world. Confusion ruled my life.

I commented to one of my girlfriends, "I'd think I was pregnant, except I don't have a boyfriend and haven't slept with anyone." I even surprised myself with this statement and it stuck in my mind with the deteriorating eyesight memory. It was truth enmeshed in a bundle of words.

We meditated as a group on my eyesight.

"I see images of castle times and hot pokers thrust into my eyes. A magician is involved - I may have been an apprentice. Then I see myself lying in a stone room in a castle with my eyes being taken out of the sockets and cut from my body."

Another participant shared his vision: it was the same scene, only with pokers going into my eye sockets. It seems that my eyes had been removed in medieval times, on possibly more than one occasion. Maybe I was not meant to know some secrets. Whatever the reason, I came into this life with a pattern of losing my eyesight.

Still, I wanted to know what caused my visual shut down at seventeen. Something important eluded me, so I put poor eyesight on line for healing again and again - for months. Eventually, the answer came.

It was evening and Verna had been told by Spirit to question Daniel.

"What does 'four plus one' mean?"

At this stage of our course we knew it was pointless to say, 'I don't know.' Everyone realized his or her consciousness stored everything ever experienced. Thinking 'I don't know' was a cop out. We had to search within to find our answer.

Daniel's body started to react with its usual cramping to the three words. He knew he'd better start searching his memory banks to avoid excruciating pain.

"Four plus one," Verna repeated. A wave of fear passes through my body now as I type this.

Daniel spoke quickly.

"When I was about eighteen there was a group of guys I hung around with."

He had already slipped to the floor and had the look of terror that came with the pain of not releasing the memory.

"We'd spend our weekends drinking and were often drunk."

His body was sweating. He needed to say more.

"I'm not quite sure why they were friendly with me. They came from wealthy families. The father of one of the guys liked me. He'd often help me get work."

"Four plus one. Maybe it could be two plus three. They both equal five," Verna continued.

"We took drugs too!"

My body started to react. I could sense my fear. Did this 'four plus one' mean something to me as well, or did Daniel's fear trigger me?

"Maybe it could be one plus four," Verna continued, in an attempt to prod Daniel's memory. She didn't know the reason Spirit had told her to say 'four plus one,' only that this was a key to something locked in his subconscious.

Internally I wanted to scream, *No, don't say that*, to the twisting of the words, but I kept my mouth shut. My body involuntarily stretched out and I balanced precariously on the chair.

"How about three plus two? It's the same sum," Verna said.

"No. Don't you get it?" I yelled, "The answer isn't five. It has no answer."

The misuse of words infuriated me. Daniel's hands were tightly clenched; his conscious mind couldn't release the grip. He was in pain with the muscular contractions that always came when he wasn't speaking enough of his memories.

"These guys regularly took drugs. I thought some were dealers. They knew some of the bigger dealers, people well known in the community."

I couldn't concentrate on his story anymore, too much was happening with my body. It shook and I could hear my heart pounding as I slipped out of my chair onto the floor.

Rebecca noticed and came over.

"How old were you Mum?"

"Seventeen."

The age just popped out of my mouth. It wasn't something I'd considered as I felt my body contort over the words 'four plus one', but that age was the most pertinent clue to discovering eyesight failure. Knowing the time of this trauma was highly significant as I could then tie it in with my conscious memories. Something big clicked in my mind – a lock had been released.

Earlier in the day, walking amongst the trees in a peaceful hollow on the mountain I'd become aware of individual pine needles on the ground and several straight sticks lying by the path. It was a pretty scene with damp soil, soft moss, rocks and scattered twigs. I'd felt a moment of *deja vu* as my eyes imprinted this scene of the forest floor in my mind. I wondered why I had perceived it so clearly. Now I started to sense there was greater meaning as the scene revealed itself to me again. My thoughts returned to the room.

"Four plus one Daniel? Maybe it could be one plus four?" Verna prodded.

"No," I yelled again. "It's sacrilegious to say the wrong numbers. Stop saying the wrong combination of words. It's grating to my body."

I re-experienced a moment in life as a seventeen-year-old lying naked on a pine forest floor, carefully positioned in a pentagram made of sticks.

Again, Verna asked, "Well, what does 'four plus one' mean?" She truly had no idea.

"Maybe it's the third eye, the heart, the throat. Do you think it is the chakras," Daniel suggested.

He wasn't totally confident but it sounded like a possibility.

"What do you think it is, Christina?"

I'd first thought of my feet and hands before Daniel started.

"Probably the chakras…" The words stumbled out as I followed Daniel's lead. It didn't sound right as I fumbled in my mind checking the meaning, for I didn't want to be wrong.

"No, No, No. That's not it. "

I looked again at the way I had been placed on the pentacle.

"You know what it is Christina," Rhonda encouraged me.

I did. I remembered.

"Four plus one isn't a sum. It's a code…It represents the two feet and two hands. Two feet and two hands make the four and the head is the one. Each part is in a point of the pentagram made of sticks. I think my feet are tied to the ground – and my hands also. The soles of my feet are on the ground, stretched there in my lying position. They are grounded, for more reasons than tying me to the ground. It is to do with bringing the energy out of the earth up through my body. Or it could be to take the energy down to the earth. It is significant to have the soles of my feet flat on the ground." I took a breath as I surveyed my internal pictures for more information.

"The pentagram is made of sticks. They are uniform in length and width. Each point of the star is joined to the next with another straight stick. I don't think it's doweling they've used, they seem like very nice, carefully selected natural sticks. They are straight and cut to even lengths."

Lying on the floor, more images came to me.

"I am lying on my back. I see a group of men in robes step out from the trees. They're holding something in their hands and move quietly around me. There are only men here and they are not raving mad, like usual. This is a quiet and special ceremony. It's different. They have an order and are walking in single file. It is silent and methodical. Their robes seem to be brown, like monks' robes, with something tied around their waist. They have hoods over their heads, extending beyond their face, hiding their profiles. It's solemn. The object they're holding could be a candleholder, it looks that size but I don't think they are candles. It looks as though it tapers in the middle. I don't know what it is, or what it is for. I'm fearful and numb in my body as they cut a pentacle on my forehead or throat. I think it is the forehead, maybe both."

"My guides inform me that this is a fertility ceremony held in May," the psychic Helen said.

"That's it! They're right." I exclaimed.

Oh, yes. Yes, thank you Spirit, thank you for this clarity. This explains so much.

It was the timing. May was the month my eyesight went. It was true; I knew it in every cell of my body. I was pregnant for four or five months when I was seventeen, not just depressed.

"I am out of body, I don't remember being raped. A ceremonial rattle was shaken over my lower abdomen, over the sexual chakra, ovaries and uterus. Special words are said. I see someone standing out from the other men. He's holding his hands like there is a book in them. I thought they had to know all the incantations by heart? Maybe it isn't a book, just a special positioning of the hands. This is a somber ceremony. I don't remember experiencing such a quiet and orderly ceremony. It seems almost religious; maybe everything had to be done precisely to ensure pregnancy."

Well…it worked. Their incantations, rattling and raping successfully impregnated me.

"I sense there was a very small window of time in astrological terms for this ceremony to be performed. Half an hour comes into my head. The timing had to be within a specific half-hour for all conditions to be fulfilled. There is something about the moon. Is it a new moon? Everything had to be set up perfectly for this ceremony to take place at the absolute correct time."

I searched for more information.

"I can't see any more - I've left my body. I can't get back there…"

It's true. I didn't want to see anymore. It was nicer being out of body, floating in the warmth of bliss, with no stress, no responsibility and no pain.

I hate these men for my inadequacies, lack of confidence, fear and for not achieving highly in my study during college – the very time of this ceremony. I remember who some of them were – including Dad.

No wonder I dislike people shaking musical rattles near me - also feathers, bones and dead animal hides. There are a lot of things I find abhorrent that were used in ceremonies. Candles are one. Sometimes I can tolerate them if deemed necessary by others. Indian dream catchers decorated with small bones make me shudder, as do any skulls, bones or antlers used as spiritual tools. My mind was busy looking at every possible effect of this ceremony on my life. It was a pivotal time, with such trauma that my eyesight plummeted.

What goes through the minds of these men as they prepare for their orgies? Do they think they are important? Although they are also victims under mind control, can't they take some responsibility for their actions, even if someone at the 'top' uses them as mere pawns? What is ritual abuse all about? Is it to provide wealth for a created elite, with enough sexual revelry and drugs to keep the plebeians happy?

I am so grateful for finding this memory. It explains my enigma of being seventeen and is the key to the treasure I was looking for. It laid open the absolute truth of ritual abuse in my life, the lock which inhibited me from finding my genuine self. That treasure of authenticity, my soul.

How could I possibly ever want a sexual relationship with a man again? Respecting men is difficult and mostly I look at men as sexual abusers. These are my prejudiced thoughts, a total reflection of my past. But I have to let these thought forms flow. When they stop appearing I will know that part of me with such anger towards men is healed. Being a nun currently holds quite an appeal.

The 'four plus one fertility ceremony' and failed eyesight are tied together. As a seventeen-year-old, I gave up. In hindsight it was so obvious. It was reflected in my study and exam results. Desperate to do well at university, I studied every night and weekends to get good grades. My parents pressured me not to study late but that was impossible for the amount of information I needed to memorize. After May, only three months into the year, my concentration failed. I couldn't remember my work and no longer found it exciting. Although I managed to pass exams the reason behind my inability to concentrate and learn easily eluded me. I knew this memory was absolute truth.

Thirty years of cogitating and wondering about eyesight and missed periods were answered. Here one episode of my surreal life memory finally matched the timing of my normal life. Recalling the incidents myself helped my body release and heal more swiftly. I may never have recalled this ceremony if 'four plus one' hadn't been said in the group.

My 'four plus one' ceremony was held in the grounds of a Catholic boy's orphanage. It was in a nice isolated pine forest close to town. We often drove past there in my childhood and I wondered what went on amongst the trees. I imagined wolves and Red Riding Hood's dilemma, a fairy tale akin to my own life.

In the past decade, there have been newspaper reports of charges of molestation against the men of cloth, from men who were raised in this and other orphanages. Some Brothers were imprisoned twenty-five years after the event. Other Brothers from similar places were even imprisoned on their own admission of guilt, not remembering who the molested boys were. I wondered if there was more than molestation going on.

In later recall I saw myself in a church on these grounds. There was a sizeable group of children gathered in a circle for classes from the black-robed priest. We stood in a circle around a coffin being taught the significance of the five-pointed star.

There is something strange about these memories as I tie them in with feature television from the past decade, which uncovered terrible deceit about child migrants to Australia in the fifties and sixties. Although many of these children were brought from Britain as orphans to live in institutions, it was found that this status was not always true. Some of these middle-aged men and women have now been reunited with their distraught, aged parents in Britain who had wondered what happened to their children for forty or so years. The children were abducted or deceived about their family's status. This is the beginning of exposure of more lies perpetrated through our society. It seems that there may be hidden reasons for that travesty of forced child migration.

We leave our body because of fear, and feeling unsupported.

Chapter fifteen

An opportunity to participate in extra groups arose. Summer workshops were an annual event on Blue Mountain. Placed in between our Year Long groups, they were ideal for continued growth work and meeting new people. Melissa and I decided to participate.

Having a different group with a new focus was refreshing. People from around the country gathered and we transported them from the airport. Chatting in the car was a great way to meet a few people at a time.

Apart from our inward search, a highlight of the week was to participate in a sweat lodge.

Although I had heard of sweat lodges, I hadn't realized how small the structures actually were. There wasn't much room to move inside and I wondered how twenty people could fit into such a close space.
Late afternoon sunlight filtered through the pine trees onto the circle forming around the fire pit. Everyone came with naked bodies wrapped with a towel or sheet. Daniel had built the fire earlier in the afternoon. Now there were just hot, glowing embers left, ready to heat the lava rocks. Prayers were said for every stone placed in the fire and the four directions were acknowledged.

Anticipation grew, as we stood around the heating rocks in the developing sacredness. A bunch of fresh sage was handed to everyone as they entered through the sweat lodge's small opening. Awkwardly I crawled around the edge of the cool dirt floor, right to left, following the previous person circling the central pit. I sat between two men. What irony placed me between two of the three men in the group? Waiting, I held the sage to my nose – the air was already stuffy inside. Hot stones placed into the pit sizzled when water was thrown over them. It was hot, humid and hard to breathe. I wondered how I was going to cope with several hours of this overwhelming heat. My hand edged toward the side of the lodge. Once I felt the canvas cover, my hand slipped under the layers of coverings to the outside. This was freedom to have my fingertips out in the cool evening air. I could cope knowing there was a way out.

The rounds of prayer started: first to our forefathers. Whoever wished to say a prayer participated. Slowly I realized there was virtually no visibility in the blackness of the lodge. I loosened my towel from around my body and covered my face with one end to reduce the searing heat on my skin; a flash of recognition of the use of fire by the cult. But I was safe here. I pressed the sage against my nose. This environment required stamina.

My towel was saturated with sweat. I wrung it out and the water streamed onto the dirt floor. People's prayers were deep, touching and meaningful. Self-consciousness dropped away in this environment and everyone was open and sincere. The air was filled with trust and safety. There was something special about the evening, but I was relieved to leave the sweat lodge. The elemental heat, darkness and cramped space were overwhelming. I rushed to shower. Water the temperature of the cool evening shocked my body. My skin felt smooth, cleansed and vitalized. I sparkled inside.

A light dinner was served. Everyone seemed peaceful and happy. This had been a sacred, cleansing ceremony.

I felt quite different after the sweat lodge. Although an agonizingly long test of endurance, the end result was wonderful. I preferred it to the fire walk six months earlier. I felt cleansed by the sweat lodge. The fire walk took a mind shift to acknowledge my achievement.

During time between workshops I continued having bodywork. Often memories would come as stored tension was released.

My Rolfer explained. "I work with the soft tissue to balance your structure. As your body is released from the old patterns, sometimes the emotions you've hidden away are discharged. That's what you're experiencing."

These sessions were significant in helping liberate stored energy from my body, often with visual memory. My Rolfer's intuition and skills in knowing where to work and release stress were astounding. As her hands hovered around my heart with a degree of uncertainty, she commented, "I have a feeling to work in this area, but I'm not quite sure why."

My body responded by shaking; every square millimeter.

"Oh no. This is fear," I said.

I recognized this familiar energy immediately. Even my teeth chattered, so I shut my eyes and breathed through the discharge of this emotion – and I started into memory…

"They are cutting my heart out. Lying here, I am well aware it was a trick - but it fooled me at the time. They show me my heart. It's a big one and there is a little heart next to it. They tell me, 'We have your heart and your baby's heart.' Those two fresh, red-blooded hearts disappeared as they show me a tainted, greenish heart that was ready to be put back into my own heart space. 'This is your heart now; it's a bad heart because you are evil. A child of Satan.'

Although this was a created deception, I believed what they told me. Obviously, my heart wasn't cut out. However, in a drugged and fearful state, clarity of thinking wasn't possible. These cult masters were powerful illusionists and magicians of horror.

I lay quietly on the massage table. Tears filled my eyes and ran down my cheeks with grief of my loss. Where was that baby? Where did it go? How old was I? Why hadn't I remembered before?

More revelations of my family's dysfunction came during workshops as Verna invited Melissa to let her personalities out.

What? I thought there was just one other person who came to the workshop with multiple personalities: Cassandra, the red haired woman who had supported Melissa's memory of Michael sexually abusing her. Cassandra knew her different personalities well and they often talked to me. How could Melissa be categorized as having different personalities as well? She didn't have obvious people who wanted to dress in their own style and act differently.

I didn't want to know anymore. Not my daughter. MPD: multiple personality disorder, DID: Dissociative Identity Disorder. They seemed to be the same to me, resulting from severe abuse.

A bigger shock came when Melissa responded to Verna, totally understanding. A personality came forth and Melissa spoke for her. Verna and Melissa had a conversation. How did Melissa know? How did Verna know? How can Verna take all these things so calmly? Nothing seems to startle her.

More to the point, why didn't *I* know? How did Melissa get to this point of splitting her personality? How come I didn't even know what went on in my family's life?

"This part of me is Felicity and she is sixteen." The Melissa I thought I knew continued. "She loves sex and longs to go to cult meetings. She's allowed me to speak for her."

I couldn't think. Absolutely nothing entered my mind as I sat there, shocked at Melissa's honesty discussing one of her promiscuous cult personalities. Even with the despair of confronting these horrors, I am grateful we are finding out. Hiding problems is no help to us.

Melissa explained to me later that she often wondered what the different voices in her head were. "Mum, do you remember when I told you last year that I thought I had ADD?"

"Yes. I didn't know why you would consider that possibility."

"I'd searched the college medical library looking for something to explain the way I felt. There were these different voices in my head and I didn't know what they were."

"I didn't think you were hyperactive," I said. "I thought kids with ADD are uncontrollable, usually exhibiting wild behavior."

"It defined my symptoms. Anyway, it was reassuring for me to categorize what was happening inside me."

"Did you realize Cassandra's different personalities were the same way you felt about yourself?"

"No. But after a few workshops I realized DID could explain my different voices."

I had been ignorant about DID. When I studied nutrition at university, I'd read about a child who had one personality allergic to orange juice, but another wasn't. That was the limit of my understanding. When I met Cassandra and was introduced to her kids, I assumed multiple personality was obvious. The people within her took on a very different demeanor when they emerged. Each had a name, distinct characteristics and could even be male in her female body. Gradually, I learned from Cassandra that these little people had developed from abuse. Until then, I'd assumed DID was a congenital disorder.

My mind was challenged constantly with the effect of trauma on humans. I had to face up to how abused people skillfully adapted their different personalities so the general population wouldn't even recognize them.

It took observation and awareness to recognize DID and a lot of trust for the personalities to reveal themselves. Mostly they were not obvious. I looked at my daughter. Slowly I recalled how she sometimes acted like a baby. Occasionally she'd snuggle up and put her head on my lap, suck her thumb and pull my hand down to stroke her head. There was always something odd about this. There were other times when something about her eyes changed simultaneously with her behavior. That was when we witnessed a switch.

Melissa knew several of her personalities – the ones prepared to communicate with her and allow her to know their actions. When one she knew came out, she – Melissa - was aware of what happened and what she did. It didn't appear that she experienced missing time with these parts.

My steep denial of Melissa's abuse was pointed out to me from another source when she had been fifteen: about the time she told me she'd been sexually abused. I couldn't tie the pieces together then. I had regularly spent time with Lynette, a dowser, as she taught a group the art of medical dowsing. We dowsed together for Melissa's medical condition. I recently found the paper in my folders.

Healing to initiate for Melissa
1 Abused: Allergies: Congestion: Dental Malocclusion:
Multiple personalities.
2 Health: Ovaries, inflammation and growths.
Respiratory infections: Skin tone- rash, burns, disease, dehydration.
3 Behavior: Unconscious hostility : feels put upon.

*4 Childhood patterns: A 'doesn't belong child': Balance with magical child, gifted, innocent child.
5 General needs: Bio-energetic exercises: Oil essences – lemon grass-
She needs highest of divine light beings from Arcturis to help her.*

What a shock eight years later to find that I'd been given more clues along the way, but hadn't known how to pursue them.

Many torturous acts are perpetrated in the cult to fill victims with terror. But from the Spirit Doctors' healing session I learned about the use of knives. At every workshop we had a visit from the Spirit Doctor team on the last evening. Healing in this mode is usually gentle and loving. Although these caring energies were around me this evening I felt immediate pain in my ovaries. Some indefinable discomfort was in both ovaries. I lay down but it was several hours before I could move and even more time before the pain subsided enough to sleep.

I had no idea of why my ovaries needed healing so asked Indira the next day.

There were blades that were very fine, so fine that they could be thrust into the ovaries and solar plexus and turned slightly. It wasn't an inexperienced person who did this. The knives had blades like acupuncture needles. Doing this can wreak havoc inside the body without external scarring that would be noticed on the skin. They used the knives in your head, your solar plexus, under the ribs and in the ovaries. In the head the knives created a creepiness.

The knives were not always used. They had to wait a while before being able to use them again because there was great danger of killing someone. These are torture instruments and there is a big part of you that doesn't want to ever remember something like this. Be cognizant when you speak with others that there are such potentials of torture. These knives are available and they were used. Sometimes they were used when you had done something wrong but mostly they were used just to let you know who was in charge. And you weren't.

I wondered how I was still able to bear children after the things that had done to my body. I was lucky. It seems it isn't uncommon for women who have been ritually abused to have fertility problems.

The healing of my ovaries continued for another year. Often pain and heat would bring them to my attention for a day or two. The first response to my own question, 'What is happening here?' was rage for the violation inflicted on them. I spent several months clearing that. When that layer healed, I felt ready for Rolfing on this area. Deeper healing occurred as fascia surrounding my ovaries, released tension.

Within another few months, I remembered syringes and something clicked. I called Rhonda

"Did you know they took human eggs and experimented with in-vitro fertilization?"

"Yeah. But they didn't do it properly. Probably didn't have all the necessary equipment. But what I remember is from years ago, maybe twenty years, so it could have changed since then. I don't remember them even mixing eggs with sperm."

"It seems to me that that they mixed sperm with eggs and tried placing the solution into a woman's vagina. I've got this vision of a salt solution in a syringe being used to collect the eggs somehow. I can't put a time period on that memory though. The only way I can place times are when I was little or if I see Melissa or Rebecca."

Having a friend to discuss memories with always felt assuring and confirming.

"You're not the only person who's called me about this. A young woman told me much the same as you. They'd withdrawn eggs from her ovaries. I think they keep up with modern technology that could be useful to them."

"Evidently highly trained doctors are involved."

"Well, that seems totally obvious."

Indira confirmed the extraction of human eggs.

Attempts failed because of the incorrect environment. You don't have any children living that you don't know about.

This is not the case for everyone. Rhonda later recalled having a live baby induced, in her early teens. Her parents had arranged for this child to be sold. Records were easily created to register him as the birth son of his purchasers. All that was needed was the cult doctor's signature for the certificate.

Then she realized what caused her inability to have a baby when she was a married adult. Her husband was Rh positive and she was Rh negative. The doctors were confused by her adamant response to their questions, that she had never been pregnant before, yet her blood was fully of antibodies. Because of all the babies she bred for the cult, continually building the antibodies to Rh positive, there was no chance now of her having a live birth.

During this round of healing sessions I recalled having been tied up, hung upside down and pinned down by a vice holding my head and fingers.

The pressure in my head during these memories was so uncomfortable I wanted to take medication to reduce the pain. Every bone felt displaced as though they had been moved and not put back correctly. It was another evening of healing from the Spirit Doctors which set off the motion in my head. I looked into my memory.

"I am small, lying on a wooden workbench with my father and some of his workmen standing around the edge. This place seemed familiar. It could be the garage next door... Now I remember - I think it was a large shed in the back yard. That's funny – I remember being told never to go near there. It is behind the chicken coop – away from any nosy neighbors. Any sounds could probably be drowned out by machinery noise. My head feels tight with the restriction – and I think my hands and feet are tied also. From the corner of my eye I see one of the men come forward. It is the same man I remember raping me. I think he is being taught anatomy – or how to administer chloroform and the limits not to exceed when torturing. I'm being used for study or experimentation. He has a drill or screwdriver in his hand and puts it in my ear. Why? Whoa – they have splashed something on my face – it is to revive me. My father calls my name, and shakes me to get me to respond. I think they over dosed me with chloroform."

I'm sure this vice wasn't used just once; probably many times to inflict fear in my psyche. That may explain my intense dislike of anything tight on my fingers and head and my speed at removing rings quickly if my fingers swell. I recalled my fear as we removed patterns associated with the use of a vice on our heads, fingers and toes.

This was the type of cruelty used to create the extreme fear necessary for implanting mind control. Threat of death, watching torture or killing of others insured we knew we were powerless. It also meant suggestions could be implanted. Families perpetuated the programming.

Everyone involved in multi-generational ritual abuse has been programmed from birth. Pain and torture is used to create personality splits, then these personalities are trained to be activated by a cue word or signal to do cult work. Specific words easily hidden in conversation make us react in a certain cult defined way. One personality may be trained to sexually please men during ceremonies, or an expert at seduction and acting for pornographic pictures. Another may hold memory of pregnancies.

It appeared the cult was knowledgeable about torture and brainwashing techniques. I was shocked by my ignorance about brain washing, although I knew from war stories it was used to force prisoners to accept the philosophies, rules or regulations of a regime. I thought of my childhood image of prisoner re-education. I had imagined them sitting in a classroom repeating slogans their captors wanted to instill in their brains. I fantasized about me being involved and not taking on others' beliefs by pretending to be brainwashed - while all the time holding onto my own truth. How naïve I was. And how odd that as a young teenager I would even think about my possible reaction. Brainwashing uses cruelty and torture to open the subconscious to horror programming. In computer terms, a virus is fed into the hard drive; in humans it is fed into the mind to alter and block our thinking and action.

'These are not your children,' programmed me to not protect my daughters. It kept me compliant in circles for I believed I was powerless. Obediently, I obeyed cult orders. A converse program given to children was, 'Your parents won't save you'. This was clever programming to break family bonds and trust and ingrain reliance on the cult for security.

Everyday words, phrases and actions guaranteed that no link implanted in our consciousness was weakened. We were kept active and alive for the cult. Types of words used in my family's programming were 'coming home', 'when are you coming again', and 'family'. I started to recognize some words from the clues my body had in response to them.

When we visited our relatives, these words were used unconsciously to keep our programming activated. I remember the heavy feeling invoked when they were said as part of our good-byes. Words came to me during the workshops. Even typing them and thinking them causes a mixed emotional response of anger, cutting off and wanting to run.

Indira warned me of danger.

Search with yourself to find the words used for programming. Don't say these words to yourself for they can reactivate you. Reading them is not as powerful as hearing them.

Verna's deprogramming used healing techniques with sound, one of the methods used to implant the programs. Penetrating and unexpected sounds break through the energy obstructions built by the programming. I felt my shields shatter and my body respond with the deprogramming sounds. The sound waves penetrated through to my core. Sometimes further techniques were needed because a deeper program needed removal of other patterns first. Programs protecting programs: a multi-layered system with virus protectors, malfunction scanners and continual reprogramming.

It was a pleasantly cool evening in the dome. Deprogramming was the focus, using sound. The words used for program healing are carefully stated. For example, it would be removal of patterns of programming associated with 'coming home', not just 'removal of patterns or programming that came up for people today'. I still can't remember the programming words Verna worked with this night - that is significant - but I do remember my automatic response when she voiced the words of the program up for removal. I whispered, "You're not going to get me." I hadn't experienced this response before. I had felt my energy block the sound from resonating through my body for some program removal but this conscious thought of resistance had never entered my mind previously. Then the sound started. I hid my face in my hands because I wanted to laugh. I didn't want to break the effect of the sound for anyone else who needed this program removed but I couldn't hold back my chuckles.

Melissa laughed. Then Rhonda. Earlier I'd noticed Rhonda hiding her face, I guess with the same response as me, not wanting to disturb anybody. Rebecca soon joined us. The four of us were hysterical. Our laughter was crazy, with no apparent reason. I sat on the floor where it seemed more comfortable to move with the unconstrained ripples of laughter running through my body. Melissa collapsed on the floor too.

The sounds stopped. We stopped laughing. Verna looked around, fascinated.

"We've found a core program," she said.

So what? I didn't care. What the hell was a core program anyway? There was nothing funny about this, but I giggled anyway. Except we now had an explainable reason for our spontaneous, eerie reaction.

The deprogramming resumed and we all laughed again. With four women who were ritually abused responding like this, there was no stopping. Each person stimulated the other. Russell was agitated.

"Stop it!" he screamed.

This was a useless order for people who had been programmed to block any attempt to remove this program with laughter.

"Shut up. Stop being so ridiculous. You're putting this on," he yelled.

Our behavior annoyed Russell but we didn't care.

Helen understood what was happening and explained to him.

"Your response is exactly what they want anyone trying to deprogram them to have. They don't want us to continue."

Melissa, Rebecca and I rolled on the floor in hysteria, blocking any deprogramming. Someone recited the twenty-third psalm. Now everyone in the dome was involved in this strange event.

Verna wouldn't give up. She intended to clear this program. I heard what others were saying but couldn't relate to it because I was engrossed in laughter. Someone sang. My God, that was annoying, asking the cherubim and seraphim for protection and help! Obviously I wasn't the only one bothered.

"Shut up," Rhonda yelled. "Stop singing that thing."

The singing didn't stop. It grew louder as more people joined in.

"Shut-up!"

"Keep singing," Verna encouraged.

I wished they would shut up too. Stupid religious song. I didn't think singing would help us remove programs. I chortled between coughing fits, oblivious of my surroundings except for sound. I knew I didn't want to know about the program removal or what was going on, and I had no desire to try and let the healing energies in. I forgot what the program was. That was important to the cult. The religious stuff irritated me. What was so special about it?

Rhonda flipped into another memory. "My grandfather took me to the cathedral. I'm tied up in a church."

That explained why the songs affected her so much. She crawled on the floor, out of the reality of being a young woman in the dome into her childhood state, trying to escape the abuse in her memory. Her mind focused to get out the door, away from craziness, prayers, religious songs and abuse.

"They're laughing at me," Rhonda sobbed. "They say I look like a popsicle, tied up with my legs in the air."

She crawled out the door crying. Verna followed. She asked us all to come outside for a few minutes to let the energy change in the dome before going back inside for healing.

There was far more going on at many different levels in the dome than I was aware of. People told me later how they felt drained by sending out healing energy to help remove the marasmas exuded by the four of us.

Michael and Daniel were unaffected by the program removal. Why? Was it that only women had this programming? Did men have different programming? I didn't know.

What was the resolution of this session for me? A deeper understanding of programming; the awareness that there were barriers built into our consciousness to resist attempts to remove the core programs. Just because we didn't feel a response to some of the deprogramming sounds didn't mean that we didn't have that program.

Earlier in the workshops Melissa and Rebecca discovered they had received cult messages over the telephone. Instructions for their cult personalities were given when they answered the phone. One word, and they knew what to do and when. Then the normal phone conversation could continue. Neither of them liked to use the phone.

I don't know how I received my instructions for going to meetings. Possibly from Michael, or maybe the children, but I do know there was a command that would get me out my front door and to a meeting. Right on time, never late. Punishment for tardiness was severe.

An 'age of return' program appeared common for everyone involved in ritual abuse. When a particular age is reached the program is activated internally to remind a person to return to their group. Such a delay in program activation gives people the opportunity to go elsewhere for education and jobs for years, without forgetting their first loyalty - the bondage to the cult. This age seems to vary somewhere between thirty-five and fifty years and is indicated by an intense, irrational desire to move back to one's childhood area, or reconnect with family.

The universe supports us to reach our destiny.

Chapter sixteen

I had a trance channel reading with Katar who channeled Tsen Tsing. I wanted to know if there were more insights for me about ritual abuse, and how my life would be when I returned to Australia.

Who could we trust? I was in so much confusion and wanted guidance.

How are you feeling this day in your body Hmmm? I know you have been feeling a lot of inner stresses and agony in the body, and so I bless these with you now.

I also want to ask you a question first. "Do you love yourself?"

The tears and sadness this brought up indicated to me, that it was probably, "No."

Do you? Right now you don't know. You know you ought to, and there are loveable parts. You have found them before, but right now there is such a void. You feel the void of love in your own being : in all the things that you have surrounding you: with family and husband.

All are supposed to love you. You feel as though you're blown into little fractions and scattered away. Who you are, standing in all of the scattering, you don't know.

You would say to me, " I don't know what's loveable about me. I have done despicable things that I don't know about, and that I do know about. Also, I have so much anger and rage in me for others, how could that make me loving?" And you'd also tell me, "I also feel so impatient and so completely disgusted and annoyed with those around me!"

Yes. I see through your thoughts!

Then you'd say, "Well, how can I love myself? How selfish of me?"

But that is exactly what you need right now. Some selfishness! You have not 'selfished' yourself quite enough most of your life, have you? You have given and given. You sacrificed your own desires for fulfillment for the good of the family, for the good of your business, for the good of your husband's work, for the good of everyone. Whether it was for your family before your children, or for your children.

In spite of whatever you may, or may not have done, in these abuse circumstances, you, in your own conscious mind and body, let go of many and most of your dreams and desires. You even let go of your own physical possessions that you liked, for the sake of your family. You don't know self love so well. Selfishness is not easy on your plate. I tell you there is a very high selfishness with a big 'S' you need to practice more. It is good timing now as you search out, "Who am I and how can I be loveable." You will come to understand, " I don't owe anybody anything, I don't owe anything to my husband, I don't owe anything to my children."

That is not easy for you to say, but the truth is, you don't owe them anything.

Now you and Michael are trying to come together, and wonder where all this ritual abuse is coming from. You want to hurry up, but it is a long healing process. You are not done yet. Don't pretend that it hasn't occurred - but proceed patiently.

What was your childhood family situation? It was ritualistic and very distorted. That is my interpretation. Go into your own memory to see. But to help you launch deeper into your memories, I see that it went on and on and on, in various forms. Using and abusing girls and women. It was sexual and very distorted.

Was my mother involved as well?

She did some manipulation with you. Mostly she was being abused. So for her own survival, like many, she did what she was told. She was brainwashed to believe that was the only way to survive.

Did I really see an animal being dissected?

Oh yes. This was just playfulness, like men going to the woods. They were play-acting being big brave men.

Were my sisters involved?
Yes. They just used everyone until there was no more to give.
Was I ever pregnant?
Yes you were. Didn't you feel that when you had Melissa that it wasn't your first pregnancy?
No, I didn't know.
But in terms of your sexuality, loosing your virginity and so forth, didn't you know? There was never the usual loosing your virginity for you. "Oh my gosh, I thought it was supposed to be painful, I thought I was supposed to bleed." These type of things. Of course all this had been done many, many, many years earlier, when you were just an infant.
I had no idea at that time. Since then I've seen them abusing me when I was just a baby.
Yes, you were just an infant, a baby. Before that, there was manipulation by touching and as you got closer to the age of two, it was penetration. I tell you this because you kept repressing and repressing your knowing of that level of abuse, and trying to lead a normal life so much, that you forgot it even was true for you.

There is a certain vibration that you attracted someone like Michael into your life. He also had experienced abusive situations. You both came from family backgrounds that were very warped. Not how you would like to think they were.
Can I go home?
You could, except but there are still some fragments that are related to Melissa there. Because of her training, she is being trailed and connected in the States. I don't want to say it's not safe going home because of that. You want to just really watch, if that's where you choose to be. Don't go anywhere near Michael's family. However, you were all around the city when the abuse was going on.

How do you suppose it was that you were already a grown woman and had children, and all these activities going on and you don't recall them?
I think the brain washing is more powerful than I realized.
Yes. The brainwashing, drugs, and power of the human psyche to survive. It has very clear mental shutdowns. Many horrible things occurred. Yet, what would make it less painful now? Acknowledge everything, because it happened as a pattern, not just specific incidents.

Even if you did these horrible things, are you loveable? Of course you are, because you are more than that. You are not just an individual that did things that were murderous or incestuous. You were a person who lived with the consciousness of spirit.

You danced and laughed with the great spiritual teachings. You gave reverence and your life to God and spirit. That was a big healing for you when you did this, when you went to be a sannyasin. That was one of the most healing things you did for your self. You realized, there was a group of God. You were loved and supported, and felt completely safe. I know there was sadness, when you had to let pieces of that experience go.

You deserved all that love you experienced there. That love, you truly are, as a soul. It is your God nature. With your group you found a completely safe place to express your love and joy. This other abuse doesn't take that away. Although the abuse was hidden, it still needed to be dealt with.

You are God's loving soul, whose only desire is to be, serve, and experience the joy of God's love. It is the most incredible irony, you would know such joy and love with people from the light, and now see this other side.

But it isn't who you are, that participated in the abusive things.

Yes, what are you? It was your responsibility to the whole, but that doesn't diminish you. Prior to revealing this abuse in your own family, you had thoughts, that even Hitler can be loved, because he had more than that lifetime. You forgave all kinds of horrific energies, and it's time to give it to yourself as well.

Well then, you hit your daughter with a spoon. Your first session started out with such a little thing yes? And you want to blame yourself for being a bad mother, because you hit her with a spoon? Or whether it's you observed her having sexual intercourse with her father and you didn't stop it?

Both acts are coming from part of the self, which is in pain. You understand all your own inner violence. It comes from all the abuse you experienced as a young child. You had no defense, and even when you were a teenage woman, you had already figured, don't ever tell anyone. So you stopped telling yourself, didn't you? You had to get focused on some part of life, or be insane.

What would your girlfriends at school think if they thought all this was going on? Christina was so stable. Yes, you were a rock, and you were so reliable. If only they knew how much pain you had from this other life. Your shame cut it off, as if it weren't really true. In your pre-teen years you fantasized a different life and made that real. It is no wonder you have no memory of that part. You know how to block out these memories and when you were exposed again through marriage, you let the drugs help you block it again.

It sounds like you are hanging around all the time, to see what's going on.

Oh yes, I pay very close attention to all that you are doing. I don't have to hang around, because I am all things. I'm merged into my God consciousness. At any moment I see the hologram of your experiences. I'm there, anyway, because time is all one and right now I am with you and I look into the hologram of your whole life experiences, and it is as if I was there. Do you think I can tell you what to do? You don't want that. How can I help you sort this out?

Should I tell my mother and sisters about this?

No I wouldn't. You can tell them about some memories of sexual abuse, but they are not ready to hear all this other stuff and may not be ready to believe you. Your consciousness says it is willing to handle it and it's even still difficult for you.

Melissa is not entirely safe from the cult at this timing, because she is so totally raw and not very clear. She has many issues she is not looking at.
We want you and her to know that there is safety in Spirit. She is conscious enough to know that, but she is not sure that she wants that…because there are parts of her personality which are drawn into the cult. They are tempted… Very easily tempted to be drawn into that, because she feels powerless in any other role …So that is why she has been still active… Not so much during the school year, but bits and pieces during the breaks …She has had some activity trying to draw some other people in from school.   This is not in her conscious memory …I know it would be convenient for her to finish schooling there… but I would try to negotiate her finishing school somewhere else. It could be traumatic for her trying to readjust to other living circumstances, but give her moral support… Make sure that is what she wants, and be there to support her…

What part of the country would be better to live in?

(Laughter from Tsen Tsing.) There every where aren't they?   So that is part of the concern. The abuse ring is so massively big that where could she ever go to be completely free of temptations, or triggers drawing her back into it? So she needs someplace where she has the illusion of not being where the entrapments are as big.

What other parts did I play in the abuse?
I'll let you see those.
How does it feel to hold a knife?
Which hand did I use?
(I knew what he meant – stabbing.)

I think you tried doing it with your left hand so you weren't so conscious of it...

I know part of you is homesick, but you can never go back home again, can you? You can go back there, but you will make a new thing out of it.

Was I carrying out some things on Melissa that were done to me?

Yes... you made these little inner vows, "When I get bigger I'm going to be the one in power." So you wonder why you were sadistic to this little innocent child. It came from your own inner child...

Tell me something about the garage next to my early childhood home?

Your father is learning as you learn. Even you didn't know that you had so many things to forgive him for. Even though he was as mean to you as he was, he still loved you, in a very bizarre way. And as a soul, he obviously let you come through.

There is the probable dissolution of your marriage.

As I look upon the way you are maneuvering your energies at this time, I am witnessing you becoming free. So I only say this word probable, to give you free choice. You are becoming free. Not because Michael was abusive, or did these things to you or your girls. He is no longer there for your need to grow.

It is still your choice. This affects the girls and in some ways they will be cheerful about this. Right now they are confused. It is up to them to be completely responsible for their relationship with their father, and you will support them to have a good relationship now. So they are supported one hundred percent and do not to have to take sides. They no longer know how to perceive this man who caused some of their pain. There is no reason why there cannot be love and healing for the four of you.

When you return to Australia, watch the energies. If you are going to settle there, watch the energies...Don't be paranoid of everyone.

If you don't remember doing these things, does it mean everyone else is a perpetrator as well? Don't start looking for spiders, you may hurt yourself.

Christina, know you are loveable and loved by God...

So, Christina was my name in my last life too! - (I had thought this was so a few months earlier.)

Yes, you came in with the same vibrations....

The energy vibrations coming from spirit during a channeling are so loving, that it almost doesn't matter what they tell you. Being surrounded by this love for an hour is a love bath of eternity ...even re-listening to the tapes brings back those same energies.

What did I remember from that session with Tsen Tsing?

I was shocked when I listened to the tape again to write this book. For what I remember hearing and what was said were often different. I had filtered out what I didn't want to know and recreated what I was able to cope with.

I heard that Melissa was being followed, but assumed she would be safe in another part of Australia.

I heard, but soon blocked out, that it was my choice if I wanted my marriage to finish.

I selectively heard that my family weren't involved in ritual abuse, just sexual abuse and concluded that my relations were not the bad guys.

I had filtered what I wanted to hear, and interpreted what Tsen Tsing said in a manner I could manage psychologically.

I was upset because of Melissa's involvement and I was sad that shame stopped me questioning what was going on in my body during my whole life. I didn't mention my predicted marriage collapse to anybody. I couldn't handle the thought myself so promptly forgot it.

My life was chaotic and I was barely coping.

"Be prepared for anything! The last days have a habit of bringing up unexpected circumstances."

Chapter seventeen

We took a short visit to the Western Slope between workshops and drove directly from there to Blue Mountain for our last group. The trip was a nine-hour drive along unfamiliar roads so we watched out for distinct signposts to ensure no wrong turns were taken. Driving in the United States was always something of a challenge for us because we had driven on the left-hand side of the road for nearly thirty years. My judgment for the right hand side of the car was tenuous and staying accurately between the white lines took concentrated attention. Lights, indicators and windshield wipers were reversed from our Australian vehicle and often caused confusion. If my reflexes responded before conscious thought, I'd watch the windscreen wipers start instead of signal lights. A quick reaction hurriedly made me switch to the correct gadget.

Even the positioning of traffic lights was foreign, for in Australia they are usually at eye level on intersection corners. Occasionally I delayed looking upward to check the hanging American signals and had to brake suddenly for a red light. I needed to be fully alert on these roads to make up for delayed and reversed reflexes. Michael niggled about my driving.

"You're too close to the edge of the road."

I immediately retaliated.

"Your driving is no better than mine."

"Yeah Dad, you drive close to the edge of the road too," Melissa said.

Michael ignored us. Obviously brooding with his own anger filled thoughts, he looked out the window. He appeared so emotionally distant. I didn't know how to placate him nor did I know why he was so irritated. He wouldn't share his feelings. Although he had accused me for bad driving, it seemed there was more to it than my road skills.

We drove a few more hours till reaching crossroads where there were two alternative routes to our destination. Melissa, an accurate map-reader like her father, directed us down a main highway.

"Who chose this route?" Michael demanded, "It's miles longer than the other way."

"Why don't you look at the map yourself then?" I said, quite aware of Michael's anger. "Melissa, can you see the other route Michael wants?" I asked, although, to me, it didn't seem an important issue. I just couldn't understand his fury.

"This highway will get us there," Melissa said. "On the map it looked easier to follow from the last turnoff. What does it matter anyway?"

"We always arrive early," I added. "We'll be there on time. Everyone else is usually late. We don't have to stress ourselves about this."

But Michael was clearly furious about something beyond our arrival time at the workshop and he blamed the females in his life.

We arrived in a town and I couldn't see the road-sign for the turnoff.

"Do you know how to get there?" I asked as I looked around, wondering where to go. The street was lined with shops and it was hard to see anything.

"You're driving." Michael said. "You find the place."

Michael's spiteful response shocked me. Somehow I remained detached from his emotion. This anger was entirely his and I knew further attack from him wouldn't stir me.

"I don't know where to go. Can you ask someone for me if I drive into a parking lot?"

He didn't answer. I braked at a stop sign and Michael scooted out of the car. Stunned at his behavior I could only laugh.

"Where are you going?" I called after him.

He slammed the car door, headed down the pavement and crossed a road. I followed in the car, rolling down the passenger's side window as he proceeded over a small bridge.

"What are you doing? We're going to a workshop on healing. That's what we're here for. Use the workshop - it's the perfect forum. Running away isn't serving any purpose."

Michael's mouth tightened. Although his eyes filled with hate, he didn't speak. Instead he opened the car door and got back in. We drove on in total silence. What were his thoughts? All I could see was a man immersed in withdrawal and blame. Whatever was stirring him, he kept it a secret. It was a relief to ignore him. I didn't want to become part of the thoughts brewing inside him. Instead, I found my way and continued on the now recognizable road to Blue Mountain.

I wondered what was going on inside Michael's head. His parents had occasionally walked out in a huff from family gatherings without communicating their frustration. Was he throwing a similar tantrum? I felt he blamed me for something but didn't want to pursue reasons for his behavior while driving. He'd consented to come to the workshop, that was enough for now. He didn't mention what was bugging him and his complaint about my driving and poor map reading were superficial issues. His real anger stemmed from something deeper. We arrived with time to spare, as usual.

Michael didn't raise his anger issue at all in this group. I was confused but didn't really want to know what the source was. We both let it sit until a few days into the group when Verna initiated some process work for us.

Even though I was fearful of what could happen or be said, it was a relief to have the opportunity to vent my feelings. Verna encouraged us to communicate. This seems so basic now. To talk about more than our nightmare of ritual abuse, more than where we were going to live, more than what we were going to do after the Year Long. No, not those things that seemed easy and acted as safety zones: seemingly important but screaming of avoidance. She wanted us to talk about our feelings, our hurts and misunderstandings.

However, Michael still refused to contribute his concerns or to look at our issues. He was distant and disdainful toward me, ignoring me during breaks in the workshop. He hardly spoke, even though we shared the same tent. I felt subservient, even more so because I'd always felt on some level that men were superior to women.

Twenty-two years of marriage; how easy it is to stop sharing feelings. In fact I wondered if we had ever talked about them. Shame and fear of abandonment stopped me discussing my pain. I hated the thought of confrontation. Plus there were also things I had learned never to mention. It was useless to ask for help from Michael: I knew it wouldn't come. Any possibility of discussion was cast away when he took on his authoritarian role and dictated to me what he wanted done. With no counsel together, we had created an unequal partnership.

I loved Michael but love wasn't always my strongest feeling. It was often submerged under the murkiness of everyday living. My spirit took solace with friendships within the group and the joy of having Melissa and Rebecca with us. But this support also helped me avoid voicing my anxiety about Michael and me.

Water for the camp came from a well a mile away. When it was hot and there was a large group of people, we'd collect it daily. This was done in the morning, using the truck and filling a huge water bed bladder and other smaller containers. It wasn't a difficult job but took time waiting to fill everything and then offloading them.

When Verna suggested Michael and I talk, I volunteered to go with him to collect water. That gave us half an hour of privacy without Melissa and Rebecca. The noise of the generator and some work filling the bottles and bladder acted as a cover when we went beyond our comfort zones. Keeping busy was an avoidance technique I excelled in.

I don't know what Michael's feelings were, for as always, I initiated any conversation. He was certainly one for keeping everything to himself. His introspection was difficult to deal with because it was accompanied by a lot of derision. I tended to say anything - idle thoughts or bits of conversations, trying to understand my life and relationships. Though I wanted to share things, he remained silent and withdrawn. I was frustrated by Michael's lack of contribution in the workshops. When we had general issues he seldom shared his experiences or thoughts; he rarely expressed his inner visions. I felt the workshop's opportunity for change drifted by him without him embracing and utilizing them. He didn't participate enough for full value.

I presumed he wanted to change our relationship into something better. I commented about this to him, although I was afraid he would raise something - I had no idea what - to prove whatever problems we had were my fault. I wasn't able to talk through my own shame and heal either. We both put up barriers to our mutual growth.

I hadn't talked much with Michael about his molestation of Melissa and Rebecca. The only time he let it surface was when we traveled and shared a motel room as a family. He would just direct me with his index finger to the side of the double bed closest to Melissa and Rebecca's beds in the motel room so he was further from them than me. I obliged, but his non-verbal order hurt me.

I hadn't recall Michael's abuse of the girls, but channeling from Tsen Tsing and Indira said it happened - and I believed Melissa.

Families have patterns. My own little inner child told me about my father hurting me to get at my mother, and because there was incest in my family, it is quite probable my children would also incur sexual abuse unless I broke the pattern. My mother didn't protect me and I didn't protect my children because of our denial and programming. Also, there was definitely an air of sexual perversion about Michael and his mother. With ritual abuse running in our family, everyone's sexuality was skewed.

I presumed his abuse of the girls happened when they were young and was shocked during channeling when Tsen Tsing informed me that I stood and watched without doing anything about it.

This incestuous part of our family life puzzled me and I was appalled by my lack of courage to fight for my children. I couldn't remember what happened and didn't want to talk about it, beyond asking Michael if he thought it happened.

"I can't remember. I feel accused of a heinous crime," he said and never raised the topic again.

Incest is not a topic that families want to discuss. Who would want to admit to this crime? Denial by creating a mental block is the easiest way out of confronting this abuse, followed by blaming daughters for 'enticing' their father to perpetrate the sexual act.

"Christina, I don't understand why you are not furious at Michael. Incest is one of the worst things a father could do to his daughters," Verna chided me. I was confused, probably because the same thing had happened to me.

"My Mom belted me when she caught Dad sexually abusing me when I was older," Cassandra told me. "She screamed and blamed me for taking him from her."

"Dad's a sexual pervert," Rebecca commented. "I saw him stare at Melissa's butt as she reached to pick up her shoes."

The meaning of these words still didn't penetrate.

When Melissa recalled Michael's sexual abuse outside the cult circles during the workshops two months ago, he was unable to express regret.

"Can you see your daughter's distress?" Verna asked him at the time. "She needs an apology."

All Michael said, "What about me? I was hurt too." He had no notion of his choice of action as an adult, and didn't apologize.

Although the group spent some time with him over this abuse he was unable to say sorry to Melissa. His ability to take responsibility for his action was blocked by his own pain, although the abuse had been committed to demonstrate his dominant power over his family. What a pity he hadn't participated in the group enough to clear some of his own mistreatment. Then he could have helped with his daughter's healing.

Even Russell had raised the issue of Michael's sexual perversion in our group a few months earlier.

"I saw you stare at my girlfriend's breasts when she lent forward," he accused Michael.

Back then I had wanted to defend Michael. I didn't believe he looked at other women in a sexual manner, but Russell's stance indicated he was ready to fight over it.

"You fucking bastard!" he taunted.

Michael, the non-aggressor, shrugged it off.

"You're not getting away with this one!" Russell threw a punching bag for Michael to hold. Michael stood up and held the strong foam bag in front of his chest for Russell to strike at. Russell vented his feelings and thoughts on Michael's lusting, then gave Michael a turn to hit back on the punching bag.

I didn't understand then. I thought it was simply a false accusation. But Melissa and Rebecca knew the truth.

"I would never leave one of my girlfriends alone near Dad," Rebecca had said.

Michael and I talked a little the first morning while pumping water. The conversation wasn't about anything important. I wanted to know what his plans for us were when we left America. He hedged around the question, saying nothing definite. I felt I was on assignment - the interviewer questioning - not knowing what the response would be. We were able to get through our first half-hour together reasonably well. The water flowed fast and we were back at the campsite quickly to fill the storage tank. Conversing was difficult and work came as an easy distraction from delving into intimacy.

I still hadn't mentioned to anyone that Tsen Tsing had told me two months previously to prepare to get rid of my possessions pending the probable dissolution of my marriage. That prospect was too distressing to consider, so I'd already pushed the thought away. Nor did I share messages from my higher self that repeatedly told me I needed to leave Michael.

Actually, I'd totally forgotten all the above because the idea of separation upset me. I didn't want to act on the content. Only the tape recording from the session with Tsen Tsing reminded me many months later that I had already been warned.

The second morning pumping water from the well, I asked Michael the same thing I asked Tsen Tsing several months earlier.

"What happened in Asia?"

He looked at me with a 'serves you right for being who you are scorn'. "I had an affair."

I was stunned.

"Well, that's it," popped out of my mouth. Seven words and our marriage was finished. I was frozen in disbelief.

Again, I took responsibility of action and completed our status. Michael, obviously the one who wanted separation, said nothing.

At last he'd achieved his desire without having to do anything. He'd even saved himself the bother of saying the concluding words.

I couldn't believe Michael would do something like that. There was no way I wanted to compete with another woman for a man. I never wanted to fight for a man. Why bother? I only wanted to share, care, love and be able to work with my husband.

But our goals and desires were obviously different.

So I stood, 8000 feet above sea level, on a small, grassy flat area beside a steep, pine-covered slope, in the Rocky Mountains of America and realized my marriage had finished.

I mumbled nonsensical sounds to myself as I looked at the trees. This was reality.

The man I'd spent twenty-two years with had finally confessed the reason he had treated me with so much disdain for the past three years. Michael leaned on the opposite side of the truck from me. I looked over the tray and heard him start with his excuse.

"I was lonely," he said. He didn't want to wait three months before I moved to Singapore. "You sent me to Asia."

Something started to stir inside me.

"Hey, wait just a minute. You're a grown man. I didn't force you to do anything. We discussed the prospect of working in Asia together. What I remember is you actually left for Asia as soon as you could, without considering the impact on the girls and their schooling. I believe I recollect you saying, 'If I don't go now, I won't get the job'."

My impression of Michael altered, albeit slowly. I began to see him differently. The veil I'd created lifted before my eyes. I noticed he didn't speak full truth and twisted words to suit his purpose. He had lied to me for years. This man I thought was my confidant, was actually sneaky and dishonest.

It was eight o'clock in the morning; the sun glowed pleasantly warm in this peaceful area and I had just become another negative marriage statistic.

I didn't know what to say. Michael obviously wasn't asking for forgiveness, nor was he showing any desire to spend any more time with me. He didn't care. Now that his secret was exposed, I was unceremoniously dumped.

Michael said nothing.

I couldn't comprehend it all. Didn't Michael understand that I too had been lonely while he was in Singapore? I had dismantled our Australian home and stored our possessions so we could join him. I had felt unsupported, but accepted it as my part in his work and our marriage. Didn't he understand what a shock it was for a woman to leave work to care for her baby? I had felt incredibly lonely when I first left work to care for Melissa. Was loneliness a real excuse for his behavior?

But now it dawned on me why he had been so distant and rude to us when we arrived in Asia. We went out to dinner the first night. He sat Melissa, Rebecca and me at a table and waited for an Australian colleague to arrive. He hardly spoke to us, but as soon as his friend arrived, became animated.

"Don't remember that," he said.

I was so naïve. That first night in the bedroom in Singapore when he looked at me, proclaiming that he was celibate now and something about how long it was since he'd had sex that he wasn't interested anymore. That wasn't the Michael I knew. But I had believed him and didn't even consider he may have had a new girlfriend.

"I'd forgotten about that," Michael acknowledged.

More feelings started to penetrate through the initial shock. I was hurt and angry. More lies in my life? I'd encountered so many lies I couldn't help but wonder if Christina was actually real? Thank God we had a few more days of the workshop so I could sort some of this out.

"How could you leave an issue as important as wanting to leave a marriage to the third last day of a Year Long program? We'd done all those workshops with no mention of your desire to be off with your girlfriend."

What a waste!

"What were your plans?" I questioned. "If you expected to marry her, how did you intend to get rid of me? How can you expect a relationship based on betrayal, lies and deceit to work? She has to be manipulative as well. That is one thing I am not, Michael. Your relationships are not healthy. You made no effort to heal your issues so it will all come back again."

No wonder Michael didn't talk about anything much during the workshops. He was so busy hiding his other life from us that he wouldn't dare talk about anything in case he slipped into talking about his affair.

His brewing anger and silence in the car as we drove to the mountain had also been related to the affair. He hadn't had an opportunity to speak to his girlfriend for the week we'd been away.

"She worries about me if I don't call," he said.

He had no comprehension of the loneliness I had endured when he forced me to stay in America with minimal communication from him.

"The basis of your relationship with her has to be shaky, Michael. You're both deceitful. You might be united, scheming against me. But what other commonality is there to hold you together apart from sex? No wonder you forced me to stay in America last year. You did that as a punishment."

He nodded his head.

We drove back to offload the water at the camp. I walked slowly down to the kitchen carrying water bottles, hoping not to see anyone. I wanted to be alone for a while. This was a big thing to integrate. Michael needed to raise it in the group, not me. My responsibility for 'us' had finished. I wasn't taking care of anything that was Michael's stuff ever again.

Rhonda was in the kitchen, completing breakfast cleanup. As I carried in some water containers, she noticed my teary eyes.

"What's wrong?"

"Michael had a girlfriend in Asia before I even arrived there," I blurted.

"A girlfriend? Well, that explains a lot." She leaned across the wooden bench top "I often wondered why he didn't say much in the group. I guess he didn't want this to slip out." Then she added, "It's not much fun finding out, is it?"

Rhonda hugged me, which prompted more tears. She was surprised too.

Everything happening to everyone in the group seemed unreal. We empathized with the revelations that seemed to come in every possible way throughout the workshops to each of us. Although each story was different, the emotions were the same.

I decided to shower. The running water soothed my skin as I stood under the outlet, crying. I wanted to change the prickly energy on my body and feel fresh. The water calmed me. I had no desire to hurry to the group meeting. I preferred to be alone, so I sauntered down the pathway to my tent.

Totally, simply, with absolutely no inkling, the entire rug had been pulled out from under my feet. Every piece of my life's foundation had gone. I was finished. Nothing left. The lies of my life had opened up in the last sixteen months like leprosy and had eaten my flesh away. So much seemed incomprehensible: my childhood sexual abuse; my daughters' incest; participation in ritual abuse and my husband's affairs. I was left only with pain, agony and despair.

Verna was on the pathway. I wanted and needed her support. She listened silently to my story, standing with me for a few minutes, not judging. When I had finished, she was astonished and said, "Michael doesn't act like a lady's man."

I didn't think he was either, or I may have suspected earlier in our marriage and then put it into denial. Hold on, I remembered moving the family to a new home because I believed he had too many female friends in the old location and I saw the lustful excitement in his eyes when he was around other women. He had already created tension by spending an evening with my best friend, ten years earlier. It was me who decided to stay in denial for twelve years. Why did I do that to myself?

I couldn't concentrate on anything. Thoughts of Michael's betrayal circulated, twirled and twisted in my head. I felt battered. Blow after blow after blow.

I went into the first workshop nearly twelve months ago thinking my life was a lie. Was I right! My entire life was full of falseness. Where was the part of me that was a flame of something positive or good? Was there anything of my life that was real?

Something was. My emotion. I felt so much grief, so much sadness. Was this the only reality? Pain, grief and tears?

I had thought I was working to get myself together, but in every workshop more of myself shattered.

Was this personal growth? It was getting pretty tough to continue confronting everything as my life was thrown into my face. Had I been so arrogant to think I actually had a place in this world?

As a ten-year old I learned about the solar system at school. My teacher took the class outside and lined up students, holding various sized balls. Earth was a well-used tennis ball, small and isolated in the lineup – as were the other token planets. I related the size of the ball to the size of the asphalt playground we stood on. This was an important point in my life as the insignificance of humanity dawned on me. It seemed we were smaller than ants and less meaningful than a grain of sand. The feeling of that revelation returned, I felt only the negative side of humanity's existence; pathetic, insignificant, feeble, useless, and purposeless.

Betrayal: a pattern I had brought in from previous lifetimes. My most vivid memory of my brother, a Nazi officer, sitting in an office with his boots on the desk jeering at me. I'd been caught working for the resistance and stood in terror in front of his desk, assured of death. Already the memories of ritual abuse, incest, and rape had shown me constant betrayal in this life and now it emerged again, from the man I loved.

I sat with my own thoughts in the dome, oblivious of anyone else. At lunchtime Verna videotaped a brief interview with a few of us. We had already done this several times through the year to see changes in ourselves.

"What understandings and changes have you made through the year?"

"I believe my life was saved several times by angels and other beings and today my marriage has finished."

The three other people in the dome stopped what they were doing and looked at me, aghast. The family doing this course sure was in rapid deterioration. I had already told Melissa and Rebecca. They accepted this the same way as everything else that had come to the surface during the year, unemotionally.

Nothing surprised them now.

"You're better off without him, Mum," Melissa consoled me. "I don't know why you married him in the first place."

So many strange occurrences had happened that seemed to explain our weird lives, anything seemed believable. Another spanner in the works wasn't going to make any difference to their perceptions.

After lunch, the group did some anger release. Outside among the trees we could scream, hit, thump and yell as much as we wanted. Michael got into his own anger. Holding a bat in his hand he hit a tree stump.

"I feel sexually aroused when I'm angry…that gives me power…In the circles, I got what I wanted. I was powerful…"

He talked, but I couldn't bear to hear anything he said. He spoke of things I felt too terrified to hear - his sexuality, his power, and his girlfriend.

"Trisha, I can't listen to this anymore. Come to the kitchen with me and prepare dinner," I said.

I didn't want to feel ridiculed and I didn't want to know about Michael's affair. I also knew I would have vented my own anger towards him if I'd had the support of others in the group - and I did. I wanted to fight him, punch, kick and scream my anger at him. I wanted to put curses on him and cut him into little pieces.

I wanted to avoid anything that involved confrontation with Michael again. I was too weak to acknowledge my fears, let alone face Michael's anger and abhorrence toward me. I was a coward. Here was one of the most important issues in my life and I couldn't face it. Somehow it seemed easier to say I was a murderer than to look at my inability to be able to maintain a loving relationship. I'd failed Marriage 101.

I recalled the first night of the workshop series when Verna said to me, "You created and are responsible for everything in your life."

I hadn't wanted to face that responsibility. Definitely I didn't want to admit my own part in the collapse of our marriage.

"His affair is still continuing, Mum," Rebecca told me later at dinner. "He's calling her in the Philippines regularly when you're working…He uses phone cards. Then it's not on the phone account."

I was so stupid. A regular phone bill would have allowed me to see the itemized account. Michael was too smart to leave that trail. I had noticed several used phone cards around the house. I just thought that was something Michael liked to have. I didn't consider what they were used for.

Betrayal had continued, even during our course. How could Michael be with me, sleep in the same bed and lead this double life? No wonder he'd had an intestinal complaint so serious he spent time in an Asian hospital. Nothing had been found from all the tests, despite intense investigations in hospital two years before.

"When you return to Australia, get a referral to a gastroenterologist there," the young specialist advised. "We can't find any reason for your pain."

An elderly Australian gastroenterologist who had looked at Michael's X-rays and colcoscopy video said, "There's nothing wrong with your intestines. Go home and sort out your family problems."

Michael told me this part but he didn't attempt to clean up his family matters. He had avoided helping Melissa and Rebecca in their dilemma in Australia at that time and left me alone when he rushed back to Asia to be with his girlfriend and job. No wonder he was unpleasant most of the time over the past three years: criticizing me, refusing to help or share in household responsibilities. While in America, Michael didn't help in the house even on the days I was working. Yes, he was objecting to me by blaming and condemning. That's what I had felt, but I hadn't understood why he behaved that way. Now I did.

"Will you do an exercise together?" Verna asked.

"What is it?" I asked, nervous to take another unknown step.

"If I tell you, the impact is lost."

We agreed.

"Sit facing each other and speak for ten minutes each with no interruption from anyone. One at a time use the words 'on the completion of our marriage' as the beginning of every sentence."

Michael started,

"On the completion of our marriage, I should have left at least ten years ago.

On the completion of our marriage, I felt lower than the dogs.

On the completion of our marriage I hated living with you.

On the completion of our marriage, you didn't give me what I wanted."

Suddenly I stood at the door of the dome. My legs had carried me there, like a protective reflex. I wasn't in control of my body's action. His words had cut me deeply. I stepped outside, not quite knowing what to do. I wanted to run away but there was nowhere to go.

"Come back, Christina…"

But I rushed blindly along the path away from the dome, going nowhere in particular. Where could this body which contained 'me' hide? I reached the bathroom. Ronda followed. She sat and encouraged me.

"Come back to the dome…we're here to heal ourselves. It's important to finish this."

"I know," I replied. "I couldn't stop my legs taking me outside. Then I didn't know what to do. I don't want to be here…I wish I was dead."

I had to face up to the truth, my life, and my deeds…. And I hadn't vaporized; there was no atomic explosion to rescue me from my internal agony. There was nowhere else to be. I returned to the dome.

"On the completion of our marriage," it was my turn, "I still love you…"

On the completion of our marriage I feel betrayed.

On the completion of our marriage, I feel sad.

On the completion of our marriage, I love Rebecca and Melissa.

On the completion of our marriage, your girlfriend didn't even clean the bathroom when she stayed with you in our home.

On the completion of our marriage I find this all unbelievable."

I slept in the same tent with Michael that night. He didn't volunteer to move and I didn't really care, or so I thought. I was sad and angry.

"Why did you lie to me? How could you come here for a year's healing and not mention your problem of one partner too many, till the end of the course? Why didn't you talk with Verna earlier?" I asked. "She wouldn't have told me – but would have helped you. How could you wait for a year? Its unbelievable!"

It was why? Why? Why? How could you!

Blah, blah, blah.

I got no answer.

My head echoed all night, *On the completion of our marriage…on the completion of our marriage.* Reverberating down the hallways of my consciousness. Another failure, the completion of our marriage, haunting me through my sleep state. Completion of our marriage. Was this the end of loss? I still had two incredible daughters – but felt stripped down to almost nothing. Completion of our marriage.

I didn't sleep in our tent the next night. I took my bedding out.

"When we return home, I'm having the main bedroom. You can sleep on a mattress in the basement and take all your things down with you."

Michael consented with a shrug.

"You need to take care of yourself, do your own washing and clean up after yourself. I'm not doing anything for you. Seeing we're in the same house, we can share meals. But you need to contribute physically, cooking and cleaning. I'm not going to be your prostitute and maid anymore."

I slept with Melissa and Candy that night in their large tent out on the ridge. We put crystals out in the moonlight to cleanse. I was safe, in the midst of friends and Spirit.

My whole life was cult-influenced. It was a shock to see my marriage with Michael had been partially arranged.

His father's cult decision was, "She'll do," when our relationship became serious. When my friendship with Michael developed I was already so mind controlled that I obligingly went to meetings with his family in my robotic state.

For all the cruelty at cult activities, there is a sense of family loyalty and protection.

Rebecca recalled Michael protecting her from group torture. Tears poured down my face as I recollected my re-initiation by Michael's family group. I endured the torture but felt despair that my own father wasn't there to protect me. Dissociation doesn't mean there is no physical and mental anguish. It minimizes the pain to a level that the mind and body can tolerate. The cellular memory and subconscious mind still store everything.

Under the bowl I recalled part of my initiation

Michael's family took me to a secret ceremonial room. I think this room was left set up. In a cult that is so clever with hiding evidence, this seems unusual. It is dark, maybe underground, a type of temple full of Egyptian magic. There are books of incantations and methodology. Ceremony is important and Egyptian artifacts are used, including the Ankh.

Cult leaders use this ancient knowledge to search past lives and associations their members have had with each other. This gives the group understanding of knowledge, skills and wisdom available for their use and clues about their members so they can use their special skills in ceremonies.

Astrological knowledge is widely used in the cult but this method was used to find abilities from past times. They could see my association with Melissa with our many lives together. They were after her knowledge of power, including Egyptian times.

I saw Melissa sitting on a throne in ancient Egypt. I wasn't sure if she was male or female but she was magnificent and powerful. Her aura was golden. There were many people surrounding her, including Poppa and me. That was the life that appealed to them.

The Priest assessing me was excited when he unraveled this. I was a good find for his group because Melissa was what they wanted.

Melissa was trained to do this work when she was mature enough in this lifetime. I saw her there, working over a person's body, dressed ceremonially and using the Egyptian magic. How can they use the

Ankh, the symbol of new life?

Melissa was aware of being trained for a role as priestess in the cult. They knew her abilities from the astrological charts of this lifetime and her past life knowledge. Knowledge can be used for internal power within self or external power over another. It seemed to me after sensing the Egyptian power that the cult of ritual abuse uses secret knowledge handed down through the ages to maintain power over others: external power.

I wondered if books of incantations, Egyptian scholarship of the laws of the underworld and other secrets such as Nazi experiments on mind control were accumulated by the cult. It seemed someone knew this knowledge.

The last days of the workshop were a celebration of our commitment and completion. A time for the ceremony was set on the mountain. These activities distracted me somewhat from my further changed status. My year of personal growth, moved me from victim to perpetrator to losing the family I came to heal.

In many ways I was one of the luckiest women alive to have friends constantly around me, even though my personal reality had collapsed. The support was genuine. Not one person laid any blame on Michael or me. It was obvious Michael's sexuality was perverted from ritual abuse. We had seen the surrealness of our lives and understood that everyone contributes fully to the course of their own life. The outcome wasn't what my conscious mind had planned. But as I had seen from this year's investigation into my life, my conscious mind was oblivious to so much. It had no idea of the big picture I had created before incarnating and failed to take heed of indicators along the path.

Before we all left our group, Indira gave us parting words.

Although you think there is the parting of the ways, you are deeply connected. You have done higher work not only for yourselves but also for ending of sacrifice on the planet. You will move forward in certain ways and identify with others. This will become a domino effect. It will not only be the ending of ritual abuse but also the subtleties in which people sacrifice themselves.

Act in gentleness and kindness to one another. There will come a time when many of you will have the opportunity to help others when they are going through energies they are unaccustomed to.

There are small beads of light from our side to your side. Come and take a few beads. They are endless, so there shan't be a lack. You are not taking anyone else's beads. Remember this for some of you feel a lack. These beads are going into the entirety of the cosmos. Take as many as you like. The strands of light are to go to your hearts and to be shared with the hearts of others. Blessings will be constantly with you. Know that if you ask, always you shall receive. I come with love and gratitude. I shall walk with you in ways you know and in ways you will not know. I shall stand with you in your own divinity.

Christina, underneath the pools of sadness are pools of joy. And it doesn't matter how thick the pools of sadness are, for they will fill from time to time, there are always pools of joy.

Everyone whose gifts of psychic readings had come forth through this program then gave others their intuitive readings. We felt warmth and compassionate love. Rhonda's message to me was,

"Spirit is acknowledging the courage you have and even though you don't think you have much courage at this time, and you can't recognize the bravery of your actions, they are applauding you. You will have to use your courage further in the next twelve to eighteen months and they will help you to look deeply within yourself. There will be people there to help if only you will ask. You have the tendency to forget to ask. They encourage you to look deeply inside".

Tsen Tsing gave a final appearance for us. He addressed me, saying,

Beloved soul, among this confusion you are spinning around, you still want to take responsibility for your potentially 'ex'?

Michael, do you think she is still trying to be responsible for you?

A little! It really comes from deep love.

Isn't it amazing how much deep love is there, even though there are so many wounds to the ego?

You are surprised, aren't you? "I'd rather hate you," she thinks, "But I can't." It would be so convenient, but it's not easy when you see the essence of a soul and you still respect it. I acknowledge that you see this, Christina and I want you to trust that by letting go, this soul will still get his 'God Presence' work. And your love and support is there without trying to figure it out, how to get it for him too. And remember, love will help you heal that hurt. It doesn't make the hurt wrong. If somebody says something that they meant or didn't mean to hurt you, the ego feels bruised because of the expectations and other levels of layers of pain you have had before.

You were given a gift, although it doesn't feel like a nice present; it showed your pain. It demonstrated a place for you to go deeper in love and healing. And I know that is how you feel. You went so deep you hit pain but you also hit the place where you are letting go and are finding that, yes, there is love in you and for this man still.

Michael, you will keep growing, won't you? But you must be fully responsible for this!"

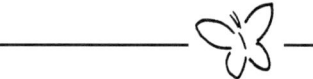

Spirit is the source, it is love, it is all.

Chapter eighteen

The Year Long had finished. I hadn't. Now that Michael's illicit relationship was revealed, we separated. Back home from the mountain Michael responded to my request and moved his possessions into the basement. I was still shocked from the unexpected outcome of my year. It seemed incredible that my intent of cohesion and healing for my family had concluded with marriage break up and discovery of heinous abuse.

How fortunate I couldn't see into the future when I started, for I may have clutched to the fraying strings holding Michael and me together instead of searching and healing patterns of dysfunction.

This tangled life of mine still needed unraveling. Part of loosening the threads was informing my family and in-laws of our separation. Michael wanted to call them immediately after our return from the mountain workshop. I argued for a delay, mainly to give me time to adjust. I felt raw, exposed and unsure of all the implications. Anyway, he'd had his three years to prepare.

I didn't feel as settled about separation as he seemed to be. It was obvious Michael had absolutely no intention of clearing anything about his relationship with me. He was free. Personal growth had no agenda for his past life or for his future. He was prepared to take on his new wife with all the baggage from the old. I could see he believed he didn't contribute to the failure of his first marriage. No, he thought he was totally a victim, the same as he believed he was a victim of abuse from his parents and a victim who committed incest. He seemed incapable of recognizing personal choice and responsibility for his life.

It was such a shock to realize the man I thought was my best friend – wasn't. I wanted to tell my family face-to-face so nothing could be left unfinished. The possibility of having a phone slammed in our ear by his father across the world wasn't a path I wanted to take. Also, I didn't want our breakup blamed on personal growth groups. Again I allowed the responsibility to inform our families to become my job, for Michael wasn't going to return to Australia. I didn't look forward to telling them.

Tricia from the Year Long stayed a week with us before her return flight to Australia. Everything seemed somewhat weird, for in our house was a visitor who knew everything about our lives. There was Michael, the former husband, slinking in the background yet sharing meals, the car and going places with us; two teenagers, Rebecca and Melissa supporting me, even though they were going through their own shock; and then there was me wondering if this was really the end of our family.

Fantasies of reconciliation flitted through my mind. However there were two dominant factors affecting this possibility. Firstly I didn't like Michael's dishonesty and secondly he didn't want to be with me. As soon as he'd divulged his secret I was tossed to the wind.

I still loved him! During my marriage I'd put my own life on hold to please Michael. I'd put him first. Now as number one in my own life I didn't know how to please myself or even know what pleased me anymore. I believed my responsibility as wife was to submit. I'd sacrificed myself. I'd been taught to obey men's orders, and Michael had been trained to believe it was his right to have women obey him.

Freedom associated with being alone, frightened me. No longer was there anyone to stand by my side as I rediscovered myself, my dreams and desires. Re-creation of myself was destined to be solitary.

"If you ever go back to Dad, I'll never speak to you again," Rebecca threatened. I guessed this reflected her fury at her father's betrayal but it cautioned me. A gift of a bracelet with the letters FREEDOM woven through it, was another message from her.

Melissa's approach was different.

"Mum, you can do whatever you want now. You're very capable and can look after yourself well."

Although both girls were angry with Michael, they were at least civil. There was no need for nastiness but I found it hard not to attack him with questions.

"Why didn't you say anything?" I'd ask as we passed in the kitchen.

"You could have talked to someone about your problems," I'd say walking down the hallway.

So many thoughts floated into my head that at times I'd run downstairs to the basement and yell.

"What about that gastro-enterologist in Australia who told you there was nothing wrong physically that couldn't be healed by getting our family relationships sorted out? Did you say anything to him? Didn't you realize what it meant?"

"How were you scheming to solve the problems you created, Michael? What was your plan?"

He always responded with a shrug of the shoulders or a non-committal, "I don't know."

The answers I needed didn't come. Michael's responses were guarded. I couldn't understand how he could do this. It was me who had verbally initiated the completion of our marriage, yet it was he who had wanted to finish our connection. He'd already planned to marry his girlfriend; he just didn't know how to get rid of his wife.

I was deeply hurt. I wanted him to say sorry and ask for forgiveness, to feel sad, but that wasn't his reality. His emotional relationship with me had finished when he pursued this clandestine affair. Our Singapore home was hers when I was in Australia. When I was in Asia, he visited her after work.

I wanted to nag, but I tried to say as little as possible. My feelings were my own. I was an unconscious part of Michael's triangle. It was just as well Melissa, Rebecca and Tricia were with us, for I would probably have continually screamed and ranted.

Michael didn't talk. I still don't know what he experienced. I only knew how I felt. Devastated. He had three years to prepare for this completion. I had a week. My grief, anger and sadness would surface again and again. If it wasn't the horror of ritual abuse, it was betrayal by my husband.

It was difficult to believe that Michael had decided to act this way. I didn't imagine he would woo another woman while I finalized our Australian affairs before joining him in Singapore. Another false belief. In my musings I recalled strange tales he had told me. Now they appeared to be false trails, laid to distract my attention from his deceit. One was of a foreign colleague who'd developed testicular cancer as a result of celibacy. "It's dangerous for a man not to have sex," Michael informed me. Why would he bother relaying this information? Was it to validate his action? When I first listened to the story it seemed distinctly odd. Now it explained some of his internalized thoughts.

In Asia, Michael also shared with me, "I was at my desk and a few women co-workers were discussing sex and female circumcision in front of me today. They didn't mind that I was listening and even asked whether I'd been with a Muslim woman. I was surprised they were so open with a man." His facial expression reenacting the story for me was a good ruse for laying another false trail.

"They stopped speaking about sex in front of me as soon as I said no."

Oh, he was so clever at dropping misleading information in my lap. No he hadn't been with a Muslim. He could say that with a clear conscience. And yes he was concerned about testicular cancer too – not enough sex and he might develop it. He justified sex to maintain good health in his genitals. Throw these little teasers of information that imply his innocence to his wife and she'll be kept off a suspicious track

I started to reflect. Maybe the long hours he worked in Asia, especially Saturdays, weren't necessarily 'work'. He looked after himself in Asia. He had a car and I was left to find other transport. He would ask me to take the car for its service on days I had other activities planned. I co-operated because he'd convince me it was the only day he'd be in the office and he needed the vehicle for site inspections the rest of the week. I didn't realize the manipulation and control I lived with for so long. I was in touch with my anger and Michael knew how to use lies, withdrawal and judgement as a method of subtle control. In my state of denial I'd thought he was a man of integrity.

It was strange living in the same house as the man I was separated from. I wanted to tell him that he was a cheat, a liar and a sexual abuser. I couldn't understand why he bothered to come and spend a year delving into his psyche. I thought we were going to heal and renew our relationship.

"Why did you come with me for healing, Michael?"

"I thought we might fix up our relationship," he said.

With so little participation from him, that was impossible.

I thought Michael hadn't achieved much during the year until I realized he got what he wanted - separation.

"I asked her to tell her boss that I was married," Michael whined.

I didn't see what difference telling her employer that her boyfriend was married would have made when obviously neither Michael nor she cared.

"Why should she tell her boss if you couldn't even inform your wife?"

I had trouble understanding Michael's logic. Now I questioned everything he said, for most of it made very little sense. Then it dawned on me; I had accepted this balderdash throughout my entire married life. My tolerance for his nonsense and lies abruptly diminished.

Rose, a Filipino maid living next door to our home had warned me as we left in December, only eight months ago.

"I watch the comings and goings of Michael while you're away." I presumed she referred to his male friends. In my pattern of not questioning I didn't even think of asking her what she really meant. I didn't delve into people's leading statements at all.

"Rose and my lady didn't like each other." Michael admitted for some reason.

I know Rose cared for me. I gave her medicine and we often talked. We gave her money for her children's schoolbooks in the Philippines. Now I thought that was a blackmail payment from Michael - so she wouldn't speak out and tell me. An unconscious bribe arranged in Michael's own mind to ease his conscience. For a while, I felt angry at all Filipinos. Then remembered some I'd been friends with some.

"Michael, didn't you know not to start a new relationship until you had cleared the old? If you want to change partners it would have been a lot better to clean up your old issues before continuing. All your psychological baggage from our marriage is still there. You'll have the same problems occurring again."

Unfortunately I couldn't drop my concern for him easily.

"She's really sorry it happened this way," Michael told me, very soon after saying they never talked about me. Some of the things he told me were unnecessary and more than I wanted to know.

Rebecca had final exams in November. It was impossible to change the location. She had to return to Australia. I didn't want to go home. I hoped extra weeks in the States would clear my confusion. My plan of a year ago, to heal and bond my family together had collapsed. I'd failed and now had to create a different life with new goals. I wanted reassurance that I was okay. Remaining in America gave me time to ground myself.

Michael decided to stay in America and sort out his new life while waiting for an American work permit. He promised to support Melissa emotional and financially. Ritual abuse wasn't healed in one intense year. She still had many issues to deal with, including integration of personalities and deprogramming.

I was terrified to return to Australia and leave my support in the USA. Any thought of the future overwhelmed me for my immediate fear was that I'd unwittingly be caught up in the cult again. Oh yes, I had received a lot of deprogramming during the course and now watched my response to words and phrases. But it wasn't as though I knew everything about programming. How could we for so much was still veiled and secret. If I didn't know about my involvement before, there was a part of me that hid my activities from my everyday self. How would I know when that hidden part would come out and go to ceremonies?

Would that programmed child part of me respond immediately to a trigger I didn't know about? Was there an adult split part as well, waiting for specific cues? It was frightening and confusing to contemplate. Until now I thought it was only Melissa who had different personalities. Hers were obvious. But maybe everyone in the cult has some degree of multiple personality, an inherent part of the inflicted trauma. Some would be more pronounced than others, depending on the degree of training, amount of abuse and individual ability to survive. Compartmentalizing *is* a survival mechanism.

Most of this theorizing came down to definition. I decided to forget the labels, even though it was reassuring to know there was a definition for how I felt and reacted. I trusted that *everything* could be healed. Though I wasn't sure how or if anything could be as quick as I wanted.

Going home didn't feel safe. I wanted more time to integrate and rest. I didn't know how to cope and wanted to stay in America as long as possible. There were still friends here who understood our dilemma. I didn't have to explain anything to them. Plus we felt safe from the cult in America. This may not have been a wise perception. We knew ritual abuse was an international organization. More highly trained people in the cult traveled within their own countries to train others. Melissa received training from people like this. Through international connections they would know where their members were and what they were doing.

Indira warned us of this. *They are well aware of where you are and what you are doing.*

We had no proof that we hadn't been to cult meetings in America. Even though we were healing, there were probably parts of us that liked certain roles in the cult. If that was the case, we hadn't remembered. We weren't necessarily watched everyday, but enough that our movements and activities were noted. I wondered about the salesman who came and talked about a vacuum cleaning system for our home when we first arrived in America. Was he using his salesmanship as cover, to see how we were living or were we suspicious about everything?

If we went home to Australia, they would know where we were. We would mix with our relations and any cross programming could kick in. Also Australian words and phrases would be continually in our daily lives again. Maybe we would be reprogrammed and not even know. How could we keep ourselves safe? I didn't think there was any way.

Glen from the Year Long came to my rescue.

"I'll come and stay with you for six weeks or so. Rhonda has a different airline ticket from me. She'll stay longer in the States. I'll be able to help you clean up your home and settle in if you want."

This was amazing. Adult male support. I knew he'd be helpful and was grateful for his offer.

Melissa was my main concern. Indira and Tsen Tsing warned us she was the family member in the most danger of returning to the cult. Her training was long and extensive, so the cult-loving parts would keep her involved in order to fulfill her cult destiny as mapped out. That plan would see her use her potential for their purposes.

By this time I had no doubt that before birth I chose my parents and part in the cult activities as my soul growth for this lifetime. The big picture as to why I did this was still unclear. But perhaps one aspect was so that I could come out the other end, survive and clear it spiritually for generations of my family and heirs into the future.

Melissa and Rebecca believed they chose us as parents knowing what they would experience and use the experience to move through and clear for themselves

Yes, I had seen several previous lives with involvement in abusive cults. Not big pictures of those lives: just awareness that this wasn't the first time. And there was no doubt in my mind that my Polish life with the Nazis had participation in cult-like activities. The Nazis were heavily into the occult and embroiled in mind control and abuse.

I returned to Australia with Melissa and Rebecca. Glen was due to arrive two days after us. It was wonderful to have another adult in the house for support and friendship. He was a great cook and prepared meals while I started cleaning up accumulations of my life and throwing everything away. It was agonizing, and heartbreaking.

I set the finality of my marriage in motion. I was going to sell everything. It was devastating.

Continuously, I wished I was dead. This was my daytime and nighttime thought companion, an unconscious mantra. Nothing seemed real. I was in despair. Even though I knew, *this too will pass*, it seemed too long for the change to start. Whatever was going to happen I wanted to move away from my home.

Though relocating anywhere else seemed a mammoth effort, beyond my capability, I needed a goal, a purpose and belief in myself. The lie I had been living was even bigger than I thought; I wondered what more would come to the surface of my unreal life.

Some things we did helped us back to normalcy. Rebecca had her exams to sit and she planned to get her driver's license. These everyday life activities were just what we needed.

Rebecca supported me greatly. Both girls were disgusted with their father. Melissa was in her own world. Although she had tremendous purity of spirit, we often didn't know who we were talking to or what type of reaction we would receive. Conversations with Melissa were a nightmare.

Fear was constantly with me. The first night the three of us slept home on our isolated property in Australia, sounds of drumming penetrated through every window and door. The whole valley resounded with the sound, making the point of origin impossible to locate. I was terrified. Were *they* around? Informing us we weren't forgotten?

I had no energy to check. I didn't sleep well. For some reason I couldn't bring myself to put sticky tape around the edge of doors. In the morning if we'd been out without remembering during the night, detached tape would be obvious. I had everything planned out, but couldn't discipline myself to do it.

I lay awake every night for hours, fearful. I didn't ever imagine I would return to Australia a single woman and I absolutely believed I would hear Melissa if she left her room. My bedroom door was left open to hear better, but my body was lead. It was impossible to jump up and check her room. I couldn't move. I wasn't taking enough care and didn't take responsibility to protect my daughters. Again.

Many in the group were deeply concerned about our return home. But what other choice was there for me? Melissa planned to return to America as quickly as possible for more healing. However she had to wait. A certain visa we needed wouldn't come through for a few months. What to do for six months? I was occupied, selling possessions. Melissa needed something to do. She wouldn't apply for a job and I thought I would go crazy with her attitudes. I was dealing with a tiny child part of her who was frightened and stubborn, as well as dealing with my own feelings.

Michael was safe in the USA. But that only lasted a few months. He soon moved off back to his job in Asia. His other life, and de-facto wife. He was totally off the hook. I was so angry I didn't want him near me. Plus he had been warned not to return home.

Tsen Tsing came through the phone while Michael was chatting with Katar in America.

Don't return home, Michael. If you have to, tell no one. Just appear the day you need to for the work permit and disappear immediately after. You can't afford to be complacent.

Spirit rarely comes through for a brief message like that just over the phone. It was a vital message, which Michael dismissed.

During this time at home, I regularly meditated with Tricia from the

Year Long. We got impressions during our meditations together. I saw Michael in quicksand with only his head out. He was smiling, thinking he was in bliss. I felt he was in great danger but totally oblivious to it. I warned him about our insights but he just scoffed in his normal manner.

I asked Indira six months later if anything had happened to Michael when he returned home for several weeks and stayed with his family.

Yes, he was drawn in. He was tortured so much. They wanted to kill him. His father stepped in and stopped that. He has no recollection of this except for strange dreams and awakening with anxiety.

Accustomed as we are to denial and because of all the programming from the cult, Michael didn't remember if this occurred.

Amongst all my anger was a desire to kill Michael. Although this may have been a fairly normal feeling for someone with such anger, I was horrified when I imagined how I would execute it; slit down the sides of his throat and let the blood drain. I'd never imagined doing that before. It was probably the way I had seen the cult perform it.

A few friends from our Year Long program came and visited one day soon after we returned home. Eight of us ate pumpkin soup and homemade bread on the front porch, surrounded by gum trees. Springtime in Australia is beautiful. It is the best growth time for plants.

Russell brought another friend, Margaret, who commented after the meal, "I've been here before. I recognized the front gate and when we got to the house, I knew the layout." She had been through cult ritual abuse too.

"Do you think your property was used for ceremonies?"

In reality she was tactfully telling me it had been. We walked over the acreage. Certain areas, especially around an old building had unpleasant energies.

"I remember participating in a ceremony here," Margaret exclaimed. Life seemed surreal again. Just when I was trying to become normal, I was thrown back into cult remembrances.

"The buildings are familiar. See the chimney? A man stood on top of it. People gathered in a circle around him," she told me. "Let's move on from here. It feels creepy."

I could barely answer.

Many years before, I had belonged to a meditation group. The women were my mentors and friends. Two of them came and visited within weeks of our move to our new home. We walked around the property together. This very building my 'ritual abuse' friend had recognized as a ceremony site, these meditation friends recognized as a site with unpleasant energy.

In fact they had said, "Let's have a ceremony up here one day we normally meditate to clear this negative energy." This was done. A crowd of twenty-five people gathered around the old building, saying prayers and asking for goodness and light to come in.

One woman said she sensed a rape occurred here. Another mentioned murder. That's funny – it was my mother who said that.

At the time, I thought rape and murder would leave the same energy – fear and violence. Yes, it could have been either. This old building was a home for people working on the railways a hundred years ago. Even then it was isolated. Either violation could have occurred and left its energy mark. The meditation group had thought cleansing by fire was best to help clear the site of the unpleasant energy. We needed strong measures to eliminate it.

Several women walked around the building, defining a perimeter of how far the negative energy extended. The rest of us gathered dead wood to lay along this line of energy. We were going to build a ring of fire. Even the trees inside the perimeter appeared contaminated. I couldn't bring myself to destroy them. They were old and had struggled without care for a lifetime. They had been forced to support murder. Maybe the ring of fire would cleanse them too. The fire burned with the help from some kerosene and the cleansing helped change the energy.

The next day one of the participants called me.

"My husband, John, drove me to your property yesterday. He waited by the shed and read the paper in the car while we did our ceremony."

I listened curiously, for I hadn't even noticed someone waiting in the car.

"At one point some movement caught his eye. He glanced out the window and saw an Aboriginal in khaki trousers. It was someone who had lived on the land maybe a century ago. This spirit said to John, "You no belong here."

Whoa! I felt freaked. We weren't alone on this land.

"What does this mean?" I asked. "Do you think he doesn't want us on the property either?"

"No. Don't worry about that. What I suggest is you and your daughters have a ceremony for him. Give him some tobacco and help him move into the light."

Melissa, Rebecca and I bought a pouch of tobacco. We made little packets of powdered milk, sugar and flour from our kitchen supplies, then purposefully went to a place behind the shed and made a small fireplace for our ceremony. We lit the fire, sat on rocks and offered our gifts.

"To our unknown Aboriginal from the 1860's, find your peace."

My meditation group was not the only ones in the past who had commented on the strange energies on our property.

Two Aboriginal men working nearby had told me, 'Bad fella land' as they pointed in the direction of the old buildings.

I didn't feel these energies unless someone pointed them out to me. I was used to them. If I was reminded, I could tune into my feeling self and usually sense the feeling. I didn't like the site of the old buildings, although they were fascinating. Often it surprised me to find bits of junk in the area moved about. I presumed local kids had visited.

On a day-to-day basis, I wasn't in tune with my feeling self. The only times I felt shivers through my body, was walking up the driveway close to the shed at night. That happened every time. Usually I was scared so I took the dogs, a flashlight and ran to do whatever I needed. I often wondered what would happen if someone pounced and killed me. There were a lot of places to hide in the bush, a lot of places to conceal weapons and bodies. Other people had been murdered and dumped in the bush around our city.

Now, a decade later, I had confirmation of the cult using my property. My friends who came for a picnic were shocked. My recall during the Year Long was validated. The block was isolated, away from streetlights but not far from the city. Unused telephone poles still stood by the shed and old buildings. Was that where I was tied and hung upside down till I became unconscious? I think so, they're a good height for hanging. Local people had reported strange things occurring in the neighborhood.

Reality of memory was thrust in my face again. I wished I could live in my fantasy world and pretend it wasn't happening. I knew things people were telling me, but didn't want to believe them - so I shoved them to the back burner of my mind. My friends were awakening me again and it wasn't pleasant.

By the time Russell drove home with everyone, I was in panic once more. How safe were we here? We had better go elsewhere, for the October ceremonies around Halloween were coming up. I suspected there were many ceremonies during October. Rehearsals for the real thing.

Melissa and Rebecca were in competition as to who was higher in the cult. I couldn't believe they would argue about this abhorrent thought and had to call them back to reality.

"Who cares? This was the worst part of your life and you want to argue about your importance?"

Rebecca felt she hadn't received as much attention as Melissa as a child. She was right. However, attention from their grandparents wasn't something to relish. Sometimes it was better to not have all the focus, particularly in this family.

At this time, about three weeks before Halloween, there was an abduction of an eleven-year-old boy on holiday at an ocean resort town. He was racing his brothers to the local shop but never arrived at the destination. Police distributed descriptions of the child far more quickly than usual in obvious concern for this boy's safety. His body was found several days later. No details were released. Something was very strange and the timing made me think of sacrifice.

I had a session with Verna over the phone. I needed some clearing of stress.

Over the phone, from the other side of the world, I felt nurturing energy surrounding me as we began the session with a prayer.

"The most awful thing has happened here," I began to tell Verna. "A young boy was murdered this week. He was abducted off the street in broad daylight."

As I related this child's death I started relaying details of how I imagined the murder, with two people involved, one far more dominantly than the other.

"I know what they did."

The words flowed out of my mouth. I hadn't seen any description on TV, no details came over the radio and the paper just told of his abduction. I described the details from my own mind. I was shocked as I related how they tied him up, cut a cross on his body and raped him. This was all totally my own projection.

"What does this child's murder mean to you?" Verna asked.

"Oh my God!"

I started to see in my mind's eye.

"Pedophilia... not me as a child...it's different."

Oh Jesus, my projection of what happened to that young boy was something I had seen before.

A robot-like voice came through my mouth.

"I-was-in-charge-of-the-children-and-I-gave-them-injections. The-drug-starts-with-P. It's-the-stuff-given-to-people-when-they-go-for-an-operation. ... Pethedine... that's it."

I saw where I was, sitting on the floor between two doors with four or so little children near me. My normal voice returned as I described the scene.

"There were quite a few children. I didn't really want to look after them. They were hard to settle, a nuisance. I didn't nurture them. There seems to be a heap of little bodies. I seem to be the only adult female here. I may have taken some pictures, I'm not sure. Pictures were taken of me, as evidence of my involvement. Something comes to mind about blackmail. Pictures taken of Michael...compromising pictures...doing things to the kids. That is the blackmail. To say we were involved. If we dared say anything they have pictures to show we were involved."

Reality struck me.

I had just described a snippet of child pornography, and I was involved.

Suppressed memory had leaked out. It took a devastating local event to release it.

Oh, no. God, had I involved my daughters in pornography?

So far I had no idea of my age. Had I actually previously seen these things done that I was describing about this boy? Is that why I knew?

"I recognize where the pornography was filmed. An educational institution in the city. A film and television studio. I see family members there – men. And Melissa. A little child. About three. Her father was sexually abusing her."

Who are these sick minds that want to be titillated by movies of adults having sex with children?

I wonder if sexual abuse was why Rebecca often said she had a sore vagina when she was about four or five?

Michael communicated with us occasionally. In the new workshops without us, he remembered his mother teaching him how to skin. This was done to humans. Alive humans. The place of training was a university laboratory.

"I remember training Melissa," he said.

Margaret came and stayed for a few weeks in our home. I set up the spare bedroom, close to the back door. Her room was separate from the other bedrooms, which were together at the other end of the house.

"Did you hear chanting outside my bedroom this morning?" Margaret asked me, a week after living with us.

"No. Are you sure it wasn't an owl? There are plenty around here. Maybe you were you dreaming?"

"No way! I know I was awake – I was too scared to go outside. It sure sounded like a child. Did either of the girls go out last night? "

"I doubt that, I'm awake a lot during the night," I said.

Surely I would have heard them, but then my body always seemed too heavy to move and check any noise I heard.

"I'm sure I would have heard something unusual," I offered.

Maybe I was sleeping more than I thought. I hadn't heard either of their doors open during the night.

I didn't want to believe what she suggested.

Margaret called a psychic friend for some personal guidance. In their long conversation, the psychic told her, "There is a child leaving the house at night. She walks to the gate and is taken somewhere by car."

Margaret stopped doubting herself.

"What I heard wasn't an owl. It was human. It has to be either Melissa or Rebecca."

I believed her.

Although we locked the house at night, anyone could leave if they wanted. I'd leave the key in the inside lock. The locking was only effective to stop someone from entering. Not from leaving.

We wondered if it was Melissa. Her behavior was difficult. If it was true she was leaving, I needed to get her away from this house altogether...but where could we go?

I was actually afraid of her at times. I thought she may be taking down all our secrets to report at a later date to the leaders.

I wasn't alert. We were in our own home, triggered by our own memories. Our unknown vocabulary could easily be spoken to us over the phone. The closer to where things happened, the more danger we were in.

We did another phone session with Verna. She emphasized the need for Melissa and Rebecca to work with Michael.

"It is important for females to clear their issues with men before starting relationships. Male issues usually begin with the father," she told us again.

This session cleared and lifted some things for me. I saw a few ritual sites in the southern parts of the state in recall. They could have been sites of ceremonies.

Sometimes, when in the pit of emptiness and agony, it is difficult to recognize gifts that manifest in our lives. Often the third dimension realities we need to clean up and live through seem overwhelming.

The third dimension was my despair about Melissa's future. She appeared incapable of living a normal life. Who would look after her? Did she need to be in a mental institution or on a disability pension? I am sure many people who have experienced trauma like her are in institutions because no one is able to heal them.

I struggled to cope with her behavior. I knew her beautiful side and her brilliance, but they weren't shining through. It was immensely difficult being with her.

Now I understand how she and Rebecca, like me, were integrating. The year of discovery and healing we'd completed needed more time to be absorbed by the body and the mind. It was only a few months since we'd finished our course and while we had a big project ahead, selling our property, we really needed time for convalescence. Our light bodies and our physical bodies needed to come into alignment. It was a readjustment we needed to become whole.

But this didn't change the pressure on us of the reality of sorting and disposing of our material goods.

The gift was Melissa's acceptance into a university in another area. The offer was unconditional, totally accepting her previous work. Perfect. This gave her a purpose and meant she could mix with her peers. Melissa needed a life with people her own age. Hopefully, being so far away from our family she would have much less chance of interaction with the cult.

Rebecca completed her exams and passed her driving test. With our obligations at home completed, we planned to move enough things to a location close to the new university for Melissa's needs. We decided to drive there a month before her course started. We would return for final business in March.

Verna spoke to me several times.

"Melissa has been programmed to do this course and she will use some of these skills back in the cult. Don't think going to another state will make her safe."

Rhonda warned, "She needs to be away from her current university. There's too much there to trigger her. Something new may break the pattern."

Melissa had already suspected some university lecturers were involved, including an international lecturer. They - the cult - would still know where she was and how to contact her.

We prepared for our journey. I pretended it was a holiday but I felt like we were refugees, running, hiding.

Several weeks after arriving, we found a flat for Melissa. She had a good place to stay and Rebecca and I were soon to return to America. Now there was the consideration of Rebecca's and my future. Both of us needed training, Rebecca for the beginning of her adult life and me for the beginning of my single life.

It was going to be difficult leaving Melissa in Australia when we returned to the USA.

The truth was dawning on me – many families could unknowingly be involved in ritual abuse. The same way love can be sent, so too can hatred and anger. We needed to protect ourselves and the best way was through awareness.

*The heart holds no shame or guilt,
only the mind judges such things.*

Chapter Nineteen

How could I have thought my marriage was healthy? I had so much subconscious anger and revulsion towards men, all of it repressed until now. God only knows what Michael's subconscious attitude toward women was.

Two adults subjected to such sexual perversions as children and who didn't remember till their mid-forties could be expected to have a difficult time creating a balanced and caring relationship.

Words describing my visual glimpses of ritual abuse gatherings are chaotic, crazy, circles, frenzy and sex. This was the overall scene. For special ceremonies there could be a certain calm. Maybe it was drug-induced but it could also be a 'trained' response: a knowing that anything done out of place would bring a violent consequence from the group, possibly torture.

Occasional screams were heard when someone was forced beyond their will, despite preparation to numb normal responses. For all the mind control and drugs inflicted by the cult leaders, there often would be a glimmer of the human spirit that struggled to bring love and sanity into some of the proceedings. A participant could let this part of her spirit come in attempt to reduce suffering. She might cry in despair, act in defiance and ignore the consequences to herself.

I believe that anyone involved in ritual abuse would have any or all of a distorted, perverted, dysfunctional and unnatural attitude toward sex. A normal, healthy, sexual relationship or feelings of equality and love for the adult brought up as an object of sexual pleasure for adults would need psychological work to overcome the obstacles of perversion. A little boy sexually abused by his mother would have confusion amongst his feelings. His violation hasn't taught him the sacredness of sexuality. As he was also taken by who ever desired, so he as an adult takes what he wants.

A little girl trained in oral masturbation remembers the erotic energy swarming over her, even though she doesn't know the implications of sex. It is easy for the cult-trained child to confuse lust with love. A small child well taught to provide sexual gratification for men and women might only remember her revulsion in one persona. She was also educated to forget. All of this perversion was accompanied by teasing and lustful remarks in a smoke-filled atmosphere of adults euphoric on mind-altering substances, and men prancing around naked, displaying their erections.

Inequality of gender in the cult also promotes the male's demand for his right to sex. This could easily drift into his everyday expectation without knowing the reason or how to control it.

Paralytic drugs forced into a teenager for the popular sport of necrophilia were only used for special occasions. The drugs, even though contaminated, were precious and experience was needed to administer the doses perfectly to keep the recipient away from death. Other sadistic games were to blindfold the female victim and tie her arms together. Give her some length for movement of her arms but have a length of rope for control by the 'oh so powerful male'. How many men could rape one girl for their night's reward? Don't worry, she's used to it.

How could a child brought up in these circumstances grow into an adult without sexual distortions or self-consciousness of some kind?

About fifteen years ago I was in a workshop with a cosmopolitan mix of people. Our facilitator related how his beautiful teenage daughter made a sexual invitation to him. He related her beauty and his own sensual attraction to her. Fortunately he realized his responsibility as a father and was grateful that in hindsight that he had declined her suggestion. Acting out her fantasy would have changed his relationship with his daughter into a category he didn't want to develop.

Although there are often past life connections between fathers and daughters as mates, lovers and beloved for each other, this is not the relationship the souls agreed to for this lifetime. The memory may be there for either or both of these past times to act out these feelings. But that creates more karma, not healing the souls may have planned.

"I know babies are sexual beings," a young South American father informed us. "When my daughter was less than a year old, I stimulated her genitals orally. It was obvious she had an orgasm."

I didn't understand the implications of this at the time. I wondered if this was the custom of his society. But something nagged me about the story. Now I understand. A baby who has been stimulated to orgasm is now a sexual being. All her sexuality was turned on like an electrical switch. Normal sexuality starts in puberty for a well-balanced, non-abused child. Hormones produced by the ovaries and testes respond to their own biological clock. This is correct timing corresponding with the time the child physically and mentally moves into adult hood.

The body of the sexually stimulated child will betray the child because the memory of sex is already implanted in his mind and senses. Sex will mean 'attention' although the context may be aggressive.

Sex with a child is savage and perverted. Touching is molestation and sexual violence towards a child is injury to the psyche and emotion of the child. Once it happens the body has sexual knowledge.

Indira once said,

Sexual abuse is invasion of the spirit. Your spirit is your very essence. As it is violated by others, so it will be self-violated. It is important to deal with the challenges of molestation because it is a very big betrayal. Even when you uncover it as an adult there is a feeling of betrayal. Work on the elements of shock, betrayal, strangulation of the soul and a sense of having lost innocence. When you bring elements of the self through for your healing, it is very important that you do it in a deep sense of safety. Do not interact with someone who wants to put you down or pretend it is not so. Maybe later you can cope with this.

Firstly it is just a question of protecting yourself. That is important.

If ever any of you are cognizant of someone in your immediate area, anyone within your midst that may be prone to desire or likely by any chance to bring a child some harm or molestation, don't allow it.

Never allow it. Never.

Don't be part of knowing and not acting.

Just because we don't believe in something, doesn't mean it does not exist.

Chapter twenty

What I have noticed about many people remembering multi generational ritual abuse is that often their parents are the last people to be recognized as participants. The concept of family involvement is too horrific. It would be easier to believe the abuse was accidental, possibly from a chance meeting with a perpetrator who kidnapped us to take along to his circles. Maybe a friend, extended family, relation by marriage, or a changed circumstance could have enticed us there. Sometimes people think their memory was a past life. Never could our immediate family have been involved. That is impossible to contemplate.

Melissa and Rebecca as younger people seemed more aware. They saw both Michael and me very quickly in their memories. Of course, we verified our participation with our own recall. But even for them, during the course of remembering it seems there were occasions where they put my participation in a softer light.

Melissa comforted me with, "Mum, they didn't like you, it wasn't your fault."

"You were just a pawn, Mum. You were used," Rebecca said.

They didn't say this of their father.

Rhonda, my supportive friend, was heartbroken when she discovered her parents' involvement.

"I believed it was my aunts taking me to meetings for a long time. Years, actually. Then I noticed a robed person hiding behind a mask continually appeared in my memory. I was devastated when I looked carefully and discovered it was my father. He was an important part of the proceedings. He was a leader."

She sobbed as she continued. "Later I sensed my mother. I loved her. She was my support. Then I remembered her programming me by whispering into my ear at night when I was small. I don't know what was worse, discovering ritual abuse or unearthing my parents' role in my abuse. It was more bearable thinking it was only my aunts taking me to meetings."

Rhonda could no longer hide her grief by denying her parents' abuse.

Although I delved deeply into ritual abuse memories, it didn't dawn on me until recently that my own father was probably implicated. A year after our workshops together, Daniel confronted me as I talked about the strange behavior of Michael's parents. Really, I was blaming them for abusing my daughters and me.

Hands resting on his thighs, Daniel leaned forward looked me directly in the eyes.

"Look Christina, when are you going to face up to the fact your father was involved?"

Oh yes, deep down I knew my father had participated in perverted activities in the garage next door when I was little. There was the smoke-filled room with the Freemason symbol, drinking urine laced with feces, along with pornographic-style pictures taken with my brother. I didn't deny that. So it actually seems odd how I accepted all these occurrences and didn't think them out of the ordinary. They explained my self-consciousness and inferiority – the very reason I was pursuing my personal growth.

I had remembered ritualistic abuse circumstances in my late teens at the time of the robed men's fertility circle. This dramatic ceremony which affected my eyesight was the first chronological time that robes, pentacles and chanting appeared in my visions.

I spent a lot of time pondering what caused this change. There *had* to be someone different or new in my life that took my father and me there. This explanation was satisfactory and supported my denial. I *knew* my family wasn't involved in ritual abuse until I was seventeen and then it was someone else's fault that we were dragged into it. There had already been enough abuse to make us good candidates to easily submit to more terror.

Daniel's impatient challenge surprised me. During the Year Long I'd come up with conclusions that suited me about my childhood. So how could he know better than I did? I thought Daniel was projecting his own involvement.

However, more than anything, I wanted to know the truth about ritual abuse and face any denial head on. Certainly, I needed to listen and acknowledge other people's perceptions to discover my blockages. I can't tell you how much I longed for someone to verify my memories and see more than I had of my corrupted childhood. What I really desired was a chronological history of what happened, month by month in my life and specific ages for my memory fragments.

Of course this was impossible. Although whatever I recalled was incomplete, there was no one to write my history except me. So it was easier to deny my early childhood as being ritual abuse than go through the agonizing pain of remembering the shadow side of my parents.

Towards the end of the Year Long, before Daniel's challenge, I had asked Indira one evening if I had been involved in ritual abuse as a child.

She replied.
Abuse is abuse, and you were abused.

At the time I thought Indira's answer was odd. Because I had already seen so much abuse in my life I expected her answer to be, 'Yes, you were involved in ritual abuse as a child.' I interpreted her reply to mean I hadn't been involved in ritual abuse from my own birth family - only through marriage. I was quite relieved with my version. I wanted to blame someone other than my parents.

Indira reported that my sisters were also involved in ritual abuse, so I assumed they had come with me into my marriage group as adults. Messages from Indira were generally accurate. Her words were usually carefully chosen to make us look for ourselves at what we were asking. For some reason, she didn't want to tell me directly that my birth family was involved. And it suited me to maintain my blame on Michael's family.

But it was quite obvious, a year later that Daniel saw I needed to face the truth.

One morning, I picked up a book at the library, *Family Secrets* by John Bradshaw. As I flicked through the contents, it opened at a page that gave a short exercise. This appeared to be an appropriate way to check if the book was suitable for me to borrow.

Draw the house that you lived in during childhood…

Images of the house layout came immediately to my mind: three interconnecting bedrooms, a common practice after the war to save building materials, the sleep-out off the back verandah, the front porch, and the kitchen. I couldn't quite remember the exact details of the bathroom and living room - they were a bit hazy - the toilet was outside. I remembered that clearly. I was terrified to go there at night for my father or brother would taunt me, telling me the witches would get me.

See your father in his room there and he will show you something…

Suddenly, in my inner vision, Dad appeared in the main bedroom holding a small bundle wrapped in black cloth in his hand. He opened the cloth and showed me the contents, a strange knife. It looked a bit like a scalpel with a fine blade, very, very sharp and with a long, deep point. The blade widened from the point into a curve, returning narrower near the handle. It was an odd-looking knife.

Well this was a surprise. My heart ached from these clear images and I was ready to put the book down. I'd discovered enough for one day. But the next answer to the instructions in this guided imagery popped into my consciousness immediately,

And your father has something to tell you…

He did.

'*I killed people,*' was the message.

Damn! I put the book down.

That was enough for today. Maybe there was much more I could discover with other exercises like this, but I needed to take it slowly.

Why would I have come up with those words? Those images?

Again and again my brain rummaged through all the possible convolutions when I discovered further verification of the lies in my family. When I returned home, I needed to experiment – just to try out what may have been the truth. Strange thoughts continued to pop into my mind and I had to test out my response to them.

My father is a murderer.

I checked this out, how it felt to know, to examine if it was true. I hand wrote this statement over several pages of paper. Big writing, printing, small writing. I tried different colors and used both hands. One was shaky and the other confident. I cried and felt angry. It felt so obscure to write these words... but there was a reason.

I had believed Dad was with a group of friends who hadn't got past the second chakra stage of their development. They'd done their war effort together and acted like little boys in men's bodies, playing their cruel sex games.

I needed to go outside, to see the world where other people moved about their seemingly normal lives. A place where our created illusion made me seem ordinary and not out of place. I need to breathe.

Was I sane? Many years ago I did a guided imagery with some friends in a weekend workshop. It was fairly typical of guided meditations.

"See yourself moving along a pleasant path. The sun shines as you move through a forest. You pass a stream, then come to a small hill." We were told we saw a house from the hill. "Go to the house. Inside is someone you need to talk with."

I opened the door and looked in. There was my father: a cardboard, photographic cutout, sitting on a chair pulled up at the kitchen table. I was baffled and cried for hours when I saw this image. I know I cried for a long time because I couldn't move off the floor where I lay. The rest of the group participants discussed the significance of their images, had a break, then meditated for an hour. I couldn't halt my outpouring of grief, nor could I share my experience. I had no notion of its meaning. Now I had the connection between these two incidents: the cardboard cutout of Dad and my father's secrets.

My cardboard cutout father was a visual image of a façade, with nothing behind. The figure looked very real, a photographic image, but had no emotion or substance. Father's secrets: the knife and murder, was the other side of the cardboard body, hidden from everyone.

This is my truth of how I saw him, a father who ignored his emotion and feelings, making them unavailable to both himself and everyone else. A man with a hidden side. An unknown dimension, presenting himself as a two-dimensional man in a three-dimensional world, with the third dimension invisible.

Writing this book was an emotional journey. At this point I felt just sadness and grief. I remembered this guided image meditation of twelve years ago and cried again. I was shocked at my father being a cardboard figure but had little concept of its meaning back then. Writing, and the huge time lapse, helped me understand.

I cried.
For the father I didn't know,
For the father I hated,
For the father I loved,
For the father I had several babies to,
For the father who tortured me,
For the father I wanted to love me, as his daughter.

I don't remember much about my parents from my childhood. We lived in several different houses and I can recall little things from most of them. I loved sitting on Dad's knee when I was seven, in the second house I lived in. He sang funny little ditties and rhymes to me that I later repeated to my children. After re-reading this chapter about a hundred times, it has finally sunk in that my brief and precious time of rhymes with Dad was probably programming. Acceptable rhymes in front of other people but altered with a word here and there to mean something quite different during cult abuse. Still, the attention felt special at the time.

His presence is in some memories I have of going to the wharf to see the cargo ships, eating fish and chips, and swimming in the ocean. As a teenager I'd ask him to sign my detention slips from school. I knew he enjoyed the *Sound of Music* the one film we saw together as a family.

But I could count conversations I had with Dad on my fingers. My lifetime of connection with him, represented by the ten digits on my hands. I didn't talk about life, school, or dreams, for these weren't conversations we had in our family. Dad was away a lot, working long hours. There was a lot of stress. Maybe it wasn't all to do with work, but I presumed he was a fairly typical father of the 1950's and 1960's when male and female roles were clearly defined. The woman stayed at home, cleaned, cooked and raised the kids. The man went to work to build a better future for his family. I thought it was normal for fathers to not interact much with their children. If I consider the terrible poverty of my father's childhood, he worked hard to give a different life with conveniences and education to his children. That was a mighty achievement in one generation.

I was with Dad when he died. I was a teenager and he wasn't an old man. His death was quick, not unexpected but still a surprise. He lay on the hallway floor in our home, unconscious.

"Talk to him while I'll call the ambulance," Mum said. "Hearing is the last sense to go."

I spoke my last words to him. "I love you." I don't ever remember saying that before.

Many years later during meditation I remembered his death again and saw a golden energy rope left his body from his solar plexus. Then a golden cord left my heart to meet his, however, my heart cord was deflected off into a magnificent deep blue. I have since learned family sitting with a dying person, often keep the soul of the dying in their body because of their love. The soul needs to be free to leave the body. My father deflected my love so I didn't hold him in his dying body.

It is funny how strong my feelings of Dad being a murderer were when I started this chapter. Now I feel guilty thinking such thoughts of someone and wanted to rationalize it away. Everything I wrote was my memory and my memory, like everyone else's, filed away things it didn't want to recall. We remember everything; it is the recall that is often difficult.

I was born into a family of ritualistic abuse. My marriage was into a family involved in ritualistic abuse. I have seen my daughters, husband and his relations in my memories. I was attracted to Michael because of similar experiences. We felt safe together with our forgotten secrets and fear. We needed each other to support the lies of our lives.

There are generations of secrets in both our families

I contemplate my family's closeted skeletons. Incest is one. Then there was an affair before my father married which produced an illegitimate child. My mother told me about this after I was married.

"She didn't look like anyone else in the family so everyone agreed she couldn't have been your Dad's child."

What a story. It makes me sick, though I bought it at the time. I guess an illegitimate child was pretty tough to contend with in the

1930's. Although this child might not have looked like the rest of the family, it could have meant she took after her mother's family in looks. No, I don't believe that this person was not related to me. She was my sibling whose name I knew long before my relationship with her. She, like me, probably had rejection and abandonment issues to work through from this life. Maybe she doesn't know what other horrors she was saved from. I wonder if she would ever read this book and recognize a sister?

It took me nearly twenty years of personal growth before I remembered sexual abuse, so I checked with my sisters to see if they had any recollection.

"Yes, that could have happened to you, Christina, but not from our father. Possibly from people working with him. There were so many men around," one sister said.

"I'm sorry that happened, I wish I could have helped you at the time," the other responded.

Neither believed they were abused physically. They considered circumstances were different for them. One was adored by Dad and she believed he wouldn't have hurt her. The other didn't live in that house. They both created explanations for not being concerned.

Indira had told me both of them were involved. I hadn't seen them in my memory and didn't tell detailed information to them. When I told them of the possibility I left it open for them to remember or not. I know I had done more deep memory search and healing work than they had. They too, may eventually discover their own secret life.

Maybe Dad's murder consciousness arose from the war. He didn't talk about his experiences, except the unnecessary death. How ironic.

So what else have I remembered about my father that might indicate murder? There was the fox dissected in front of me and the baby mice and kittens I was forced to swallow. Does that mean my father was a murderer? I remember often using the words, 'I'll kill you' and 'I'll be killed' but does that mean I witnessed my father perform the act of murder? I had pre-term babies that were sacrificed - and I still don't want to falsely accuse anyone. Was I judgmental saying my father was a murderer? I chose my family and circumstances as Spirit. I thought I could handle it. But was my father a murderer?

Sadly, yes, I believe he was.

Dad wasn't ever accused of murder. He wasn't put on trial in a court of justice. He wasn't committed for a capital crime. He wasn't incarcerated.

So where is the proof? There is no physical proof. Only my knowing: my feelings: little snippets of memory. No bodies were left around, no blood was left as evidence on the floor.

Why was I even thinking of this? As my tears welled again, I realized it was best to let them flow. I may have needed time off from writing this story, but there was obviously pain and sadness to release. I continued writing when the tears stopped.

I relate some of this accusation of my father with my own fear. Until a few years ago, I was terrified of being murdered. Constantly I felt something behind me wherever I walked. I checked behind doors, under beds, and in cupboards. I was a master of hiding and continually looked for 'safe' places to hide. I'd look for intruders in my home. This paranoia ruled me, and a week before enrolling in Verna's first workshop, before any discovery of abuse, I sought help.

Lynette, an American dowser, taught me how to program crystals and use a pendulum. Her specialty was medical dowsing, to find what virus, parasites or problem were causing an illness. She then created programs to help remove the microbial culprit. I was confused about my life asked her for guidance. Using her pendulum she quickly picked up my fear.

"I get that you are frightened of being murdered. You've brought this fear in from previous lives," Lynette said. "It seems there are many times when you were accidentally murdered. It's alright if you don't remember anything specific."

Lynette suggested I went to a Kinesiologist who could help clear this type of issue.

I arranged a session. The Kinesiologist tested my muscle reactions and confirmed my fear.

"I agree with Lynette. You are fearful of being murdered. We can work together to remove your anxiety."

She used sound, affirmations and essential oils to deprogram my fear. But nothing about the reality of the fear of being murdered this lifetime came up. It wasn't a normal fear expected in our society. However, I felt lighter after this session and less frightened.

Look at yourself first Christina, think clearly. Don't you remember the pain and tears when you first remembered murdering during the Year Long? Unstoppable crying. There were no pictures in your head, no idea of when, where or who, only inexplicable grief and sorrow. No body, no blood, only emotion. No location, no age, only anguish. Pain in your heart you hadn't met before, crying out for release.

Maybe I should have started this chapter with,

"I AM A MURDERER...."

Ah, the feeling is different from how I felt about my father being a murderer. In my heart, along with the grief and the regret, is fear.

Tears emerged with my confusion.

If God is love, what is evil? Power and control? Is ritual abuse part of the experience of God too? A choice of our God-selves to delve into darkness?

Yet it doesn't matter about the deeper meaning, because there is no way a human could truly understand the reasons for all this perversion. 'Why is there ritual abuse?' is a question akin to 'Who is God?' No one could answer the same way.

Who did my father really murder? Did he murder people I knew? I became paranoid and wondered if he murdered a woman when I was eight. There was a story in the newspaper about how she was killed near our home. Pictures on the evening newspaper's front page showed the murder implements. Why did I relate with such terror to that murder? At that time I begged my mother to let me sleep with her. She promised to set up a mattress at the foot of her bed if I told her the reason for my fear. I didn't want to tell her. But my desire to be safe near her was so great, I whispered, 'I'm scared I'll be murdered.' Was I already so familiar with murder it seemed a strong possibility in my eight-year old mind?

Indira helped me clear up my thoughts.

Your father didn't murder the people you read about in the newspapers. The cult murdered people who had no family. They were people that no one would even notice if they disappeared. They even murdered people's children. You have seen many people murdered in front of you.

As I pondered my life, I looked around and wondered if everyone in the neighborhood had been abused. I look at the tension in people's bodies and listen to words they choose. I have to be careful to not become overly suspicious and remind myself that maybe not everyone has been sexually or ritually abused.

Murder. My body told me at least a year before I was aware of involvement in ritual abuse, that I had 'murderous fury' stored inside in my liver area. It felt as though that side of my body was bulging under my ribs. I wondered if my liver was enlarged from alcohol. I wasn't a drunkard and chuckled at my children when they said, "You're an alcoholic, Mum, you drink too much."

I knew I wasn't, but was touched by their misunderstanding and concern. "Alcoholics are often drunk. They'll drink through the day. I only have a couple of glasses of wine each evening to relax. Don't worry about me," I explained to them.

My wise, sensitive children knew so much more than I did. I had inordinate anger and used alcohol to suppress emotion. I didn't understand then, so brushed aside their comments of alcoholism and continued drinking to relax. Blood ran around my body crying out for alcohol to calm my feelings, but I still didn't think of myself as an alcoholic or alcohol dependent.

When my need for alcohol stopped suddenly. I was amazed. There was nothing conscious about my decision, just my first discovery of abuse. Now I know that if I desire alcohol, there is something up, I can drink the alcohol, or look deeply behind my desire to consume the numbing, repressing substance. I listen to my body and words for the clues I need to heal.

I no longer want to be in denial or keep a lid on the reality of my life. How did my father feel? Did he have pain in his heart? Did he have regrets and anguish? Did he work hard so he could ignore his feelings? I eventually found my feelings - in a mysterious dark box - so tightly bound by metal bands and chains it took years to open. It was a black hole of grief I'd built walls around with metal bars and bands to keep it from engulfing me. I built the box to keep these parts of my life away from the light, hidden from God.

Darkness only exists without light and I'd spent years searching for those parts of myself I'd kept in darkness, not knowing what I was looking for.

Spirit is the power that breathes life into created form.
Spirit is life's true identity, the part we search for.

Chapter twenty one

I don't really want to consider the prospect of violation or betrayal by my mother even though I know that in ritual abuse everyone is involved. No one who survives is an innocent bystander. The leaders - those with more power - ensure their group members endure every side of torture as both victim and perpetrator. My mother was another pawn controlled with threats of losing me. And I am still in denial about my mother's involvement. How could such a nice, kind lady be involved in such horrendous abuse of her family?

I know more about my mother's life than my father's. Both were teenagers during the Depression. Mum came from a small family with average conditions for the times and a father who always worked. She told me they were never without food and took cases of goods on the train when they visited relations who had no income. The only girl in a very close group of children, it was her duty to help her mother with household responsibilities. A tight control was maintained on her life, with playmates selected for manners, elocution and intelligence. Apparently Grandma constantly indicated a preference for boys in front of her only daughter.

Support for Mum came in her late teens from relations who encouraged her to follow dreams of education and training. She was a nurturing person and pursued her nursing career full of compassion. I could tell how much she loved the children she worked with from her stories, which were backed up by references from the hospitals stored in her files. But how would she be attracted to my father, a widower with a small son?

Like attracts like, abuse attracts abuse and there is karma. Although there appeared to be no physical abuse in her family, Mum was psychologically abused as a child. It appears that Dad continued this form of abuse from the day of their marriage. She didn't know what to do about it at the time and through her entire married life didn't know what was really happening.

When I was a child I totally believed that somehow I pushed my parents together so I would be created. I believed this was my way of arranging to be my brother's little sister – the man I knew in my Polish life. Because of this belief, I knew my family's unhappiness and tension was my fault. I had caused it all. Since discovering my own childhood trauma, I've found out it is common amongst abused children to blame themselves for family problems. It was then, I knew that I'd chosen my family for the abuse, with physical strength to survive and resources for healing later.

Tsen Tsing confirmed this.

You chose your parents for the father's male energy of abuse and your mother to provided a suitable vehicle and nurturing.

Love from someone was necessary to endure the other extreme of my life.

I wonder if it was my mother's care that stopped me from choosing to be a violent or destructive teenager. Her example to care for other people and to look for goodness inside everyone kept me from acting on my rage and fury. I wouldn't have dared expressed my anger in her presence – or out of her presence – for although she was a loving human being, she ruled my behavior and dictated my likes and dislikes with considerable control. I wasn't given freedom of vocal self-expression so stuffed my feelings and anger deep inside.

Starting 20 years ago, several healers at different times asked me in a disparaging way, " Who were your parents? Why were they so hard on you?"

I remember responding that I was hard on myself. I had no idea then of any abuse and wondered why they couldn't see that my behavior was a result of my own harsh judgements. But being a child victim of my parents' marriage is not an issue. It was my choice. I had my own karma and life goals to work on. My purpose was to clear these patterns from my body and consciousness - quite probably from many lifetimes - to break the cycle by healing. My parents and I agreed to play out the roles together for reasons the mere 'human' part of me doesn't fully know. In the big picture of life, there is no one to blame.

Multi generational ritual abuse begins in the womb. Powerful programming using sound – including modulated chants - upsets the energy field of the fetus. The developing baby senses confusion and the pattern of fear is initiated by sound directed at the solar plexus before the child is even born. Torture to the mother then accelerates the environment of fear, preparing the baby for a life of terror in the cult. Was my mother aware of the programming for me? Was I aware of the programming happening to my unborn children? No. Another case of trained forgetfulness. Moreover, the mother helps program their developing child in the womb.

Some enjoyable time I remember from my childhood with Mum was helping her bake cookies and cakes. She spent a lot of time in the kitchen, for that was the way of the times – no fast foods or jobs for married women. I remember being around the clothesline as she hung the clothes out with the wooden dolly pegs.

I also recall my mother telling me about a learning difficulty I had in my first year of school. Apparently every letter I printed was reversed.

"You did mirror writing," Mum said. "Your teacher was concerned and said you may have to repeat the year if it didn't change. Fortunately, by the end of the year it had improved."

Both my daughters also had initial reading problems. Hereditary? No, for we discovered cult programming causing confusion, which affects learning. Dyslexia and learning difficulties are not uncommon amongst ritually abused people: induced by torturous taunting. Tied in a chair- unable to move - an electric probe or burning candle ready to apply to the child's skin.

"Show us right?"

"This is right."

"No! That's left." An electric shock reinforces the might of the torturer.

"What is left?"

Well, if that wasn't right, and they say it's left, it must be left!

"This is left."

"Wrong. That's right." Another shock on the cheek or burn to the foot.

There is no way to please them. Right is left, left is right, back is front, front is back, up is down and down is up. Left is right and right is left, front is back and back is front. On and on and on. Total confusion. Never can I presume anything or know how to please anyone. Around and around my head goes. Spinning. It feels crazy in my head. Even now, I want to scream and climb up the wall, totally disorientated, to get away. Consistency in sucking my right thumb was my secret way of knowing which was my right side.

Who was my mother? A woman in the cult not protecting me, and mother at home teaching me normal things.

As I grew older, I spoke less and less with my mother. I felt self-conscious and knew my opinions would be criticized. She probably thought I was a rude, angry and uncommunicative teenager. I just knew there was no point in sharing my thoughts. There wasn't much point in having opinions.

After the Year Long, further insights and memory came through meditation which explained some of my relationship with my mother. I didn't feel as close to her as my youngest sister did. She adored Mum and I often felt bad for not being as devoted as she was.

I received this memory fragment while meditating with friends.

I am very small, less than six…the men are there and have me hanging from rafters spanned across the ceiling of a church. Somehow I am tied by a rope: hung in space, swinging from side to side of the building. I am bad and evil covered in black ink to emphasize my attachment to the dark side. I can see the pews lined up underneath me. In the center aisle, in front of the pews, is a table with a coffin on it. The coffin is outlined with burning candles. There is a body lying in the coffin – it is my mother…dead! Dressed in a red checkered dress…I feel resigned…no hope. My mother is dead.

As a little girl I didn't know paralytic drugs or anesthesia could be used to simulate death. I only saw my mother's inability to move as another example of her being unable to rescue me from torture. I couldn't count on her protection. Why would these men subject me to such horrors? I asked Indira, who told me,

This ceremony happened to you more than once. It was a type of bonding for mother and daughter. Not that it makes a great deal of sense. It was to instill in you a fear of being alone.

I was well trained to be fearful of authority. It was ingrained in my consciousness by the creative abusive threats from these men.

Bodywork over the past few years brought memory of my relationship with my mother to the surface. Deep grief was stored in the cells of my left arm from the cruel wedges placed by my tormentors to break our mother-child bond.

My mother,

dead in the coffin,

drugged in the circles,

unable and unwilling to save me from my father's torment,

lined up with some other people to 'greet me' after my night alone in an underground box.

I soon figured out there was no one to give me solace or support during my secret life. Mum was never present in a state of consciousness to help when I needed it, or she was too scared to protect me. Consequently I severed my emotional attachment to her at a very young age. It wasn't safe or useful to pursue a deep relationship of trust with someone who didn't appear to care for me. This was exactly what the cult mind-set wanted - to create a sense of aloneness and dependency on them. The cult would be there when I wanted companionship and support.

I feel cheated of a deep relationship with my mother.

Looking back with my adult understanding, I see her fear. She was threatened with my death, further brutality and my father keeping me from her if she dared leave the marriage. She remembered some of these threats without the full context of being brainwashed and trapped.

Indira told me,

Your mother didn't protect you enough. Rummage this out. You make less of yourself than who you really are because of this.

I wondered why Indira told me this, as I was well aware of the lack of protection in the cult. Then I realized I had actually blamed myself for cutting off any intimacy with my mother.

Frequently I had to nurture myself between workshops. I tried many forms of bodywork in an effort to help move my energy, including cranio-sacral and different energy therapies. A session with Rosemarie, highly recommended by Rhonda, somehow seemed connected to my mother.

I lay on the massage table in the nurturing environment Rosemarie created. How frequently does anyone lie still and focus totally on their body? Not often - it took time to relax and sense my body and feel its strength and let it talk to me about its needs and feelings.

I felt tension in my upper arms, they ached constantly. This familiar pain only revealed itself when I relaxed. I checked other parts of my body to find where there was pain: in my lower back and sacrum. Movement in the soft tissue occurred as I lay still and calmed my muscles.

My arms didn't loosen, so I breathed into that area to investigate the tension. They felt as though they were gripped tightly, like an adult holding a child's arms in anger. Slowly a change emerged and warmth flowed into my lower arms and brought my fingers alive. The tension went and I felt vitality below my elbows.

Instantaneously my heart felt heavy, for I knew what caused the pain. The entire answer visualized the moment I asked. By blocking the feeling in my upper arms I didn't have to feel and remember what my hands had done. A necessity for my survival.

I see a face- the mouth is open and blood pours out. Oh no, the tongue has been cut out. Did I do this? Keep breathing, I tell myself, just breathe, focus on the breath. I don't want to be caught in emotions. Why is there so much cruelty? Why do we do these heinous acts on each other?

I breath faster, and hold back tears by looking at the ceiling. The light fitting takes my attention with its nothingness. It helps shut out this scene from my memory banks for I have seen enough for a few seconds.

I already knew I did this act, so why did I have to ask? I call Angels of healing to stand with me, to spread their blanket of protection over me. They come and assured me of their presence with love…I am forgiven, but can I forgive myself, a child less than ten years of age, who committed this cruelty?

When I was about six, my family went to the drive-in theatre. The move was a mediaeval setting in Europe. The only thing I remembered was when the hero said to another man, "Speak man, speak!" The man didn't reply. A friend of the mute said, "He can't speak Sire, his tongue is cut out."

The next morning I slept late. Most of the family was up and gone, so Mum gave me breakfast to eat alone – toast and strawberry jam. I remembered the toast scratching my soft palate and the taste of the jam, as my mind re-played the scene. "Speak man, speak!" over and over. Strawberry jam always brings that memory to me. It was unforgettable.

Who was the real person I saw in memory, tongue cut out and blood streaming from his mouth? Why was the tongue cut out? To silence him! A person with no tongue in our culture would still be able to read and write. He could tell his story, unlike the film I saw with uneducated men. This person is Dead Man Walking. Sentenced, after gruesome torture. So much blood, impossible to swallow. The blood was fresh, red, and like a river, flowing.

I opened my eyes again and stared blankly at the ceiling to block the images and remind myself, this is the here and now.

Rosemarie balanced my energy and said a prayer. The pain had gone. My arms felt better. They had released some of the trauma of cutting out a person's tongue.

I see how family patterns and the brainwashing of cults are handed down. As my mother was incapable of protecting me so was I unable to protect my daughters. Although both generations were in denial and controlled, there is always a level of our consciousness that knows all. As we have deprogramming and heal this pattern, my daughters hopefully will be free to protect and adore their future children as every child should be protected and loved. Healing is continual and necessary.

Lately I've become cognizant of different roles my mother played. In normal life she was as vehemently revolted by cigarette smoking as I am. Now I believe she smoked during gatherings. A rasp in her voice and reduced lung capacity bears testament to this possibility. As a child I was confused by these behaviors in Mum but because of another part of her, the tyrannical 'guardian' of me, I didn't dare mention her inconsistencies. As my female guardian she was involved in some training, but mostly ensured I was prepared for my tasks and performed well. She had total control over my thoughts, words and actions. I had to think and act the way she instructed me. Any independence of my own was squashed, and I became a puppet controlled by another puppet.

Discussing ritual abuse with my mother after my discoveries was beyond her level of acceptance. I reported my initial discovery of rape as a three-year-old to her a year after I remembered. Even though she had told me many years ago that something changed in my personality when I was about three, she didn't want to believe my recollection of what happened in our back yard.

"Don't you think it was the Gardiners? You stayed with them when I was in hospital when you were about three," she suggested. "They had several older sons who could have abused you."

But when I mentioned my father's abuse, she was adamant.

"No, not your father. He wasn't that kind of man."

She was unable to accept my version and has no idea of the degree of abuse she or I endured. I noticed a short article on false memory syndrome cut out of the paper for me to read. I didn't discuss abuse with her again.

When talking about abuse, it's not to blame the perpetrator, but to acknowledge my own reactions and release that from my body. Healing is to help clear the self, never to blame, for there are always two sides to every story and many reasons for abuse. I came into this life with the energy of sexual Nazi occult abuse from my last incarnation. The energy I had ensured the situation would be created again.

Although it isn't right for abuse to occur, it is part of the cycles of life that I created and enacted. I was playing a huge drama of many lives and many selves, and the only person who can deal with them is me. I tried to keep this in mind as I vented my fury over these men whom I thought were disgusting. I'd fantasize miserable existences for them: testicular cancer; impotency; loneliness and despair. Then I'd have to cancel my angry thoughts and hope they could also heal.

My mother has since died. She immediately visited me in Spirit as an attractively dressed, slim woman in her thirties. Her first words to me after death were, *I love you.* Then she immediately added, *I didn't know, I'm so sorry.* I was deeply touched by her acknowledgement, but know there is more for me to search out and heal in regard to my mother.

Chapter twenty two

How can I demonstrate the truth of my memories? It took *me* time to acknowledge this other part of my life and although I wanted people to believe me, I found it difficult to express my discovery because of my own confusion. My memory had unfolded in a physical and emotionally disturbing manner and I needed time to piece together the new reality of my life. I expected other people to question how we could possibly be involved in this abuse without knowing, and somehow I had to give proof of its occurrence.

Rhonda explained her experiences confidently. She was an adept speaker, unfolding her memories quietly to whom ever she addressed. Her body language embraced the listener so they felt entrusted with deep confidences.

"I don't feel offended if someone doesn't believe me. That's where they are," she told me. "If I'm put on the spot with a sticky enquiry, I answer without bringing in too much detail. I don't want to belittle anyone. It's great to have challenging opinions because they teach me how to understand someone else's thinking process."

Rhonda's memories appeared more detailed and extensive than mine. She recalled more of the hierarchy and methods used in ceremonies than anyone in my family. Well, maybe Melissa knew more than she told us. She could be quite secretive about her recollections and knowledge.

"You remember things I haven't seen. I don't know more than you, I just appear more certain," Rhonda reassured me.

"I feel defensive when I talk about ritual abuse. It's natural people don't want to believe these atrocities happen in their suburbs, but if someone makes me feel as though I'm evil, I want to challenge them to prove they aren't involved. Some people don't believe it's possible that teachers, lawyers or doctors could be perpetrators. But I don't want to be paranoid and suspect everyone," I said to her.

"It's better to only tell a little at a time. Then let it sit with them till they want to ask more," Rhonda advised.

My hunt for information proving ritual abuse existed began. The only evidence available was our memory and body, for no overt sign of rituals ever remained. Satanic activity reported in the newspaper was not done by the highly organized and secretive group I'd been born into. Our methods were too systematic and disciplined to leave any traces. The only possibility of sensing our gatherings was from a group of cars, chanting or occasional screams in hidden places.

"I've scrubbed blood off the floor with a toothbrush," Rhonda recalled. "The cleanup was always well organized and everyone knew their job was to leave no trail." She laughed, "We were a prime cleaning team."

"Everything had to be absolutely spotless. They would drop a grain of rice somewhere just to be able to check if I'd cleaned there," Melissa added. "Sometimes they'd drop another grain of rice after I'd cleaned, so I'd get into trouble anyway."

"Our incinerator was used a lot at home when I was a kid. I had to clean out the ashes and often wondered where all the little bits of bone came from," Michael remembered.

I recall putting carefully packed knives into the back of a van. No evidence that could be used as proof was left at abuse sites. Every drop of blood was meticulously cleaned. Waste was prepared for incineration and implements used were secretly ensconced away. Hiding places were secure and methodically selected. Tidy homes were used for storage.

Manufacturers of torture hardware don't have to advertise their wares, so the public is unaware of their availability and consequent use. Pornography provides money for purchase.

With no physical evidence available, factual information explaining how the body stores our biography seemed the avenue of research I needed to pursue. Although psychological literature acknowledges that denial often hides memory of childhood abuse till forty years later, there can still be the cry of false memory. Some friends believed the story of my memories for they could see changes in me. When I returned to Australia I confided my experiences with several close friends.

"Christina. What you say makes so much sense," Anita, a friend of nearly thirty years, said. "That fits in with things I couldn't place about you, your fear, inferiority and behavior."

We talked for an hour about the ideal place for ceremonies.

"There is so much bushland surrounding our cities - plenty of huge rocky areas, isolated and not difficult to get to. Ceremonies could be performed anywhere with complete privacy. No one would hear or suspect anything," she continued. "Look where I live. There's the water catchment area nearby. That's an ideal place to conceal abuse. Look how long it takes trackers to find missing bodies here." She thought a bit more, "Gosh, sometimes they don't even find missing bodies for years."

Another friend commented, "You've changed a lot. A few years ago your conversation was erratic. You'd jump from one topic to another. Now I can follow you better – you're more focused and in your body."

These friends believed me, but how could I pass on their belief of the barbarity of ritual abuse to my family and general public?

Yes, I suppose four of us from one family remembering abuse together made our recall hard to deny, but there would still be skeptics. I told Shanti, my friend from earlier meditation days, "During the workshops I did in America I recalled abuse from my father and other men. Then I saw ritual abuse."

"I always suspected you were sexually abused but do you think ritual abuse could be false memory?"

It was incomprehensible for her to consider she had friends involved in something they didn't even remember until years later.

False memory syndrome is a powerful name. It took several years before I could pick out books on this topic from the library shelves to browse through. The basis of validation within these books sparked my own inner frustration, for I found their premise inconclusive and unable to help me with proof that my memories were or were not false.

Could body memory counter false memory labels?

None of the books I read which claimed the likelihood of false memory for delayed abuse recall mentioned physical pain, illness, despair, sadness or uncontrollable body reactions. If you'd seen someone vomit blood or writhe on the floor during recall, you couldn't cry 'false memory'. Wide-eyed terror and shock shows on people's faces and in their bodies. The energy of fear is exuded. As a group, we saw and felt people's anguish during their abuse recollections. Books written on false memory may be useful for people in denial.

Articles on sacrificial worship in Australian outer suburbs have occasionally appeared in Sunday papers, along with rumors of cult like occurrences in large parks near cities. There was even whispering through community welfare departments that they are well aware of the occurrence of ritual abuse in the community. But hearsay isn't evidence and the public believes people involved in these practices are evil, not their colleagues or possibly themselves. Mind control, they would believe, did not belong to our neighborhoods and society.

Misleading information is easy for perpetrators to disseminate, particularly when the population wants to be in denial about what could be occurring next door, in schools and in churches.

I wanted something substantial to prove my story. Evidence with leading edge basis. Our family memories were often incomplete. I can't write a chronological history of the dates, places and exact torture. Melissa and Rebecca's common memories weren't mine and the swimming pool episode was the only time that the three of us remembered exactly the same situation. Consistent memory themes of torture, baby breeding, drugs and seeing the same people at gatherings wasn't enough. How was I to convince other people that this type of abuse was real?

Another avenue for checking the probability of our story was trance channeling. Again this wasn't tangible, although I occasionally used channeling to ask for confirmation of my memories. After several sessions I decided it was less expensive to trust myself. Indira and Tsen Tsing don't know everything, although I found their messages accurate and helpful. They both constantly asked me why I didn't believe what I saw. I decided that was best.

Confirmation and reassurance for me came when I discovered people from other parts of the world had recollected similar memories. I found books written by other people about their experience of ritual abuse. Then an acclaimed American author with several published books unexpectedly used a seminar to inform people of mind control and ritualistic abuse. Quite a different topic from her own published work.

However, the most powerful confirmation of abuse for me, came from body therapists who 'picked up' stories from my energetic field. Abuse clung around my aura and some sensitive and intuitive practitioners who didn't know my story before working on my body, sensed it.

The body never lies.

This was the most profound proof recognized. Our bodies are the most tangible record of how our history has shaped us. It is our autobiography, a code book of our history.

Experienced healers know this is true and work on the energetic release of trauma from the body and mind. But an amnesic victim wouldn't believe a healer reporting 'satanic abuse' in their energy field. If someone had told me six months before I discovered ritual abuse for myself that I'd been abused, I would have laughed and thought they were crazy. No one can be forced to remember. Survivors need to remember themselves. My goal became to understand storage of trauma in the body.

I began to accept my own memories and had Rolfing as a method of understanding my own reactions. Rolfing was an adjunct to my healing with Verna, for combining psychological and physical work accelerates a person's healing exponentially.

I attended courses to build my knowledge and with several friends, participated in a weekend course on understanding the body. We learned to see how the body never lies. The teacher's perception of everyone's body was an accurate acknowledgement of their life. She showed me how my memories were obvious to a body worker who understood energy.

The truth of my story is tangible and can be seen in my physical body. This was the proof I wanted.

"When I work, my intention is to support the spiritual being in her physical structure. I want the person to come alive and exist embodied."

Mimi was a Rolfer with more than twenty years experience and her words honored her method of working with clients.

"What we see in a body is not a judgement on someone's spirit. Although people have to change from within, body workers can help, as long as they don't think they are omnipotent. The body may be in trouble for it may have lived a childhood with no support, but the spirit doesn't need help, we can't better the spirit of anybody."

Our feet were the starting point. Could I see what type of childhood a person had through their feet? The concept was fascinating. How much space do they take? Too much? Too little? Does it look balanced for the size of the body? I'd never perceived foot placement this way before.

"I always want you to stand in groups of three when we look at your body, then you can support each other. One person feels vulnerable being assessed alone."

Mimi moved around three of her students. They stood as she indicated what we could discern from feet and legs. Impressions came. Feet started to have a new significance for me. Our first premise was that the left leg indicated the journey with the inner self and the right leg the relationship the person had with the outer world. I was surprised how different two legs from the same body could be. Some had stronger contact with the ground from their right foot and others with the left.

"People can change overnight. I re-assess what I see every time I work with someone. If I say the arches are high because the energy around the child wasn't safe, it is not dogma. Each person has to be looked at as a whole. However, as beginners, we just look at parts."

It was when she asked the others to look at my legs and feet that I was astounded by her accuracy.

"What do you see in Christina's feet and legs?"

"Well, I see her left foot is firmly standing on the ground. It looks strong. Her right foot isn't as in touch with the ground though," Heather, a massage therapist, said.

"Yes. Her left foot has a nice image. It has a good relationship with her inner life. Her right shows me she is accommodating. It is quite different from all the other feet lined up here. Look. The right foot is where it is going to be put and I can see I have to be careful not to be omnipotent with her because she will follow my directions.

Do you think this is true Christina?"

"Absolutely."

I was stunned anyone could tell so much from observing my feet. I knew exactly what she meant, although I'd never considered defining this habit of mine as a pattern I could change.

"Everyone keep looking. One part is not the whole person, it is just an isolated chunk. But there is more here in Christina's legs. Can you see it?"

"She seems to have anger and pain," another participant observed.

"Yes. But there is more. Look, Christina takes up enough space for herself, not too much. Observe both her legs. What does the difference between them say to you? You have noted her right foot isn't so in touch with the ground. Can you see something in the right knee?"

There was silence as the seven other students pondered and attempted to sense what my right knee indicated. I wondered too.

"I am going to have to tell you for this is difficult to see straight away. Although her feet look balanced, they show to me that this woman has done an enormous amount of work on herself to bring harmony into her life. She has worked hard. How do I know this? Look at the right knee. Knees indicate what the person has had to do to protect their spirit. On the left they have to protect their inner life and on the right, the outer life. Christina has had to rebuild herself a right leg for her right knee has collapsed. There was a point in her life when she lost hope of surviving. This is another reason I know she has done enormous work. In order to have survived - she had to!"

Mimi's words caught my breath. I felt acknowledged. She saw the truth in my body. Only knowing my name for a few hours and looking at my body, she could see evidence of a struggle to survive. My right knee gave it away.

"This is amazing. It is true. I have worked on myself for twenty years. I spent time searching and reading in order to heal myself, not even knowing what I was attempting to heal. Obviously it wasn't a waste if you can see I have made changes."

I was excited by what could be seen in the body. This was what I wanted to know. I had found the proof of the body manifesting the spirit's struggle through life. We were seeing it in each other under Mimi's guidance.

Could a living, physical body be used in a court of law? Evidence from body structure - the true story of abuse, untampered by emotion?

The pelvic floor was the next place to observe. Looking at an internal part of the body through clothing and flesh is a challenge for beginners in the healing craft. How do we know if the pelvic floor is supportive or not? Somehow, we managed to sense the internal structure.

"This is the structure of intimacy and support for the whole trunk, a place we are not supposed to look. This is a terrible taboo that we can't look at certain areas of the body. Are we supposed to forget about the support system of the body? Please look. Look at the pelvis. It is the same thing looking at a man as a woman. It is a Spirit trying to live among us as human. If you are clear in your mind what your work is about you can look with no problems and once you have been looked at you will have less problems, for it's easier to be looked at than to look."

"We have three very different pelvic floors here. They tell us their capacity to present themselves in relationship with people - friends, family and lovers. Christina's is open. From her pelvis I can tell she likes people. But it is crowded with characters and unresolved issues with people. What is going on there for you with your relationships? Do you want to say?"

Mimi totally focused on me and her nurturing energy cut to my core and found the pain I'd pushed away. In the protective space she created, she honored who I was. Barriers I created were broken as she penetrated for truth.

"I'm finding it difficult divorcing my husband and my mother is dying."

"Ah, that's it. Your whole body is full of unresolved stories, not just the pelvis."

"I'm making you all stand a long time here because the longer we stand the less we can hold an unreal position. Your bodies become more natural as they tire."

As our bodies let go our perception of each other grew.

"Here, the ziphoid process on the sternum between the breasts is indication of abandonment. Everyone standing here has it. Christina has hidden it well and you wouldn't see if you didn't look hard. You can only see if you want. There is lack of dimension between her front and back at this point. Her shoulders are collapsing too. She's handling whatever went on very well – even though they are collapsing."

Mimi coughed. "This triggers my issues of abandonment also." She moved over to another person indicating how his sternum also showed abandonment.

"Now you know why I need a minimum of eight people for a workshop. We need varying bodies to use as our learning tools."

Everyone present was fascinated by the concepts we were learning. There is an infinite number of ways bodies can organize themselves. Mapping it out is not accurate. Anything can be anywhere, although generally heads carry anxiety, kidneys hold fear and lungs hold grief.

" Listen with your hands and follow the flow. The body is a very intelligent reality, it will go with the healing intent. If you have done a lot of psychotherapy the body releases quickly."

Healing is sped up combining different modalities. Body, mind and spirit are inseparable. Mimi reinforced Verna's statements encouraging us to have bodywork with psychotherapy to speed our development.

"How did you cope with this trauma to the body?" Mimi asked me.

"It seems impossible that someone as sensitive as you could have survived,"

"I was given a gift of strength, and had supernatural help."

Memories come a lot faster now. I don't deny niggling thoughts that go on in my mind. When a reaction to words or situations arises within me, I acknowledge and store them for clearing at an appropriate time. I look deeper inside, meditate on my thoughts and talk with friends, searching for the reasons behind the thoughts bubbling in my head. I don't tell everybody about ritual abuse, nor do I tell many friends what is 'up'. I have several special friends who also watch their reactions and behavior. We talk to each other, point out habitual patterns, clear and meditate together.

Rhonda's earlier statement, 'we never finish working on ourselves' stuck with me. Growth and awareness is my priority.

I'm not shocked by memories as much now and my body releases trauma faster and easier. When emotion attached to memories is cleared, it was easier to write. However, when my feelings were stirred by writing, I was obviously not detached from the past.

I see how insidious the cult is and how many people are involved. People all over the world are remembering similar occurrences and their bodies are releasing trauma. We are part of the critical mass needed for the world to believe our stories. It will occur like the 100th monkey. Eventually, so many people will remember that denial of ritual abuse by our society can no longer be sustained. It needs a change in human consciousness. As survivors tell their stories, the rest of the population will gradually acknowledge that this abuse occurs.

Evil exists on this planet in the form of mind control.

Epilogue

Several years have passed since my discovery of ritual abuse. Although I have chronicled many of my memories and insights to date, there are still gaps.

My search to prove the body never lies was the missing piece that substantiated the truth of my involvement. If I hadn't seen how a skilled person could read trauma in my body, I may have questioned my memories and be vulnerable to continued participation in the cult.

There is a happy ending to my story, one of transformation, knowing, and helping others as well as my own family. Clearing myself of patterns of ritual abuse opens up many other delightful possibilities for my own life. Melissa and Rebecca, through awareness of their own past are changing many dysfunctional ways. Their possible futures are more expansive because they pursue their own healing.

Healing is excruciating. I understand why people could choose to stay in denial, in their comfort zone of familiarity. Initially, the pain of looking at my wounds was beyond the confusion and internal agitation I had lived with. Nevertheless, it was worth the initial devastating emotional cost, to come through and free myself of the bondage of ritual abuse to find peace, happiness and freedom.

However, I believe it is difficult to heal in the environment in which ritual abuse occurred. There is so much programming that anyone involved could continue to attend meetings without conscious awareness. This makes healing tricky.

I am still grappling with Michael's sexual abuse of Melissa and Rebecca outside of the circles. I don't know whether he has grasped the significance of this act. It was different, a betrayal beyond the multi-generational ritual abuse, done in calculated consciousness. Melissa and Rebecca have contact with Michael and want to heal their relationship with him. They love him, for he is their father and there were good times. He has remarried and works out of Australia without his partner.

Melissa had a harder time than Rebecca in healing because of extra training and programming for her leadership role. She completed her medical science course but was terrified of the implications her programming to do this profession. For her own safety she decided not work in that field. There was too much chance of further programming and reaction to her memories. This was a heartbreaking realization and she felt cheated of five years of tertiary study and struggle. She is rebuilding her confidence and opening herself to other possibilities.

Rebecca works in the field she trained in. Her life is active as she establishes herself in her profession and socializes with contemporaries. She appears happy, competent and very capable.

My issues of betrayal, lies and manipulation are still in process of healing. A lifetime of programming and torture takes more than four or five years to amend. However, I feel more peaceful and content. I continue with my healing.

What have I learned from this life experience?

I have learned that my freedom comes from healing and letting go of what I perceive to be a wrong doing to me. Hanging onto righteousness delays my growth, and keeps me bound to the past. Blaming anyone is a restriction that also encloses my own consciousness. It limits my future and keeps me bound in the cycle of karma. I pray to let go of the past, with gratitude.

Many people have heard of ritual abuse, but are not aware of the large scale of its occurrence, or that it occurs in their cities. Nor do they deeply understand the torture and sacrifice involved. This will change as more people speak out.

My message to survivors is one of hope: know there is goodness and peace that comes with healing. Remember that the despair, heaviness and tears are all part of the process, and diminish with healing, although there are many ups and downs in the process.

A premier support group doing excellent work is ASCA – the Advocates for Survivors of Childhood Abuse, based in Australia. Although we are totally responsible for our own healing, and no one else can do it for us, support is essential.

Glossary

Advocates for Survivors of Childhood Abuse

An Australian Organization founded by Liz Mullinar to take on the task of advocacy, support and education for men and women who experienced any type of abuse during childhood. Check the website, www.ASCA.org.au

Or write to ASCA, Mayumari, Coney Creek Lane, Quorrobolong, New South Wales 2325, Australia.

Aum

Sacred sound of the highest realms from ancient Sanskrit.

Aura

Layers of energy around the physical body. The atmic, monadic, egoic and lagoic are specific layers of the aura.

Blue Mountain Center

Blue Mountain Center is eighty acres in the Rocky Mountains south of Colorado Springs. It is a sacred area, on the ley lines tying the great Pyramids in Gizeh and Machu Picchu in Peru. Takawa, an Indian Chief in Spirit, whose etheric drumming can be heard at night, is a guardian of the land. Fund raising has started to finance a Center of Light and Sound on the land. Donations can be made to the Spiritual Sciences Institute. email: ARIDON@bluemountaincenter.com

Catharsis

Is the physical and mental release of deeply embedded emotions.

Chakras

Are centers of energy. There are seven major chakras and many minor ones throughout the body.

Christina

For further copies of this book, sequel of many people's experiences, and speaking engagements, contact Christina. email: hiddensecrets2002@hotmail.com or write to Hidden Secrets, Box 38502 Colorado Springs 80937-8502, CO, USA.

Clearing

This is the opportunity to release old patterns, vows, curses, and influences. Changes in the old stored energy can be initiated by physical bodywork such as Rolfing, sound healing, psychological and energy work. Combinations of different therapies are usually more effective to help with clearing than one alone.

Creating a space

Creating a space relates to energy work. Personal intent and Spirit build a spiritual energy field. When the space is contained there is greater possibility for focus to move through the emotion. Within a group, every person contributes to create this space.

Denial

This is the ability of the conscious mind to blot out recognition and remembrance of a past action or deed.

Goose Bumps

These are an indicator of truth.

Grounding

This is bringing our energy field fully into the body, right down to our toes.

Healing

Opening and releasing the wounds within a person and filling the space with golden light. It is the process to create a free, uninhibited energy flow throughout the body.

Indira Latari

Indira is a sacred teacher in the Spirit realms and speaks through Dr Yater. She uses the resources of the Spirit realm to give messages of enlightenment and encouragement in directing people on their soul's purpose and journey.

Integrity

Is acting in total truth to your own self, absolutely all the time.

Intention

Conscious thought given focus for energy to direct toward manifestation.

Karma

Is the law of cause and effect. It is the energy we create through our actions. Once we recognize our patterns, take responsible action and heal the energy surrounding our actions, karmic patterns dissipate.

Katar Schoenstadt
Runs workshops and spiritual healing sessions.
Available by writing to 4718 E Cactus Rd #190, Phoenix, Arizona 85032.
Email: ocru@cox.net

Multiple personality, or Dissociative identity disorder
Is the result of trauma which is too much for the psyche to cope with. As a result of the trauma, a personality aspect splits. Each aspect of the personality is distinct and can be male or female. These personalities have an age and may seem totally different from the core person. Different personalities take on different trauma as it occurs, or a certain type of trauma. By splitting, the main personality is able to grow and mature. Multiple personality is common in cult abused people.

On Line
This is the term we often use in a workshop, to put out a pattern, thought form, or emotion that we are dealing with and want to heal. Someone may say, "I want to put 'blows to the head' on line." By speaking our intent, the commitment for healing is acknowledged. Then we can go under the bowl or use sound as a focus on what has been put on line.

Out of Body
Is not keeping our spirit fully in the body. Terms like… "beside yourself",… " head in the clouds",… "out of it" and "scattered" describe how people who see auras, notice someone out of body. Most people can sense this even if they don't visually see it. People are out of body, because they don't feel safe in the body.

Past lives
Life is a continuum. Although the human body dies, spirit is eternal. In our linear understanding of time, we have lived many lives. Memories come from an energetic level. Often people carry emotion and patterns from other lifetimes and these also need clearing and healing. In the true understanding of time, All-Time is now.

Patterns
Behavior that rules our life is called a pattern. It is a consistent, often unconscious reaction to situations and circumstances. Our patterns come from observation of our family and society, situations in childhood and past life influences. Because our patterns are unconscious, we are not free in our choices until the patterns are recognized and cleared. Examples are arrogance, abandonment, subservience, anger and procrastination.

Processing

This term is used for a person going into memory and letting the trauma of the memory release. It is important to not interfere physically or energetically with a person processing. The energy created at the time of remembering can be disrupted by touch and the full process aborted.

Programming

Cult people are heavily programmed by mind control techniques for many aspects, including to forget involvement, to go to cult meetings and to kill themselves if they ever talk. Many words used to access the program are simple every day words.

Resistance

Building a barrier around oneself, physically, emotionally or energetically, so energies won't, don't or can't move through, is resistance.

Sannyasin

This was the Sanskrit word used by Bhagwan Shree Rajneesh (later Osho) for his followers.

Sound Healing

Sound is a pure form of healing. Healing sounds resonate in the body to release energy blockages and fill missing vibrations.

Spirit Doctors

These are beings that were either healers or physicians on the earth plane. They undertake further training in the Spirit realm to be able to come and work on our third dimensional bodies.

Support

Someone there to listen and share their energy with a person who is in an emotion they are working on healing.

Touch

When someone is touched while in process - or not - there is an immediate change in his or her energy field. When someone is processing it is important that they can remain in the energy which they have created - or has been created - otherwise the healing that may take place will be short-circuited. Also when people are hugged they may be getting sensory feed which is very likely not what they experienced when the original information that they are working with occurred. Processing and healing is a very delicate process and can be short circuited very easily - even movement in the room can short-circuit the energy and hence the process.

Triggering

This happens when a stimulus brings up memory or emotion in another person. Triggering happens from sounds, energy, environment and many other situations and possibilities.

Under the bowl

The sound vibration from the crystal bowl brings people into a deeper state of relaxation. Then by using patterns, for example, anger, abandonment and control, participants can search at deeper levels to find reasons for these issues in their lives. Past life and this life reasons rise to the surface of the mind. With awareness, healing is initiated.

Workshop or group

A session with a facilitator and group of people intent on changing their patterns and creating wholeness in their lives

Verna. V Aridon Yater Ph. D.

A spiritual healer and trance channel of more than twenty years experience. She has facilitated workshops in the United States, Australia and Europe. Dr Yater is a founder of the Spiritual Sciences Institute's Blue Mountain Center near Colorado Springs. Check the website at www.bluemountaincenter.com

Year Long Program

For 6 years Dr Yater conducted a Year Long Transformational Training Program. The program needed intense commitment from participants to reach maximum spiritual and personal expansion It consisted of seven day workshops, coaching and studies on the nature of consciousness. People from Australia, Europe and the USA came together for the year.

Christina is a Certified Rolfer® and trained in pattern removal level one with Verna V. Aridon Yater Ph D.

One of her current projects is to help others form branches of Advocates for Survivors of Childhood Abuse in America and have a retreat similar to ASCA's Mayumarri in Australia. Another is to spend three weeks annually expanding an orchard on Blue Mountain, in southern Colorado.

Her life commitment is to her personal clearing, education and fun. She enjoys travel, gardening and listening to classical music.

For speaking engagements, contact Christina on email at Hiddensecrets2002@hotmail.com

Order Form For
'Hidden Secrets, Fragments of a Double Life'

NAME:_____

ADDRESS:_____

CITY: _____ zip / post code:_____

STATE:_____COUNTRY:_____

PHONE (   )_____ FAX (   )_____

Email:_____

COST:

    $16.95 ea.   in US Funds.

    Tax _____ (Colorado residents only 6.2%)

    Postage _____ ($5.00 USA : $10.00 in US Funds elsewhere.)

    Total: _____

METHOD OF PAYMENT

    Check / cheque _____

    Postal or Money order _____

Allow six weeks for delivery overseas
Allow four weeks for delivery within the USA.

POST TO

Hidden Secrets
PO Box: 38502,
Colorado Springs
CO 80937-8502

Email address: Hiddensecrets2002@hotmail.com
Check for further publications.

Order Form For
'Hidden Secrets, Fragments of a Double Life'

NAME:_____

ADDRESS:_____

CITY: _____ zip / post code:_____

STATE:_____COUNTRY:_____

PHONE (   )_____ FAX (   )_____

Email:_____

COST:

    $16.95 ea.   in US Funds.

    Tax _____ (Colorado residents only 6.2%)

    Postage _____ ($5.00 USA : $10.00 in US Funds elsewhere.)

    Total: _____

METHOD OF PAYMENT

    Check / cheque _____

    Postal or Money order _____

Allow six weeks for delivery overseas
Allow four weeks for delivery within the USA.

POST TO

Hidden Secrets
PO Box: 38502,
Colorado Springs
CO 80937-8502

Email address: Hiddensecrets2002@hotmail.com
Check for further publications.